Professor R. Alan Cole calls the book of Exodus "the centre of the Old Testament." It recounts the supreme Old Testament example of the saving acts of God, narrates the instituting of Israel's greatest festival, the passover, and enshrines the giving of God's law. It portrays Moses, the prototype of all prophets in Israel, and Aaron, the first high priest. "The exodus from Egypt," Cole maintains, "dominated all the thought of later Israel."

The book of Exodus is especially important to Christians because Christ fulfilled its great themes: He accomplished God's *greatest* act of deliverance. He became the passover lamb. He sealed a new covenant with his blood. "No book therefore will more repay careful study, if we wish to understand the central message of the New Testament, than this book."

Extended introductory essays, including one on "The Theology of Exodus," precede a passage-by-passage commentary on the Exodus text.

Professor R. Alan Cole, Ph.D., is Master of Robert Menzies College, Macquarie University in Australia.

The Tyndale Old Testament Commentaries

General Editor:

PROFESSOR D. J. WISEMAN, O.B.E., M.A., D.LIT., F.B.A., F.S.A.

EXODUS

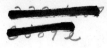

EXODUS

AN INTRODUCTION AND COMMENTARY

by

R. ALAN COLE, PH.D.
Master of Robert Menzies College, Macquarie University

INTER-VARSITY PRESS
Downers Grove, Ill. 60515

InterVarsity Press is the
book publishing division of
Inter-Varsity Christian Fellowship.

ISBN 0-87784-865-3
Library of Congress Catalog Card Number: 72-97952

Printed in the United States of America

GENERAL PREFACE

THE aim of this series of *Tyndale Old Testament Commentaries*, as it was in the companion volumes on the New Testament, is to provide the student of the Bible with a handy, up-to-date commentary on each book, with the primary emphasis on exegesis. Major critical questions are discussed in the introductions and additional notes, while undue technicalities have been avoided.

In this series individual authors are, of course, free to make their own distinct contributions and express their own point of view on all controversial issues. Within the necessary limits of space they frequently draw attention to interpretations which they themselves do not hold but which represent the stated conclusions of sincere fellow Christians. Thus, for example, the author does not put particular stress on such debated questions as the date of the revelation of the divine name or of the departure of the Hebrews from Egypt. His aim is rather to point out the profound part these crucial historical events played in the life and theology of the Hebrews and thus of the whole of the Old (and later New) Testament. The book has many lessons for our own day.

In the Old Testament in particular no single English translation is adequate to reflect the original text. The authors of these commentaries freely quote various versions, therefore, or give their own translation, in the endeavour to make the more difficult passages or words meaningful today. Where necessary, words from the Hebrew (and Aramaic) Text underlying their studies are transliterated. This will help the reader who may be unfamiliar with the Semitic languages to identify the word under discussion and thus to follow the argument. It is assumed throughout that the reader will have ready access to one, or more, reliable rendering of the Bible in English.

Interest in the meaning and message of the Old Testament continues undiminished and it is hoped that this series will thus further the systematic study of the revelation of God and His will and ways as seen in these records. It is the prayer of the editor and publisher, as of the authors, that these books will help many to understand, and to respond to, the Word of God today.

D. J. WISEMAN

5

CONTENTS

AUTHOR'S PREFACE

IT is with mixed feelings that I bid farewell to *Exodus*, for I feel as if I am parting with an old friend. I am sure that the editorial staff of the Tyndale Press, who have borne patiently with my delays over the last few years, will agree with this estimate, though their feelings may be less mixed. To me, it is a happy augury that this commentary was begun at Trinity College, Singapore; finished at Moore College, Sydney; and that this Preface is finally sent to the press from Robert Menzies College, Macquarie University. If it had a dedication, I should dedicate it to all three.

I am well aware (none more so) of the deficiencies of this commentary. I have deliberately striven to be explanatory and exegetic throughout, rather than devotional, judging that to be the main aim of the present series. It is not that I disagree in any way with the devotional use of the Old Testament (far from it), but that I must leave this task to others.

One thing I do ask is that readers will turn first to the introductory section on 'The Theology of Exodus' (pages 19ff.): this is designed to give the framework upon which the whole of the rest hangs. A prior reading of this section will not only mean that the reader will get more out of the commentary, but also more out of the book of Exodus itself (which is far more important). It is only fair to say that even this theological introduction arose from one of the many helpful suggestions made by far better scholars than I, when they read the typescript at an earlier stage. I shall not mention their names: but it is no exaggeration to say that, if this book has any good points, it is due to their kindly suggestions. For the remaining obscurities and imperfections, I must be held wholly responsible myself.

October 1972   R. ALAN COLE

CHIEF ABBREVIATIONS

AV	English Authorized Version (King James), 1611.
BDB	*Hebrew–English Lexicon of the Old Testament* by F. Brown, S. R. Driver and C. A. Briggs, 1907.
Bright	*History of Israel* by J. Bright, 1960.
Buber	*Moses* by M. Buber, 1946.
Cross	'The Priestly Tabernacle' by F. M. Cross in *Biblical Archaeologist*, 1947.
Cross and Freedman	'The Song of Miriam' by F. M. Cross and D. N. Freedman in *JNES*, 1955.
Daube	*The Exodus Pattern in the Bible* by D. Daube, 1963.
Davies	*Exodus* by G. Henton Davies, 1967.
Driver	*Exodus* by S. R. Driver, 1911.
Eissfeldt	*The Old Testament: an Introduction* by O. Eissfeldt, Eng. tr. 1965.
Fohrer	*Introduction to the Old Testament* by G. Fohrer, Eng. tr. 1970.
Gooding	*The Account of the Tabernacle: Translation and Textual Problems of the Greek Exodus* by D. W. Gooding, 1959.
Grollenberg	*Atlas of the Bible* by L. H. Grollenberg, 1957.
Harrison	*Introduction to the Old Testament* by R. K. Harrison, 1970.
Hyatt	*Commentary on Exodus* by J. P. Hyatt (*New Century Bible*), 1971.
IDB	*The Interpreter's Dictionary of the Bible*, 4 vols., 1962.
JB	Jerusalem Bible, 1966.
JNES	*Journal of Near Eastern Studies.*
Kitchen	*Ancient Orient and Old Testament* by K. A. Kitchen, 1966.
LXX	The Septuagint (pre-Christian Greek version of the Old Testament).
Mendenhall	*Law and Covenant in Israel and the Ancient Near East* by G. E. Mendenhall, 1955.
MT	Massoretic Text.

Napier	*Exodus* by B. D. Napier, 1963.
NEB	*The New English Bible Old Testament*, 1970.
North	'Pentateuchal Criticism' by C. R. North in *The Old Testament and Modern Study*, ed. H. H. Rowley, 1951.
Noth	*Exodus* by M. Noth, 1962.
Rothenberg	*God's Wilderness* by B. Rothenberg, 1961.
Rowley	*From Joseph to Joshua* by H. H. Rowley, 1950.
RSV	American Revised Standard Version, 1952.
RV	English Revised Version, 1881.
Simpson	*The Early Traditions of Israel* by C. A. Simpson, 1948.
Stamm and Andrew	*The Ten Commandments in Recent Research* by J. J. Stamm and M. E. Andrew, 1967.
SVT	Supplement to *Vetus Testamentum.*
Thompson	'Moses and the Law in a Century since Graf' by R. J. Thompson, *SVT* 19, 1970.
Weiser	*Introduction to the Old Testament* by A. Weiser, 1961.
Wright	*Westminster Historical Atlas of the Bible* by G. E. Wright, 1946.
Wright	'Book of Exodus' and 'Route of Exodus' by G. E. Wright in *IDB*, 1962.

INTRODUCTION

I. THE CONTENTS OF EXODUS

THE book of Exodus derives its English name, not from the Hebrew (which simply calls it 'These-are-the-names' from its opening words) but from the Septuagint, the Greek translation made in Egypt in the third century before Christ. Yet it is a good title, if a late one, for the 'exodus' or 'going out' of God's people is the central message of the book. Exodus begins with Israel as helpless slaves in Egypt: it shows the quiet preparation of God's deliverer, and his confrontation of the pharaoh. Then comes the violent clash between the God of Israel and all the false gods of Egypt, with plague after plague descending on stubborn pharaoh and the Egypt which he rules. Chapter 12 brings the passover festival, and the death of Egypt's first-born: Israel goes free at last. This is one of the high points of the book, continued in the crossing of the Red Sea, and the overwhelming of pharaoh's chariots in its waves. Moses' song of triumph in chapter 15, celebrating these saving acts of God, is a fit culmination of all that has gone before, and a transition to what will follow.

But this is only half the story. As proof that she had been redeemed, Israel was yet to worship God at the very Mount Sinai where Moses, the deliverer, had received his initial call (Ex. 3:12). So through the desert to Sinai she presses, still making her 'exodus' from the old life. She will need water, food, protection and guidance. All these God will give her, but already Israel makes her own true nature clear by her ceaseless grumblings and rebellions. At last she stands on the plain before Sinai and, amid thunder and lightning, hears the voice of God, and trembles. Here the covenant is made (Ex. 24:8): here Israel, as a nation, is born. This is the second high point of the book, not alone in the making of the covenant, but in the giving of the 'covenant law' that accompanies it. Summarized in the ten commandments (Ex. 20), amplified in the 'book of the covenant' (Ex. 21–23), God's very nature is expressed in moral terms, and the consequent demands on Israel are outlined. The exodus from the old ways will be harder than the exodus from the old land, but at least the true way is plain now.

But a third peak is yet to come. In subsequent chapters, slowly and lovingly, every detail full of rich symbolic meaning, there is outlined the structure known to older translators as 'the tabernacle', with all its furnishings (Ex. 25–31). God is to dwell with men: a fitting tent for His dwelling must be constructed, but, for the time being, we have only a priestly blueprint, the bare instructions for subsequent making, as in the book of Ezekiel (40–43).

Before the third peak comes a trough. With Moses still at the height of his experience up the mountain, speaking face to face with God, Israel reaches her lowest point: she makes and worships the golden calf (Ex. 32). Where is her glorious covenant now? Shattered to pieces, along with the stone tablets at the foot of the mountain? Is her new relationship with God gone for evermore? No: there is intercession by Moses and forgiveness by God, although there is stern punishment, too, in which Levi, by its faithfulness, wins its right to be the priestly tribe. So now there must be a reiteration of the covenant: step by step, the same stages are rehearsed, with the priestly love of repetition (Ex. 34–39). These chapters contain the story of the actual building of the 'tabernacle': meticulously, the craftsmen carry out every detail of the instructions already given by God to Moses on the mountain-top. At last all is ready: the final chapter contains the account of dedication of the Tabernacle, and the dwelling of God with men (Ex. 40). To this, in a sense, the whole of the rest of the book has led: this is the true climax of Exodus.

II. EXODUS AS A PART OF THE PENTATEUCH

Having said this, we may now turn to the rest of the Pentateuch, of which Exodus is a part, and indeed in some ways an artificially-severed limb. The opening verses of Exodus show a deliberate connection with the closing verses of Genesis, while the priestly instructions given in the closing chapters of Exodus run on into Leviticus and Numbers. In the Pentateuch, considered as a whole, there are only five major themes: God's promise to the patriarchs; the exodus; God's Self-revelation in covenant and law at Sinai; the wandering in the wilderness; the entrance into Canaan. Three of these five major themes are treated at length in the book of Exodus and, in addition, it looks back to the first theme and on to the last. Moses' vision and call at Mount Sinai are deliberately shown as a fulfilment of God's promise to Israel's forefathers, while the book ends with a promise of God's leading till Canaan is reached. Therefore, while Exodus is only part of a wider and far larger whole, it is a real part and, in a sense, enshrines the heart of the whole pentateuchal revelation. Of all the books of the Law, it is the one that has the greatest right to be called *Heilsgeschichte*, 'history of salvation'. Even the legal matter which it contains is rightly called *Heilsgesetze*, 'law of salvation', for it is set in the context of the covenant made with the redeemed nation, and the obligations thus brought (see Davies).

III. EXODUS AND PENTATEUCHAL 'SOURCES'

In earlier days it was held to be axiomatic that Moses himself wrote the whole book of Exodus, virtually in the form in which we have it, with the exception of a few verses written by Joshua after Moses' death. By the end of the nineteenth century, the dominant critical hypothesis had instead reduced Exodus to a mosaic of documents of different dates (but all long after Moses). The very historicity of Moses was doubted: Martin Noth, for instance, suggested that he was some unknown desert sheikh whose grave was remembered by Israel, and who thus entered her tradition from the outside. For such scholars, to speak of 'Mosaic authorship' in any meaningful sense was impossible. Where does the truth lie? Probably, at neither extreme. The old and tidy 'documentary hypothesis' has largely failed by its own success,[1] with ever smaller and smaller units, or unconnected fragments postulated by scholars, instead of major and continuous written sources. Scandinavian scholars instead have stressed the importance and reliability of oral tradition. They would not have us speak of written 'documents' at all, but of great complexes of oral tradition, which nevertheless, in final form, turn out to have almost the fixity of documents. Form Criticism had already taught us to classify and describe the varied biblical material by its form. It too dealt with much smaller units than the old 'documentary' hypothesis, and was concerned to

[1] Simpson represents the situation taken to its logical conclusion, in complete fragmentation. This may be correct, but is only an analysis, not an explanation of the book's present form.

see the living situations in which such units arose. More recently, some German scholars have taught us to look at 'the history of tradition', to see the possible stages by which the account of any given incident took its present form. All these are not only intellectually interesting: they also help us to realize the complexity of the process that lies behind our present text, and the great antiquity of the material contained there.

But, when all is said and done, the task of the Bible commentator is to comment on the final product, which is the text before him, and that is what the present writer has tried to do. In a commentary of this size, it is quite impossible to enter into such questions in detail, interesting though they may be. Many of these problems can only be profitably studied in relation to the Hebrew text, and to larger commentaries on the Hebrew text those interested are therefore directed. Suffice it to say that for Exodus, in spite of the so-called 'critical revolution' and widespread rejection of the documentary hypothesis in its old form, many scholars still make use of signs like J, E, D and P to indicate presumed written sources of the Pentateuch.[1] If these signs are regarded simply as descriptions of types and blocks of material, rather than as judgments as to dates of origin, the use is perhaps fair. However, even if the same symbols are used today, there is an important difference. Modern scholars no longer regard J as a work originating in, say, the ninth century in the Southern Kingdom. Instead they regard it as a ninth-century writing-down of traditions that had been current in Judah for many centuries, and were indeed only 'fossilized' when the collection was made at that date. Similarly they would regard E as a collection of Ephraimite traditions, equally old in themselves, but collected and written down a century or so later than J. The position is thus a very different one, though the symbols are the same.

Further, they would now say that even J and E (supposing we allow their independent existence and reality) are only differing formulations of substantially the same Mosaic tradition, denoted by the sign G (standing for *Grundlage* or 'basic layer'). In turn, D is seen to be a still later collection and explanation of early laws, in many cases laws supplementing those of the 'book of the covenant' (Ex. 20–23). Even P, once

[1] Contrast North (1951) with Thompson (1970) as general summaries of the position in their times.

seen as latest and least reliable of the 'documents', is now seen as conserving, with priestly meticulousness, archaisms lost elsewhere.

In other words, it is widely recognized today that the date of a document (supposing that such a document ever existed, and that we knew its date of compilation) is not nearly as important as the date of its contents. In short, in modern pentateuchal studies, we are not far removed from the New Testament position, where we have four Gospels, all alike preserving early traditions of the sayings and deeds of Jesus, although the Gospels themselves are of different and later dates. We may of course reject on principle any such form of source analysis: or we may preserve a reverent agnosticism, recognizing that some sources there must have been, but not wishing to be dogmatic as to their nature. We may simply deal with the text before us, unless some exegetic difficulty makes us probe deeper. But whether we do any or all of these, it is well to remember the greatly changed climate of Old Testament scholarship today. The essential historicity of Moses and of his work (at least in broad outline) would now be widely accepted. Many scholars of different schools would allow the ten commandments (perhaps in shortened form) to be of Mosaic date,[1] and recognize the material of the 'book of the covenant' to be Bronze Age. We may not be personally satisfied with this, and may want to go much further, but at least we should note this changed position and be thankful for it.

IV. PROBLEMS OF THE BOOK OF EXODUS

That there are problems in Exodus, not even the most conservative of scholars would wish to deny: but many of them are geographic or historical and few of them, if any, affect the theological message of the book. Most of these problems will be discussed briefly on their first occurrence. Some few will be examined at greater length, where a more detailed treatment seemed appropriate. But for the rest, recourse must be had to larger commentaries, such as that by Hyatt, in the *New Century Bible*.

[1] So, for example, Rowley (*Moses and the Decalogue*, 1951): but not Mowinckel (*Le Décalogue*, 1927) or Alt (*Ursprung des Israelitischen Rechts*, 1934). For a modern summary, see Stamm and Andrew.

To give examples: we do not know how long Israel was in Egypt; some would even say that we do not know whether all of Israel was ever there. We do not know the exact date of the exodus (although from archaeology we can give a close approximation), nor the route that Israel took, nor even the exact site of Sinai. These are only a selection: it is possible to collect over a hundred unanswered (and, at this stage of our knowledge, unanswerable) queries rising from the book of Exodus. Yet not one of these affects the main theological issue, and therefore we must not allow them to loom too large in our thinking. It is not essential that we know the numbers, or route, or date of the exodus. It is enough that, with later Israel, we know and believe that such an event happened, and that we too interpret it as a saving act of God. Indeed, to Israel, it was the saving act of God which overshadowed all others, since, in a sense, it was the act of Israel's creation. All God's subsequent saving acts were measured by this, the heart of Israel's creed. What the cross of Christ is to the Christian, the exodus was to the Israelite: yet we know neither the exact date nor the exact place of the crucifixion, any more than Israel knew the exact date or location of Sinai. The very existence of these problems in our minds only shows that we are scientifically-minded Westerners. Indeed, in one sense, we are importing our own problems into the Scriptures, and then blaming the Scriptures because we do not find answers there. Assuredly, to the original writers, these were no problems, or they would have framed their accounts differently. We are not to blame for being 'scientific man', any more than the Hebrews are to blame for being 'pre-scientific man', but we must learn not to ask of Scripture the answers which it is not written to give. If we must ask these questions, then we can only guess at the answers.

V. RELEVANCE OF THE BOOK OF EXODUS

It is very difficult to say which book stands at the heart of the Old Testament: but certainly the claims of Exodus are hard to match. To those who see theology as essentially the recital of the saving acts of God, Exodus 1–15 gives the supreme example, around which the rest of the biblical narrative can be assembled. To those who see the Old Testament as the product of the worshipping life of the community, at the heart of the book of Exodus lies the account of the institution of the passover, greatest and most characteristic of Israel's festivals. Indeed, the Exodus narrative may be seen as the explanation of the origin of that festival, recited or read aloud (as today) during its celebration. To those who see God's *tôrâ*, His law, as central to the life and thinking of later Israel, Exodus enshrines the law giving and contains the very kernel of the law in the form of the ten commandments. To later Jewish writers of priestly interests, who saw the maintenance of worship in the temple as one of the pillars of the universe, Exodus contained the account of the building of the Tabernacle, forerunner of the Temple. Yet, at the same time, it was not the priestly stream alone that looked back with veneration to Moses and Aaron. Moses stands also as the prototype of all prophets in Israel (Dt. 18:18), and the later prophets, while they may well search the mind of God more deeply, are best seen as essentially reformers, returning to the spirit of the Mosaic revelation, and to Israel's experience of salvation from Egypt.

It is therefore natural that the exodus from Egypt, interpreted by Israel's faith as being the supreme example of God's grace, faithfulness and power, dominated all the thought of later Israel. It even overshadowed, for a long period of Israel's history, the great events of creation and of the patriarchal days, although it will be seen that both God's creative power and His promise to Abraham are linked in thought with the exodus and indeed 'fulfilled' in part in that event. Not even the later promise to the line of David (2 Sa. 7:5–17) could obliterate the memory of the deliverance from Egypt. Instead, the exodus became a type to which later deliverances were compared. When the exiles came streaming home from Babylon, it was no wonder that this return was seen as a second and mightier exodus (Je. 23:7–8), another leaving of another Egypt.

But if the event of exodus, and therefore the book of Exodus, was precious to the Jew, it became doubly precious to the Christian. When Moses and Elijah are portrayed as discussing Christ's coming death, in the story of the transfiguration, the Evangelist deliberately uses the Greek word *exodos* to describe that death (Lk. 9:31). Whatever the exact day of Christ's death, it was clearly in the general context of the great passover feast (Lk. 22:13). Paul makes this identification specific by calling Christ the passover lamb (1 Cor. 5:7). John, in his allusive way, hints at the same identification by stressing that no bone of Christ was broken on the cross (Jn. 19:33, 36), just as no bone of the passover lamb might be broken (Ex. 12:46). From then on, throughout the whole of the New Testament, the allusions flow thick and fast. Passover introduced the week-long feast of unleavened bread: so the Christian must eat his 'unleavened bread' of sincerity and truth, free from sin's corruption (1 Cor. 5:6–8).

That this association of exodus with redemption was not a later invention of the church, but sprang from the very mind of Christ Himself, can be seen by the way in which, as reported by Paul, He views His death as a new covenant sacrifice (1 Cor. 11:25) sealing by blood God's new covenant just as, long ago in Exodus, blood had sealed the old covenant between God and Israel (Ex. 24:6). If the old covenant led to the law, then this new covenant, prophesied by Jeremiah (Je. 31:31), will lead to the law of love, explained in detail in many New Testament Epistles (*e.g.* Rom. 13:8). From whatever angle we study it, the great themes of Exodus have been, like the rest of the 'Old Covenant' (which draws its name from the events of this book), not destroyed but fulfilled in Christ (Mt. 5:17). That is why, when the song of the redeemed rises in heaven, it is the song of Moses and the Lamb (Rev. 15:3). No book therefore will more repay careful study, if we wish to understand the central message of the New Testament, than this book, the centre of the Old Testament and the record of the establishment of the Old Covenant.

THE THEOLOGY OF EXODUS

It would be hard to find a single major topic of Old, or even New, Testament that is not exemplified in the book of Exodus. Many of the themes, used later in the Bible, actually take their rise in this book, in the interpreted experience of Israel, through the great events that led to her foundation as a people. In this Theological Introduction we shall consider a few salient points under the headings of aspects of God's nature. This treatment is not intended to be exhaustive. It is simply intended as a meagre introduction to the theological riches of the book.

THE GOD WHO CONTROLS HISTORY

God is the unseen controller of all history and all circumstances. This is seen in Exodus 1, although God's name is not even mentioned until verse 20. This omission does not mean that the Hebrew was irreligious, but that, in contrast to us, he saw the hand of God in every circumstance of life, not merely at high moments in those signal acts of God that we call 'miracles'. Nothing is beyond His power and control – not even the stubbornness of a pharaoh (Ex. 4:21). It was this same conviction that made the Hebrews see the exodus as the supreme fact of all history, and as God's act of salvation for Israel. That it happened, no Israelite could doubt, for they had indeed been saved from Egypt: and the only possible explanation of this impossibility was that God had done it, since all things were under His control. But this invincible power of God over history is not exercised arbitrarily or purposelessly. He over-rules all events for the ultimate good of His children, whatever the immediate effects. This is demonstrated in the opening chapter of Exodus; the very measures designed to repress the Israelites only made them multiply more (Ex. 1:12). God's loving providence is again seen in the preservation of Moses' life and in his adoption by pharaoh's daughter (Ex. 2:10), as it is in the fortunes of the Hebrew midwives (Ex. 1:21). It might be argued that the midwives had deserved such gracious treatment, by their faithfulness to God (Ex. 1:17), and that the infant Moses had at least done nothing to forfeit such care. But God shows the same love to Moses when, by his own rash act, he is a penniless fugitive in Midian (Ex. 2:15-22). None could say that thankless Israel merited such treatment, if we study her subsequent history (*e.g.* Ex. 16:3), and no doubt she had been just as undeserving in Egypt as she was after the exodus. So, what had begun as a doctrine of providence now proves to be a doctrine of God's grace, His undeserved favour and love, showered upon the unworthy object of His choice.

I AM YHWH

God is YHWH. Exodus 3:13-15 makes plain that the revelation of God under this name was fundamental to the theology of the Mosaic age. As to pre-Mosaic days, there are various views. Some hold that the name YHWH was neither known nor used before the time of Moses (Ex. 6:3) and that its present use in earlier parts of the Old Testament is simply designed to show the complete identity of the God of the patriarchs with the God known and revealed to Moses. (However, on the whole question, see Harrison, *Introduction to the Old Testament*, pp. 578-582.) Others, relying on texts such as Genesis 4:26, maintain that the name itself was known long before Moses, to some at least of Israel's ancestors, and that this knowledge accounts for the free use of the name in the earlier Genesis texts. They would further say that Exodus 6:3 refers to a revelation as to the meaning of the name, which is now discovered to have new depths. The question is not, however, of importance in connection with the theology of Exodus. The significant thing is that God has a name, and is thus fully personal.

To the Hebrew, 'name' is shorthand for 'character'. Therefore to know God's 'name' is to know Him as He is, and to 'call on his name' is to appeal to Him by His known and revealed nature (Ps. 99:6). To 'proclaim' the name of YHWH is to describe His character (Ex. 33:19). Since Israel is YHWH's people (Ex. 19:5), YHWH's 'name' is involved in all that happens to them: this becomes important in Moses' later intercession for Israel (Ex. 32:11-13). God's reputation is bound up with the Israelites. God cannot abandon them: instead, He must get glory for His name through them. If God now bears a new 'name' (and if this is the correct interpretation of Ex. 6:3), it means to the Hebrew that a new and higher revelation has taken place than that associated with the old title El-Shaddai (Gn. 17:1–8) or any other patriarchal name for God. Henceforth, for the Old Testament, the name YHWH will mean all that the name 'Jesus' means for the New Testament. It is the name that sums up in itself all past revelation (for YHWH is still the 'God of the fathers', even if under a new name), and it also lies at the very heart of their new experience of redemption and salvation. Just to say 'Jesus' is, for the Christian, to be reminded of the cross; so to say YHWH is, for the Hebrew, to be reminded of the exodus. When God describes Himself as YHWH, it is therefore natural to add the phrase 'who brought you out of the land of Egypt' (Ex. 20:2), just as it is natural for the Christian to describe Christ as the one who 'redeemed us' (Gal. 3:13).

As to the exact meaning of the name YHWH, there has been considerable controversy: see the commentary on Exodus 3 for various suggestions. However, two points should be remembered: first, Exodus 3:14 is the only place in the Old Testament where the meaning of the name is explained. Secondly, the name is clearly represented as being explicable only by God Himself. The theological implication of this is that none but God can explain what God is like: we shall learn the meaning of His 'name' from what He says and does. Whatever the exact grammatical force of Exodus 3:14, so much is clear, since the Hebrew verb 'to be' has the sense of 'to be present (and active)': it is dynamic, not static. Israel is not left, like other nations, to speculate about the problematic existence and nature of gods. Her God is a 'God who is there', active in history and revealing Himself in word and deed.

The exodus itself initially defines the nature of YHWH, as revealed in His salvation of Israel from Egypt. Israel's subsequent history will add clause after clause to this initial statement of her creed ('who brought you out of the land of Egypt') as her experience of salvation grows. YHWH will not only be confessed as the One who led out of Egypt (Ex. 20:2), but also as the One who led into Canaan (Dt. 26:9) and as the One who raised up judges (Jdg. 2:16), and so on. The promise inherent in the initial explanation of the divine name (Ex. 3:14) is being fulfilled in history, whether that explanation be understood as 'I am who I am', or 'I will be who I will be'. Since more and more of God's nature is gradually being shown

to men by His words and acts, His 'name' is continually taking
on a richer meaning. The crown and fulfilment will come in
New Testament days, when God's greatest word to man is
spoken (Jn. 1:14) and His greatest saving act is finished (Jn.
19:30). Henceforth, He will be fully known as 'the God and
Father of our Lord Jesus Christ' (Rom. 15:6) and as the giver
of the Spirit (Jn. 14:26). A new 'name' for God will now come
into use, corresponding to this new fullness of revelation. So
it will be seen that, while all biblical theology rests on a right
use of linguistics, at the last we must seek a theological, rather
than linguistic, understanding of the divine name. Indeed, the
whole of the ten commandments are this sort of theological
explanation of the significance of the name of YHWH, for
they begin with the definition of YHWH's saving act (Ex. 20:2)
and continue with an expression of His moral nature. Perhaps
the most significant addition is that which defines YHWH as
being a 'zealous God', zealous both in punishing and in keeping
covenant (Ex. 20:5, 6). With this may be compared the later
Self-proclamation of God's name to Moses (Ex. 34:5–7),
where the 'name' is understood in terms of both love and
judgment, and where God's 'zealous' nature is again stressed
(Ex. 34:14).

THE GOD WHO IS HOLY

God is holy: the very place where He revealed Himself to
Moses is (or rather becomes, by that revelation)'holy ground'
(Ex. 3:5). This is the first occasion upon which the adjective
'holy' appears in the Pentateuch, although the idea is already
to be found in Genesis (*cf.* Gn. 28:17). Later, 'holy' will be
one of the adjectives most frequently used to define the nature
and being of God, especially in Leviticus (*e.g.* Lv. 11:45).
Without entering into philological arguments, the basic idea
of the Hebrew root seems to have been 'set apart' and therefore
'different' from common things. To the Canaanite, this idea
might have no moral connotations at all. One title of the
fertility goddess Astarte, used in Egypt, was 'Qudshu' (the
Holy One), and the name of the temple prostitutes, strictly forbidden in Israel (Lv. 19:29), was literally 'holy ones'. But the
'separateness' or 'difference' of God from men is not merely
that of two different orders of being. It is in His moral nature
that the God of Israel is different: therefore 'holiness' in

Israel has a moral content. That is why He will reveal Himself in the 'ten words', which are a moral rather than an intellectual revelation, although they have an intellectual content. Israel's ongoing experience of God, after her salvation from Egypt, was also to be a gradually deepening moral experience: it was her conscience rather than her intellect that was continually challenged. So it is that, in the new covenant, God 'reveals' His ways to babes and 'hides' them from the wise (Mt. 11:25), for there is nothing hard to understand in a moral imperative, no matter how hard it may be to obey. Basically, our stumbling-blocks are not so much intellectual as moral: the root of our opposition to God lies in our will.

Since God is 'holy', since He is so 'different', then anything associated with Him, or devoted to His service, partakes of this characteristic. If it is an inanimate object (such as oil for anointing), this may mean only that it is forbidden for common use (Ex. 30:32). It may even convey the idea of some mysterious danger on manual contact (Ex. 19:12, 13). But since God's holiness is defined as being moral, to be a 'holy people' (as Israel was called to be, Ex. 19:6) meant that stern moral demands are made of her. Outside the book of Exodus, the requirements are put bluntly: 'You shall be holy; for I YHWH your God am holy' (Lv. 19:2). It can be stated still more succinctly: the motivation for a moral command may be simply 'I am YHWH your God' (Lv. 19:3). Since YHWH is holy, there is no need for more explanation: the new relationship, brought about by grace, makes inexorable moral demands.

Within Exodus itself, it could be said that the whole 'book of the covenant' (roughly, Exodus 21–23) is an attempt to define what it means to be God's people, a holy people. Therefore holiness is, in the deepest sense, a definition of God's nature as He expects to find it reflected in His children. It is this concept of God's holiness which, in turn, is mirrored and portrayed in the very construction of the meeting-tent, with its 'holiest place of all' far within, and with metals and materials in gradually lessening degrees of preciousness as they are further from this centre. If the law was a verbal expression of God's holiness, the Tent was a visible parable of it, and the nation of Israel was intended to be a walking illustration of it. It would perhaps be true to say that the whole concept of sin-offering (Ex. 29:14), so basic to Israel's religious practice, springs from this concept of the holiness of God, understood in moral, not merely ritual, terms. This aspect however is better discussed under another heading.

THE GOD WHO REMEMBERS

YHWH is also the God who remembers (Ex. 2:24). Specifically, He is the God who 'remembered his covenant with Abraham' and with the other patriarchs. This is of course not to say that God can forget (except in so far as 'forgetting' is a metaphor, to describe His forgiveness of sin; *cf.* Is. 64:9). To say that God 'remembers' is an anthropomorphism (or, more correctly, an anthropopathism) to express the changelessness of God. There is nothing arbitrary about Him: anything learned about Him from His past relationships with men will be equally valid for present and future relationships. This is in utter contrast with the gods of paganism, who shared all the whims and tantrums of their human creators. It is this divine consistency and this alone that makes an ongoing process of revelation possible. It is in accordance with this principle that Israel will measure all her subsequent history, and understand every later happening, in terms of the exodus. This principle will be the measure of her hope for the darkest days of the future. For, in her turn, God will call upon Israel to 'remember' what He has done for her in the covenant. From this, she will draw assurance that His gracious purpose for her will continue. In addition, 'remembering' will be the spur and goad to keeping His commands (Ex. 20:2). As has been well said, only this 'remembering' can join gospel and law in one: Israel keeps the law because she 'remembers' the gospel of salvation.

To Hebrew thought 'to remember' is 'to act'; this too is equally applicable to God or to Israel. Again, this is not new. God, says Scripture, 'remembered Noah' (Gn. 8:1); that is to say, God acted in such a way to Noah as to show the consistency of His character. There too it was God's grace that was consistent (Gn. 6:8), as it was for Israel in the present instance. So, to say that God 'remembers' is to assert that He repeats His acts of saving grace towards His people Israel again and again, and in this way fulfils His promises, and shows His own self-consistency.

But there is an even deeper thought here: it is God's

'covenant' that He remembers. Now we are at the very heart of Exodus and its theology, for the covenant made by God with Israel at Sinai (Ex. 24:3–8) dominates, not only the thought of this book, but all of subsequent Israelite thought. Every time that we speak of 'the Old Testament', that is 'the Old Covenant', we give unconscious assent to this fact. True, in later days the covenant at Sinai so overshadowed the covenant with Abraham that the latter is rarely mentioned again until exilic times (Ezk. 33:23, 24). But, in the text of Exodus, the whole movement of salvation that culminates in the Sinai covenant is a fulfilment of divine promises stemming from the covenant with Abraham (Ex. 3:15–17). Indeed the whole biblical history of salvation is seen in terms of promise and fulfilment: this is what gives the Sinaitic covenant depth and roots in the past, since, in giving it, God is 'remembering' His covenant with Abraham, and thus, in a sense, reiterating it. To Paul, the covenant made with Abraham is actually deeper and more fundamental than that made with Israel at Siniai (Gal. 3:17). It is the former covenant, not the latter, to which he turns for an illustration of justification by faith. In either case, the 'Old Covenant' has given the terminology for the 'New Covenant' prophesied by Jeremiah (Je. 31:31), the introduction of which by the death of the Messiah was symbolized by Christ at the Last Supper (1 Cor. 11:25).

There is no need to stress how important 'covenant' is, as a category of explanation used by both Old and New Testaments. Terms like 'covenant blood', 'covenant sacrifice' are basic for the understanding of the plan of God and the work of Christ, since a covenant was usually sealed by the blood of a victim. 'Covenant' was indeed a natural form of expression of mutual obligation at the time. It covered relationships both individual (Gn. 21:32) and collective (Jos. 9:15), and could even be used metaphorically of non-human elements (Jb. 31:1). There is some argument as to whether 'covenant' was originally a trader's term: certainly it included the meaning of our word 'contract', and covered matters that were fully secular (Gn. 21:32) as well as religious. Some secular covenants were between equals: some, like Israel's, were between a superior and an inferior. The closest (non-religious) parallel to Israel's 'covenant' with God is the unilateral 'sovereignty' type of treaty between a monarch and a subject people whom he was graciously bringing under his sovereign protection. Particularly good examples are found in treaties made by Hittite and Assyrian kings. The king would first outline what he had done for the people; then, after that exhibition of grace, he would lay down, as of right, consequent demands and obligations upon them. We may see here the beginning of an understanding of the relationship between grace (the origin) and law (the resultant). Such early 'suzerainty treaties' usually included, at the end, a list of blessings and curses on those who either kept or broke the covenant respectively. The similarities between this structure and the format of Israel's covenant at Sinai or indeed of Abraham's covenant (Gn. 15:7–21) are obvious, but should not be overstressed. For instance, YHWH is not actually described in the law of Moses as 'king' of Israel, although this concept is probably involved in Exodus 20:5, 6, and was certainly expressed later (Jdg. 8:23). Therefore it is not probable that we have here a direct borrowing by Israel: rather, a new relationship to God is expressed in terminology already familiar to them from the general cultural background.

There is yet another point to be considered under this heading. God is the 'God of the fathers', in that He declares Himself to be the God of Abraham, Isaac and Jacob (Ex. 3:6). This is, in one sense, a statement of the consistency and continuity of divine revelation: in another sense, it is an assertion of the lasting quality of the relationship that God establishes with man. The first is a truth which is very clear in Genesis, where Abraham's servant prays to the God of Abraham, not just as a name for God, but as describing a divine character of faithfulness and mercy shown to Abraham and as claiming these qualities for himself (Gn. 24:12). The second sense is even more significant for later theology: any relationship established by God is lasting. In the New Testament, on the lips of Christ, this has become an argument for what we might call the 'personal immortality' of the patriarchs (Mt. 22:31, 32). By virtue of establishing a relationship with them, God has assured to that relationship an abiding quality which in itself guarantees the continued existence of the human participants. In New Testament terms, eternal life is to know God (Jn. 17:3), not merely in that the whole quality of worldly life alters when we enter a relationship with God, but that such a relationship, by the nature of the One with whom we have it, can never pass away. Put in simplest terms, if God still 'remembers' the patriarchs, then they must still exist. Here, then, early and unself-conscious though it is, is the beginning of the revelation of life after death. It is ultimately this relationship to which the psalmist will reach out in hope (Ps. 17:15) or Job, in despair (Jb. 19:25–27).

At a wider level, this stress on God's relationship with the patriarchs is an emphasis on the essentially historical nature of the faith of Israel. Abraham, Isaac and Jacob were seen as real men, with a real experience of God. It was this same stubborn insistence on historicity that led Israel to look back again and again to the event of the exodus in later days. She knew that God's grace and power, as shown in the exodus, had been a fact: her present existence proved it. So too, in the New Covenant, Luke stubbornly insists on the historicity of the facts of the Christian faith (Lk. 1:1–4). That was the great strength of Israel's creed: it was neither a philosophy nor a mysticism nor an initiation nor a 'religion of feeling', but a 'religion of fact'. It was essentially a consistent interpretation of experienced history and, while man might deny the interpretation, no man could deny the history. That was why Israel could see God as a 'God who acts', and could wait, in confident faith, for Him to act again, in accordance with His word of promise.

THE GOD WHO ACTS IN SALVATION

Unlike the gods of Canaan (1 Ki. 18:27), God is a living God (Dt. 5:26), a God who acts. Above all, He is the God who acts in salvation: 'I have come down to deliver them' is His word for Moses to bear to the Israelites (Ex. 3:8). This introduces the biblical concept of salvation, an area where later biblical passages are largely indebted to the book of Exodus for language and imagery. The idea of salvation is of course present far earlier than Exodus in the stories of Noah (Gn. 8) and of Lot (Gn. 19), for instance. In both of these cases, the word used of God is not 'save' but 'remember', but as mentioned already, 'remember' has essentially an active significance. 'Bring up' (Ex. 3:8) and 'bring forth' (Ex. 3:10) are also virtual synonyms for salvation, arising from the historical circumstances in which Israel found herself, a slave in an alien land. 'Redeem' is another synonym which has a rich history in both Old and New Testaments, but the main verb (*gā'al*) is comparatively rarely used in Exodus. (For a full discussion, see the Tyndale Commentary on *Ruth* by Leon Morris.) The verb often, by its use in land-transactions, comes to have the sense of 'pay the purchase-price' (although this more properly belongs to the rarer verb *pādâh*). Exodus 6:6 and 15:13 do however use this verb (*gā'al*) of God's redemptive activity towards Israel. It literally means 'act the part of the redeemer-kinsman', as exemplified in Ruth and as defined in Leviticus 25:25. The verb is used very frequently in the second part of Isaiah to describe God's coming great redemption of His people from Babylon, seen as a second exodus (*e.g.* Is. 43:1). As at first, Israel, His people, were slaves in a foreign land, helpless to move, and it was God's purpose to save them from that slavery.

Salvation, whatever the word employed, is therefore seen as the characteristic activity of God: it is His very nature to rescue the oppressed and helpless. In later Old Testament terms, this activity is seen as part of God's judicial 'righteousness' (Is. 11:4). All through the law, His active care for the widow, fatherless, captive and stranger is stressed (Ex. 22:21–24). More, because God cares for the helpless, Israel must care for them too (Ex. 22:21, 22). The memory of God's salvation, which she has already experienced, and the memory of her own helplessness before that salvation, must make her, in turn, a 'saviour' of others. To do this is truly to 'know' God, to know what He is like, and to show that knowledge by action.

It was not enough that God should save His people from the slave-pen of Egypt: by a succession of mighty saving acts, He led, protected and fed them in the wilderness. Even this is not enough: finally, God is the God who acts to bring His redeemed into a rich heritage. This had been promised to Abraham (Gn. 12:7), and again promised to Moses in Exodus 3:8, the first of many passages telling of the lush wealth of Canaan. From this stems the growing consciousness of the inheritance of blessing that God has prepared for His chosen ones, the great theme of Deuteronomy. In the Old Testament, such blessings largely remain this-worldly, although increasingly they are translated into an ideal future (Is. 11:6–9). In the New Testament, the promised inheritance has become a matter of spiritual treasures (1 Pet. 1:4), but that does not mean that it has become a less real part of salvation, or a lesser manifestation of God's power to act for His people.

Nevertheless, in spite of the manifold nature of the saving activity of God, it was always the experiences of the exodus itself to which Israel turned back as the supreme example. If we must isolate one moment, it was the crossing of the sea (Ex. 14:30, 31) that was decisive, because it was then that Israel knew that she had passed from death to new life. There are those who see in the great triumph-story of Exodus 15 echoes of some old mythological battle of creation, by which God triumphs over His enemy, *Yām*, the sea-monster. The Exodus poem may well use faded metaphors drawn from such mythology, as poetry has done in all ages, but the sea is not an enemy here, as it would have been in a myth. It is only God's agent, doing His will: it is not even personified. The true enemy is the stubborn pharaoh (Ex. 15:4), the man who has tried to pit himself against God (Ex. 5:2), and it is over him that God triumphs gloriously.

Pharaoh stands for the height of human power, ranged against God and the people of God: therefore his fall is a fitting symbol for all time of the impossibility of striving against God, or of thwarting His plans. That is why the crossing of the sea became such a fitting symbol of God's act of salvation for Israel. It was to Israel what the resurrection of Christ is to the Christian church: the sign that the powers of darkness had been decisively defeated, and that salvation was now secure and certain (Ex. 14:30). Just as the appeal to God in the New Testament was on the basis of His greatest act in Christ (Rom. 8:32), so in the Old Testament the appeal to God is always on the basis of what He has done at the exodus (Jdg. 6:13), His greatest act on behalf of Israel. This too is what makes the crossing of the 'Sea of Reeds' such a fitting symbol of baptism for Paul (1 Cor. 10:1, 2): the waters of judgment are past, and salvation has been entered upon.

Nevertheless, if we may press the New Testament analogy a little further, the resurrection was but the proclamation of the triumph of God; the actual work of salvation was done on the cross (Col. 2:14,15). So too, in Old Testament days, it was the passover night that marked the actual redemption of Israel from Egypt (Ex. 12:29–32), and the passover must therefore be reckoned among the 'mighty acts' of God. While there is frequent allusion in the other parts of the Old Testament to Israel's salvation from Egypt, there are surprisingly few direct references to the passover. But it has yielded rich symbolism for the New Covenant, principally through the concept of the death of the passover lamb, seen by Paul (1 Cor. 5:7) as fulfilled in Christ. It is probable that the same idea partly at least underlies the title 'Lamb of God', given to Christ by the Baptist (Jn. 1:29). Whatever the exact calendar day, Christ's death on the cross was certainly in the general context of passover, making the fulfilment plain (Lk. 22:8). Indeed, the Last Supper, the symbol of His death (Lk. 22:1), if not an actual passover meal, was certainly closely connected with it.

While the passover was not exactly a sacrifice in the full legal sense of the word, still less a sin-offering (these aspects of Christ's work fulfil the sacrificial system of Israel, not the passover), yet passover was associated with a blood-ritual, as was sacrifice (Ex. 12:7). Moreover, it had not only an 'apotropaic' aspect (averting harm), but also a substitutionary element, in that a victim must die, if the first-born of the house was to live (Ex. 12:13). It might also be said to be propitiatory, in that it turned aside God's wrath (expressed in terms of the angel of death) from the Israelite houses. All this fitted passover uniquely to be a category of understanding for the cross (1 Cor. 5:7), that mightiest act of God for man's redemption, by the blood of Christ.

THE GOD WHO ACTS IN JUDGMENT

God is a God who acts, but His activity is not limited to salvation. He is also a God who can be angry, even with His own servants (Ex. 4:14). This is an important aspect of all theology, New Testament (Jn. 3:36) as well as Old. Certainly this is an anthropomorphism, but it corresponds to a reality, as great a reality as God's grace: it represents God's unchanging attitude of judgment on sin (and therefore on the sinner, unless he repents). Characteristically, the Old Testament does not speak of attitudes but of acts. God's anger is shown by the judgments that He brings on those that 'hate' Him (Ex. 20:5), as surely as He shows His 'steadfast love' to those who love Him (Ex. 20:6). If God's anger burns hot against His own people, He will consume even them (Ex. 32:10). The slaughter of rebellious Israel by the Levites after the making of the golden calf (Ex. 32:28), and the plague that followed (Ex. 32:35), were alike the outward manifestations of God's anger towards His own people. The plagues of Egypt and the overthrow of the chariots at the Red Sea were signs of His wrath towards His foes.

This again is typical of Israel's faith, seen as an interpretation of historical events. The slaughter and the plague took place, and the apostasy against God had previously taken place: that was incontrovertible. To interpret these events, Israel simply applied the same yardstick to disaster as she had done to triumph. If one was the salvation of God, the other was His punishment: the principle must be as valid one way as it was the other. Both are alike aspects of God's 'judgment', that activity of God which brings salvation to the oppressed, but punishment to the oppressor (Lk. 1:52). So, while Israel crosses the Sea of Reeds in safety, Egypt's chariots are overwhelmed in the waters (Ex. 14:28,29). Just as in all her subsequent history, Israel will interpret every victory in terms of God's saving activity, so she will interpret all her disasters in terms of God's anger. It was this system of interpretation which alone enabled her to accept her later history without losing her faith in God. Disaster was no longer meaningless: it had its place in the purpose of God for Israel, even if it was a disciplinary purpose.

However, God's anger is never arbitrary, as that of Baal might be: we can tell what things anger Him, just as we can tell what things please Him and, as the history of revelation moves on, these areas become clearer and clearer. Normally it is stubborn opposition to Him that arouses His anger in the case of His enemies (Ex. 14:4), while it is unfaithfulness to Him that arouses His anger in the case of His own servants (Ex. 32:7–10). Both principles are expressed succinctly in the 'ten words' (Ex. 20:5,6). It is because of this aspect of God's nature that He can describe Himself as a 'jealous God' (Ex. 20:4 and 34:14) or 'zealous God', to use a word less liable to modern misunderstanding. He saves because He loves, and punishes His people because the exclusive bond of that love has been outraged. In the later pages of the Old Testament, the implications of the covenant between YHWH and Israel will be worked out in terms of the marriage bond by Hosea, Jeremiah and Ezekiel. While the actual marriage-metaphor is not used in Exodus to describe the relationship between God and His people, the seed thought is already there. So sin against God may be described as adultery (Ho. 2:2), unfaithfulness to the marriage bond. Since marriage is a form of covenant to Hebrew thought (Mal. 2:14), this is a most appropriate metaphor. What evokes God's anger is therefore a breach of personal relationships, and since God has revealed Himself primarily in moral terms, this breach is normally a failure to keep His moral law, obedience to which is the greatest test of love (Ex. 20:6). Indeed, the whole moral law can be summed up, within Old Testament as New, as love to God (Dt. 6:5) and love to neighbour (Lv. 19:18).

Nowhere in the whole Old Testament is God's wrath more stressed than in the context of the revelation at Sinai (Ex. 19:16–19), at the very moment when God's grace is most in men's minds. Therefore, much of the stock symbolism, used in later days to describe God's anger, is drawn from the actual circumstances of Sinai: fire, darkness, mountains quaking (Ps. 18:7–15) – all are used. Even in New Testament days it is still so, as can be seen from Hebrews 12:18,19. Yet, in a sense, even this wrathful aspect of God was part of His glory (Ex. 24:17): God is glorified by His acts, whether of salvation or of judgment.

In the face of God's anger, it is not surprising that Israel was afraid (Ex. 20:19). Such fear was at once an appreciation of God's true nature, and a realization of Israel's own sinfulness. When God's holiness and man's sin were brought together, some violent reaction seemed inevitable. So their fear became, at its best, a godly 'fear of YHWH', a fear of disobedience and of its consequences. This sort of godly fear is commended in Exodus 20:20. From this time onwards, the 'fear of YHWH' becomes the Old Testament synonym for a life spent in obedience to Him (Ps. 111:10). Seen in this light, there is no contradiction between the Old Testament virtue of 'fear of YHWH' and the New Testament dictum that perfect love expels fear (1 Jn. 4:18). This is the more true, in that the very God who is angry has provided for Israel the means by which His anger can be averted: He does not delight to punish, but to save.

THE GOD WHOSE ANGER MAY BE AVERTED

YHWH is also the God whose wrath can be turned aside (Ex. 32:30–34). Repentance (even at times repentance of a shallow kind, like that of pharaoh) can avert it, as can intercessory prayer (Ex. 8:8). Sin-offering, too, can turn it aside (Ex. 29:10–14), though Leviticus is richer in examples of this. The supreme example of God's anger being averted is by the noble intercessory prayer of Moses after the episode of the Golden Calf (Ex. 32:32), where he identifies himself with his people in a readiness to share their very judgment (*cf.* Paul in Rom. 9:3). In other religions, men also believed that the anger of the gods could be averted by prayer or offering: but such prayer had for them a magical or quantitative efficacy. If we look at the contents of Moses' prayer (Ex. 32:11–14) we see the distinctiveness of Israel's faith. Moses appeals to God by His own nature revealed in past saving act and in promise of blessing. Long before, in his prayer for Sodom, Abraham had done the same (Gn. 18:22–33). This is no extortion of forgiveness from one who is unwilling to give it: this is the claiming of the loving purpose that God has already revealed. When we read later of YHWH's Self-revelation of His own nature, we see that He is not a God who delights in wrath and judgment: His delight is in mercy (Ex. 34:6), as is made explicit in later parts of the Old Testament (Ezk. 18:23). To offer such intercessory prayer (sometimes symbolized by incense, Nu. 16:46) on behalf of sinful Israel is called 'to make atonement' (Ex. 32:30). Even an offering of money to the sacred treasury may be 'an atonement' (Ex. 30:16) considered as an propitiatory offering, accepted as a ransom for the life. This leads directly to the next point.

While, as said above, God's wrath may be 'atoned' by intercessory prayer, the common use of the concept 'atonement' (usually an intensive form of the Hebrew root *kāpar*, meaning 'to cover') is in connection with animal sacrifice seen as a sin-offering. Exodus contains several instances where such animal sacrifice, and especially the blood that is shed in sacrifice, is said to 'atone' for Aaron and his sons (Ex. 29:35,36), or even to 'atone' for inanimate objects such as the altar (Ex. 29:37). The principle is thus clearly assumed in Exodus, which is stated clearly in Leviticus (17:11). It is shed blood, symbolizing life laid down, that 'atones' upon the altar and thus averts God's anger. In Exodus 29:36, 'atonement' is directly equated with 'sin-offering', so that the meaning of 'atonement' is clear: but 'atonement' also seems to bring with it in Exodus the thought of 'consecration' for a particular task or use (Ex. 29:37). As the Old Testament continues, the concept of atonement by sin-offering persists, and in the temple at Jerusalem it became a mighty system, extending into every department of life. There is little doubt that this concept of atonement by sacrifice stems from the principle of substitution, seen as early as the time of Abraham (Gn. 22:13). Other religions too had the idea of appeasing the wrath of gods by sacrifice: but Israel's concept was basically different. To Israel all sacrifice originated with God in any case (Lv. 17:11). It was He who ordained and accepted the sin-offering that made possible the atonement, just as He had provided the lamb for Abraham (Gn. 22:8). This, like the prayer of Moses for his people, was no extortion of forgiveness from an unwilling God: it was a way of approach to Him that He had graciously granted. Further, sacrifice was not mechanical in its effect: a good illustration is the fact that men could not practise 'high-handed' sin (Nu. 15:27–31), that is wilful, open defiance of God, with the thought that afterwards they could always buy forgiveness by sacrifice. For such a man, sacrifice was of no avail. Even within the Old Testament, saints realized that it was not the sacrifice itself that averted God's wrath, but the broken contrite heart that it should ideally represent (Ps. 51:16,17).

The most interesting use of this root 'to atone' in Exodus is the noun *kappōreṭ* (often translated 'mercy-seat'), used as a name for the covering of the ark (Ex. 37:6). It is only fair to say that some commentators translate the word simply as 'lid', from the literal meaning of the root, 'to cover'. If, however, it does indeed mean 'atoning-place', or 'place where sin is covered' (as the Greek translation *hilastērion* would suggest), then this would be another expression of God's willingness that His anger should be turned aside from men. The ark was the very place at which God had promised to meet men (Ex. 25:22) and where He had promised to speak to them. This 'cover' for the ark was seen as YHWH's very throne (Ps. 99:1), overshadowed by the wings of the cherubim (Ex. 25:20), the locus (if we may use the term reverently) of the very presence of God. Indeed, it was because of this that the ark was seen as the symbol of God's presence. This significance of the ark can be seen by its being placed in the 'holiest place of all' within the tent (Ex. 40:21) and by its function of leading Israel, either upon the march (Nu. 10:33), or into battle (Nu. 10:35). Therefore, at the very heart of the concept of God's presence with Israel lay the thought of atonement and forgiveness, supplied and provided by God for His sinful people.

For a brief discussion as to the actual meaning of the word *kappōreṯ*, see the commentary (on Ex. 37:6): but whatever the answer linguistically, it does not affect the wider issue of God's willingness to forgive. At best, it would be only a linguistic prop for a theological truth, discernible elsewhere throughout the whole of the Old Testament.

THE GOD WHO SPEAKS

It is noteworthy that, on the first occasion when the phrase 'the living God' occurs in the Old Testament, it is in connection with God speaking (Dt. 5:26). This is one of the ways in which He shows that He is living and active: for God is a God who speaks, a God who reveals Himself in word. Exodus 3:4-22 is an illustration of this truth, which needs restating today, to correct a modern imbalance. Our forefathers had laid so much emphasis on the concept of 'the God who speaks' that our generation has perhaps overemphasized, in an understandable reaction, the complementary biblical concept of 'the God who acts'. What both are equally asserting is that God is a God who reveals Himself to man by word and deed, that is, by explained act: as often said, in biblical theology, 'act, plus interpretation, equals revelation'. Often in the Bible, the word comes before the act: first comes the promise, then the fulfilment of that promise. To put it in abstract terms, to say that He is the God who speaks is an assertion of the principle that God's revelation is always intellectually comprehensible and communicable: it can be both understood by the recipient and preached to others. This is what makes possible the later sequence of prophets, with their interpretation of history, within Israel. Indeed, the call and experience of Moses at the burning bush sets the pattern for all later prophetic calls (Ex. 3:1-6). When any later prophet says 'Thus says YHWH' (Am. 1:3), he is asserting the same truth, like Moses, not in terms of some abstract principle, but of his own concrete personal experience. He speaks the word of YHWH because he has first heard the word of YHWH himself (Ex. 16:23).

This thought of 'the God who speaks' runs deep throughout Exodus. At Sinai, true, all Israel hears God's voice, symbolized

by the thunder (Ex. 19:19) and all Israel fears (Ex. 20:18).
The supreme mark of Moses' unique relationship is that God
'speaks' with him, face to face and openly (Ex. 33:11), unlike
the indirect way in which He may communicate with others.
When the great covenant is made at Sinai, it is on the basis of
the 'words' of God (Ex. 24:8). Indeed, what we call the 'ten
commandments' are to the Hebrew the 'ten words' of revelation from God (Ex. 20:1): it is only because they are God's
words of revelation that they become mandatory. Further,
because He is a God who speaks, He is a God who delights to
declare His own nature (Ex. 33:12–23). The beginning of this
process lies in God's revelation of the name YHWH to Moses
at the burning bush (Ex. 3:14,15). Nowhere, however, is it
brought out more clearly than in the great Self-declaration of
God's 'name' (that is, His 'nature') at Horeb (Ex. 34:6,7), in
answer to Moses' prayer that God will show him His ways, that
he may know Him (Ex. 33:13). The word of revelation that
comes is profoundly true. No man can experience God as He
is, in all His wonder: but God may be known by the marks of
His passing, by what He has done ('you shall see my back',
Ex. 33:23). So it is God as proven in Israel's experience who
will be declared, and God as Israel will yet find Him to be
in history.

This Self-revelation is in one sense a reiteration of the earlier
revelation contained in the name YHWH, and in another
sense a further amplification of it. For instance, the '*idem per
idem*' construction found here, 'I will be gracious to whom I
will be gracious, and will show mercy on whom I will show
mercy' (Ex. 33:19) is not only an explanation of the name
YHWH, but also has the same grammatical form as the earlier
explanation 'I am who I am' (Ex. 3:14). For the question as
to whether this construction is deliberately restrictive or not,
see the commentary: it certainly emphasizes both God's
activity and His complete Sovereignty in that activity. It is
striking that God's activity is primarily defined here in positive
terms, that is, in graciousness and mercy (Ex. 33:19). So
Israel had certainly proved it in her own experience. The
opening phrases of the fuller declaration in the next chapter
will describe Him in the same way (Ex. 34:6,7): but the
closing phrases of the latter verse will also give the negative
aspect of destruction ('by no means clear the guilty, visiting
the iniquity . . . '). That is needed to give the full picture of

God. The similarity, in both respects, to Exodus 20:5,6 has
often been noticed. It is not by accident that, in both cases,
this 'autokerygma', this 'Self-declaration' by God, is in the
context of commandment to His people. In Exodus 20 the
context is the moral decalogue, while in Exodus 34 the context
is the so-called 'ritual decalogue', dealing largely with Israel's
festivals. In either case, it is because of who YHWH is, and
what He has shown Himself to be in the life of Israel, that He
has the right to command.

This Self-declaration by God continues, at an ever deepening
level, throughout the revelation of the Old Testament. For
the Christian, however, it is the coming of Jesus Christ,
God's 'word' become flesh, that has made the definition of
God's nature complete and final for all time. Here God has
at last most truly declared Himself in His Son.

THE GOD WHO IS TRANSCENDENT

God is One who cannot be experienced directly in His fullness
by mortal man. The classic expression of this truth is in
Exodus 33:20: 'man shall not see me and live.' (There is
only a superficial contradiction between this and Ex. 24:11;
see commentary.) The same idea is conveyed in Exodus 3:2
by the introduction of the phrase 'angel of YHWH', better
translated as 'YHWH's messenger'. This is not the place to
enter into a discussion of biblical angelology, the more so as
we are dealing with an aspect of spiritual reality beyond our
modern experience. But Genesis 16:7–13 will serve as an
example of the same usage earlier, with the same ambiguity
as to whether what we call 'an angel' (a subordinate and
created spiritual being) is meant, or whether the phrase is
only a reverential substitute for the word 'God'. Older theologians used to explain such angelic visitations as 'theophanies',
appearances of God Himself, on earth. Indeed, many of them
used to see in such manifestations 'Christophanies', appearances of the pre-incarnate Christ. While we may not agree
with them completely, we may well see here an illustration of
the same spiritual principle as was fulfilled in the 'word made
flesh' (Jn. 1:14). This would explain the curious alternation
by which sometimes the angel appears to act independently
in his own person (Ex. 3:2), while sometimes he seems to
speak and act directly in the person of God Himself (Ex. 3:4).

But whether we regard the phrase 'angel of YHWH' in such cases as a reverential periphrasis for God, or as a separate being, in either case the wording serves to highlight the theological problem of how to combine God's transcendence and God's active participation in the world of history – indeed, His control of that history for His purpose. This antithesis, marked though it is in Exodus, is not unique to it: it is found from the very beginning of our Bibles. On the one hand, God was transcendent and almighty (Gn. 1:1), spirit and not flesh (Gn. 6:3), the One whose thoughts were far above those of men (Gn. 6:5). On the other hand, He was one possessed of full personality, who could be described in daring anthropomorphic terms (Gn. 3:8), and who was concerned with the smallest details of daily life. The introduction of 'angels' was a way, in the providence of God, in which both aspects could be asserted simultaneously.

Though God cannot be experienced directly, yet something of His presence we may know. He is a God of 'glory': it is typical of Exodus to say 'the glory of YHWH appeared in the cloud' (Ex. 16:10). Hebrew *kābôḏ* (literally 'weight', and metaphorically 'dignity') is one of the words used to denote the presence of God when manifested to men. Usually it brings with it, not only the thought of the splendour of God, but also something of His awfulness, as in this instance. Mortal men must fear when they see God's glory, as Israel feared to see even the reflected glory shining on the face of Moses, when he returned from communion with God on the mountain-top (Ex. 34:29–35). As far as we can tell, some form of brightness is intended. In Exodus 24:17, God's glory on Mount Sinai is compared to 'devouring fire', appearing in the middle of the dark cloud. Certainly something similar was conveyed by the later word '*shekinah*' (literally 'dwelling'), used to describe the visible symbol of God's presence in Tent or Temple. The link between 'glory' and 'dwelling' is that God's 'glory' is said in Exodus to 'dwell' in the completed Tent (Ex. 40:34); indeed, that is the sole object of building it.

Sometimes, therefore, when God displays His glory, it shows His favour, as in this case: sometimes however it shows His anger (Ex. 16:10). This follows directly from what has been said above ('fire' is a two-edged symbol) and may be compared with God's twofold activity in salvation and judgment. God gets glory in and by His people (Is. 49:3), but He also gets glory by overthrowing pharaoh and his army (Ex. 14:4). The word 'glory' may therefore be considered as a virtual synonym for the revealed and acknowledged presence of God as He is, in all His godhead; indeed it is a periphrasis for God's very being. So too the word seems to be used in the New Testament: that is why we see in Christ the very glory of God.

THE GOD WHO LIVES AMONG HIS PEOPLE

He is a God who will live among His people (Ex. 29:45). This aspect is sometimes called the 'theology of the presence', and is a recurrent note throughout the entire book of Exodus. We have mentioned something of it under the heading of God's 'glory', but the theme is wider still. God's basic promise to Israel is 'My presence will go with you' (Ex. 33:14). By contrast, Moses' prayer is that, if God's presence does not accompany Israel, He will not lead them to Canaan at all (Ex. 33:15). To Moses, the whole distinctiveness of Israel lies in this accompanying presence of God. So important is this 'theology of the presence' that a commentary on Exodus such as that by Henton Davies will see it as the centre of the thought of the book. Initially, the call of Moses is a confrontation with the presence of God (Ex. 3:5). It is the presence of God that enables Israel to cross the sea, but overwhelms the Egyptians, just as it is the presence of God that leads and protects Israel in the wilderness (Ex. 14:19,20). When YHWH passes before Moses and 'proclaims the name of YHWH' (Ex. 34:5) it is a proclamation of the nature of that presence. The whole process of the making of the covenant (Ex. 24:1–11) and the giving of the law (Ex. 20) is a guarantee of the reality of this presence.

Lastly, the entire aim of the construction of the Tent is so that God's presence may be experienced in the very midst of Israel (Ex. 25:8). The crowning glory of the Tent's completion is when Israel has visible proof that this has actually happened (Ex. 40:35). The book ends with the confident assurance that this same Presence will indeed continue to go with Israel, lead her into Canaan, and give her that 'rest' (Ex. 33:14) which will be the fulfilment of the promise to Abraham (Gn. 13:15). As mentioned, this Presence is emphasized by the very plan of construction of the Tent, and symbolized particularly by the ark, resting in the holiest place of all, in the very centre of God's people. In later days in Israel, the 'static' symbolism of God's dwelling at Jerusalem (Ps. 9:11), especially in Solomon's Temple (Ps. 20:2), replaced the 'dynamic' symbolism of early days, where a movable tent and a portable ark did less to 'localize' His presence. There were of course abuses possible in either case: Hophni and Phinehas thought of God's presence as automatically guaranteed by the ark (1 Sa. 4:3), just as the later Hebrews thought it automatically guaranteed by the Temple at Jerusalem (Je. 7:4). The fate of the sanctuary at Shiloh should have warned them otherwise (Je. 7:12). Yet, in spite of abuses and misunderstandings, the most prized promise of the Old Testament was still God's promise to live among His people (Is. 7:14), and, in the coming of Jesus Christ, the prophecy of a coming 'Immanuel' (God in our midst) came true at last. Henceforth, the presence of God is directly, not indirectly, among men for evermore (Rev. 21:3): type and figure have passed away, because reality has come in Christ.

EXCURSUS 1

THE DATE OF THE EXODUS

The date of the exodus is not a matter on which we can make dogmatic assertions: equally great scholars and equally devout Christians have differed, and will doubtless continue to differ here. The matter is not one of orthodoxy or conservatism, but of historical judgment in an area where evidence is scanty. Providentially, it is not a question that affects the theology of the book, provided that we accept the historic fact that the exodus took place, and the interpretation that makes it the supreme 'act of God' leading to Israel's salvation. It is doubtful if any later Hebrew knew its exact chronological date, and even more doubtful if he would have cared. Nevertheless, since we accept the historicity of the exodus, we may well enquire as to its probable date.

One of the difficulties in such enquiry is that, apart from the two store-cities built for pharaoh by Israel (Ex. 1:11), there are no proper names in the story to pin the events to known Egyptian history: even the title 'pharaoh', 'king', is anonymous throughout. All we know is that the pharaoh of the exodus was not apparently the pharaoh of the oppression (Ex. 4:19). A second difficulty is that Egyptian history makes no mention of the event at all. True, some would identify the exodus with the expulsion by the victorious Egyptians of the Hyksos, hated Semitic conquerors, in 1550 BC. But this sort of military action is worlds apart from the exodus of the biblical account. In any case, it is too early to match the archaeological evidence for the presence of Israel in Canaan. Silence is not, however, an argument against the historicity of the exodus. Egyptian monarchs were never given to recording defeats and disasters, and certainly not the loss of a chariot brigade during the pursuit of runaway slaves. However, the silence of Egyptian records means that we are without an external check-point for dating. The only possible cross-reference to Egyptian history is that contained in a triumphal poem inscribed on a stone monument set up by Pharaoh Merneptah, usually called 'Merneptah's Stele' (1220 BC). Here he refers to a successful brush with Israel (among other peoples) located somewhere in the south of Canaan, but apparently still nomadic, to judge from the form of the Egyptian hieroglyph. A few scholars see this as a distorted reference to pharaoh's vain attempt to cut Israel off at the Sea of Reeds, with defeat turned into victory for propaganda purposes. The more natural explanation, however, would be a minor Egyptian foray, unmentioned in the Bible, some time after Israel had entered Canaan. Some see reference to such a raid in Joshua 15:9, where the 'Waters of Nephtoah' may be a spring named after Merneptah. Again, we are left without any external check, except that we know that the exodus must have taken place by 1220 BC at latest, since Israel was then in the land.

At first sight the Bible seems to give us exact chronological figures both for the duration of the stay in Egypt (430 years: see Ex. 12:40) and for the date of the exodus, which is placed 480 years before the founding of Solomon's Temple (1 Ki. 6:1). If we start with the first clue, there are certain minor difficulties connected with the actual number, which will be discussed in the commentary and need not concern us here. A major difficulty, however, is that we have no 'absolute' date for the descent of Jacob's sons to Egypt, any more than we do for the migration of Abraham from Harran to Canaan. We must guess both alike from external history, archaeology and culture-patterns. Therefore, even if we knew the exact duration of the stay in Egypt, we are not necessarily any nearer an answer as to the date of the exodus. This clue, then, is valueless in our present search.

If the period of 480 years between the exodus and the founding of Solomon's Temple is taken literally and mathematically, since the Temple was built about 970 BC, the exodus would have been about 1450 BC. This date is unlikely for various historical reasons, partly in connection with Egyptian history, partly in connection with Israelite chronology (*e.g.* the very long period that it would leave for the judges, before the rise of the monarchy in Israel). Archaeological evidence for Israel's presence in Canaan so early is also lacking. We may say, if we like, that the manuscript tradition has not preserved the correct figure here, and it is certainly true that numbers seem particularly liable to manuscript confusion. But a more important consideration is that the number in question looks like a round figure of twelve 'generations' of forty years each, the usual conventional length. There is some evidence to show that Israel did count by generations in early days: and indeed, before the establishment of a monarchy, it is hard to see how they could have done otherwise. They neither had, nor could have, any 'absolute chronology' of their own, of the sort to which we have become accustomed. Further, a 'generation', assessed roughly at forty years (Ps. 95:10), appears to have been a common, if rough and ready, way of reckoning (Jdg. 5:31). Therefore it is not unreasonable to see the 480 years as a reference to the twelve generations known to have elapsed between exodus and Temple. Where family genealogies are carefully preserved, this sort of calculation was quite possible (*cf.* Mt. 1:1–16). But if men were normally between twenty and thirty (as Albright suggests) at the birth of their eldest son, the period of twelve generations would actually bring the date of the exodus to the thirteenth century BC, which is already probable on other grounds. Let us therefore examine that date as a possibility.

We know that the Israelites built for pharaoh the store-cities of Pithon and Raamses: this latter name at once suggests Ramesses II (1290–1224 BC) as the pharaoh in question. His new capital was in the Nile delta region, close to the probable site of Goshen. We know that he engaged in great building operations, and that he had numerous 'Apiru (a depressed serf-class probably including the biblical Hebrews, though not identical with them) working as labourers for him. The 'pharaoh of the oppression' could have been either he or Seti I, his father (1303–1290 BC), in whose days the move of the capital to the delta began. Previously, both pharaoh and capital had been located to the south of the delta, far up the Nile, well away from both Israelites and Goshen. Close contact between Moses and pharaoh would have thus been impossible at an earlier period.

A further piece of evidence is that, by the time of Ramesses' successor Merneptah (1224–1214 BC), Israel appears to be already in Canaan, although still reckoned apparently as a nomadic people (see the reference above to the Stele of Merneptah). This would seem to indicate that the Israelite conquest of Canaan had only recently taken place, since Israel had not yet settled down. Other pointers to this date are the fact that Edom and Moab may only have been founded as strong kingdoms in the thirteenth century BC. Had Israel appeared a century or two earlier, she might have marched through their land at will, instead of skirting their frontier fortresses as she did. Lastly, in the decades immediately before 1200 BC, numerous Canaanite towns were sacked and burnt, some never to be settled again, some to be settled gradually by a much simpler culture. Both of these aspects would well suit the biblical picture of the conquest of Canaan by the Israelites: we cannot say more.

Of course, certainty is impossible, with our present limited knowledge and lack of inscriptional evidence, but we may tentatively suggest that Israel left Egypt during the reign of Ramesses II, and was already in Canaan by the date of Merneptah's Stele (1220 BC). Since the Bible is clear that a generation was spent in the desert, they could have left Egypt in 1260 BC, or a little later, if 'forty years' is used loosely. Albright prefers to put the exodus as early as 1282 BC, because of international circumstances at the time, but the exact decade is not important, and probably not recoverable, on the basis of our present knowledge alone. We can only hope that subsequent archaeological discoveries will clarify this point to satisfy our historical interest, even if nothing theological hinges on the discovery of the actual year.

THE SITE OF THE 'RED SEA'

Once again, the exact place of Israel's crossing of the Red Sea has no direct theological importance. It does, however, have historical and geographical interest and, since we believe the crossing to be a historic event, we are bound to make some attempt to locate it, even if all such attempts are necessarily tentative. Clearly the Mosaic Hebrews themselves knew well where the spot was, for numerous place-names are given (*e.g.* Ex. 14:1,2). However, it is not at all certain that the later Hebrews knew the exact location: certainly there is no fixed tradition.

First, then, the name 'Red Sea' is misleading (coming as it does from the Greek translation of the Old Testament) if we mean by that the modern 'Red Sea', *i.e.* the main body of water between Arabia and Africa. We are probably not even to think of the narrower Gulf of Suez. The Hebrew *yām sûp* is better translated 'Sea of Reeds' (or even 'papyrus marsh', with Hyatt). It may be a definite place-name belonging to one particular spot, or it may simply be the generic term for any shallow area of water overgrown with reeds, rather as we might say 'mangrove swamp' today. In the latter case, an exact identification is impossible. This broad general description would fit many points north of the Gulf of Suez, between the Gulf and the Mediterranean coast, where there is a chain of shallow marshy lagoons, roughly along the line of the present Suez Canal. While these lagoons may well have varied a little in extent and area over the centuries, there is no evidence that the coastline at Suez itself has altered significantly in historic times. We may reject the view that a long-lost marshy northern extension of the Gulf itself was intended. Therefore the options in Mosaic days were much the same as those today, and we may consider the problem in terms of the modern geography of the region.

As in the case of the Galatians, scholars are divided between a 'Northern' and a 'Southern' theory. Those who hold to the 'Northern' theory believe that Israel crossed the southern end of Lake Menzaleh (a lagoon bordering on the Mediterranean) or possibly a marshy extension of the lake. This is certainly possible on the biblical evidence. A more extreme form of the

'Northern' view is that Israel marched along the narrow tongue of land further to the east, a sandbank separating Lake Sirbonis (another brackish lagoon) from the Mediterranean. At some point, on this view, they must have cut south-east across the corner of the lagoon: but this does not seem as likely as the first suggestion. By contrast, the 'Southern' theory (really a 'Central' theory) would place the crossing twenty miles further south, perhaps at the southern end of Lake Balah or the northern end of Lake Timsah, or perhaps marshy extensions of either lake that may have existed in early days. It is unlikely, from Israel's subsequent itinerary, that the crossing was as far south as the Bitter Lakes, and almost impossible, for the same reason, that it was at Suez itself, although both wind and tide (prominent in the story) would presumably have been more potent factors at the head of the gulf. The biblical evidence in itself is not decisive, because we can no longer identify with certainty the place-names given, meaningful though they were to the author. But God's deliberate refusal to lead Israel 'by way of the land of the Philistines' (Ex. 13:17) would seem to rule out the Lake Sirbonis route altogether, and might tell against the Lake Menzaleh route too. Both of these are too close to the usual military highway, to which Exodus is presumably referring. All depends on the exact location of the towns Pi-hahiroth, Migdol and Baal-zephon (Ex. 14:2) and, in spite of the apparent certainty of Bible Atlases, their sites are not known today. Also, much depends on the meaning of the phrase 'entangled in the land' (Ex. 14:3). Does pharaoh simply mean by these words that Israel is caught between the sea and his army, with no way out? Were they nevertheless moving in the right direction to make an escape from Egypt? Or does he mean (as some commentators hold) that the Israelites are hopelessly lost, and have been moving in quite the wrong direction? The importance of this question is that, if Israel is hopelessly lost, so are we. We cannot even begin to guess their probable route, if they were in point of fact not moving towards their stated geographical goal. However we shall assume here that they were not lost (Moses knew the wilderness) so much as trapped between the chariots and the sea.

There is another consideration, which may enter into the argument. If Mount Sinai was actually located near Kadesh-barnea, in the north of the peninsula (say, at Ğebel Halal), then a northerly crossing would certainly seem preferable, for Israel could thus reach its goal in 'three days' journey' (Ex. 3:18). However, such a view of the location of Sinai would make nonsense of the biblical list of 'stages' along the route (*e.g.* Ex. 15:22,23; 16:1). A southern location for Sinai, whether east or west of the Gulf of Aqaba, seems essential. In any case, even Gebel Halal could be reached from a 'Central' crossing, although perhaps not so easily or obviously as from the Lake Sirbonis route. Tides of any kind would of course be impossible if we follow the 'Central' theory. They would be significant, if Suez had been a conceivable site, but insignificant in either of the northern lagoons. But it is not at all certain that verses like Exodus 14:27 refer to sea tides at all. The wording may refer only to the water of the lagoon once more filling its old bed. All that the account specifically mentions is YHWH's use of 'a strong east wind' (Ex. 14:21) to dry up the lagoon-bed, and this would be applicable to any of the areas. While certainty is impossible, the balance of evidence would therefore tend to place the crossing somewhere towards the centre of the Isthmus.

EXCURSUS 3

THE SOURCES OF EXODUS

This is not the place to enter into a lengthy discussion on the history of modern Pentateuchal criticism, whether it postulates documentary sources (like the old J, E, D and P), or streams of oral tradition, or a combination of both. There is the less need, in that the subject is handled in general terms in all the standard Old Testament introductions (see Harrison, for instance) and treated at length in a previous Tyndale Commentary (*Genesis*, by Derek Kidner). Those interested are therefore referred to these books. Nevertheless a few remarks on basic principles and lines of approach may help us to clear our minds, so that we do not make the mistake of claiming more of Exodus than the book does for itself. More will be found in the Commentary.

No-one seriously doubts today that Moses could, and doubtless did, write in a variety of languages; such languages would be known to any Hebrew with an Egyptian court education. There is, however, no need to assume that he personally wrote down the whole book of Exodus, the less so as the book itself does not claim this. Possibly it is best to understand a combination of written Mosaic sources and oral Mosaic material, later combined into the book which we know as Exodus. There is no reference, for example, to contemporary written records in the opening chapters of the book, where Moses is consistently described in the third person (contrast, for example, the first-person narrative of Deuteronomy). The stories of the plagues of Egypt, for instance, may well have been preserved and told orally long before reduction to writing. Indeed, some such processs of oral narrative may be implied by the 'children's question' of Exodus 12:26, and the answer there given, although the narrative may simply be part of the educational process, not precluding the existence of written material alongside. But if the account of the historical background of the passover festival was preserved orally, so perhaps was what we may call the 'ritual' of the festival itself. As this was priestly material, we can be sure that it was preserved exactly (as distinct from an anecdote, where the wording might reasonably vary within limits), so that, as far as the fixity of the tradition went, it would matter little whether it were a written document or an oral source. It is noteworthy that the stress throughout this section is 'Moses said' (Ex. 11:4) .or 'YHWH said' (Ex. 12:1): the emphasis is thus on the spoken, not on the written word. Even where the concept of the 'written word' occurs, it is only to record the previously spoken word. Some will feel that specific oracles of YHWH (*e.g.* Ex. 3:6ff.) must have had from the first a fixity of form greater than that of the context in which they occur, and that such fixity demanded as corollary a written record from the start. This may be so, though we have no direct evidence for this in the actual text of Exodus itself. Certainly, as far as we can judge, in later prophets the actual 'word' of YHWH had a textual stability far greater than the more fluid context of biographical narrative in which it occurs. The oracle was usually in verse, while the narrative was in prose, more susceptible to change: this factor may also have entered into the formation of Exodus. Some will feel that songs, such as that of Exodus 15, must have been also recorded in writing from early days. This too may well be:

certainly books such as 'Jashar' (Jos. 10:12,13) and 'the Wars of YHWH' (Nu. 21:14-18) seem to have been written collections of such sacred songs, antedating our present Pentateuch. But a poem can keep a fixed form in oral tradition much more readily than prose, so that mere fixity of form does not in itself prove the writing of a poem. Certainly one piece of poetry recorded as being written down in Mosaic days was the curse upon Amalek (see Ex. 17:14-16). It is unlikely, to judge from the context, that the whole story of the defeat of Amalek is intended. The reference to 'writing' here seems restricted to the actual oracle of God contained in the poetic utterance of Moses, as in the case of any other prophet. No doubt the story of the battle would also be remembered and recounted as the setting of this 'Saying'.

The first reference in Exodus to contemporaneous writing-down of Mosaic material on an extended scale is in connection with the 'ten words'. The account of their 'writing' is actually in Exodus 24:12, but it clearly refers back to the commands of Exodus 20. The 'words' are of course envisaged as spoken words in the first place, and then recorded in writing for permanence, and as a perpetual witness or 'testimony' to Israel (Ex. 25:16). There are of course parallels in the history of the time for the simultaneous preservation of material in oral and written forms, especially treaties. The verbal variations between the form of the 'ten words' as found in Exodus 20:1-17 and Deuteronomy 5:6-21 suggest, however, that the original written form of the commandments may have been brief, with none of the present amplifications (usually introduced by 'for' or 'that'). Doubtless these explanations too were traditional, preserved orally at first, then written down. Nevertheless, it would be foolish to assume that nothing existed in writing before the ten commandments. For instance, the covenant seems to have been made on the basis of something more than the mere 'ten words': Moses is said to have told the people 'all the words of YHWH and all the ordinances' (Ex. 24:3). 'Words' here must surely refer to the ten commandments: 'ordinances' is usually held to cover at least the material of the so-called 'book of the covenant' (Ex. 21–23). We are next told that Moses 'wrote all the words of YHWH' (Ex. 24₄) and that he 'took the book of the covenant, and read it', (Ex. 24:7). So, whatever the matter contained in the 'book of the covenant' was, it certainly existed in writing. It may well have comprised far more than our present Exodus 21–23; for while the material there is certainly Bronze Age (therefore covering the time of Moses), it is not a complete law code in itself. It reads more like a summary of a law code, or typical samples of a wider law, and that is perhaps what it was intended to be. It has often been remarked, for instance, that Deuteronomy, in its legislation, fills up 'gaps' in this Exodus covenant 'code', adding contingencies and cases that are omitted in the 'code' itself. Another possible 'supplement' to the book of the covenant is the so-called 'ritual decalogue' of Exodus 34, where the covenant is renewed.

This exhausts the references to contemporaneous writing of Mosaic material, as recorded in Exodus. Elsewhere in the Pentateuch, Numbers 33:2 refers to the writing-down by Moses of the various stages of the journey in the desert: the laconic statistical lists certainly sound like early documents (Nu. 33:3–27). Deuteronomy 31:22 also mentions Moses as writing down a song, while Deuteronomy 31:9 refers to him writing down 'this law'; verse 24 adds 'to the very end'. Some would press this last phrase, as involving a claim that Moses at that time wrote out the whole of the law later bearing his name. This interpretation does not seem obvious, although the phrase is clearly a reference to the recording of some law in writing at the time. Deuteronomy 27:1–8 enjoins the writing of 'all the words of this law' on the wet plaster to be daubed on the altar stones at the new central sanctuary in Canaan. (See Jos. 8:32 for the fulfilment of this command: was it the common custom later at all Israelite sanctuaries?) This command could hardly refer to the whole law of Moses because of its length. It could however cover the 'ten words' and a 'covenant code', perhaps in a shorter rather than longer form: so much could easily be scratched on the wet plaster of a fairly large altar.

Nevertheless, this evidence is well outside Exodus. In the book of Exodus itself, references to written material seem restricted to the curse on Amalek; the 'ten words'; some from of the 'covenant code'; plus various divine oracles and sacred poems. We should perhaps add here, as part of the covenant code, the so-called 'ritual decalogue' of Exodus 34 (better seen as a list of sacred festivals.) As the book now stands, this passage reads superficially like fresh terms on which the covenant was renewed (Ex. 34:27). However, in view of

Exodus 34:1 and its insistence on the wording of the tablets being the same as previously, we should certainly see the covenant as being renewed upon the old basis of the 'ten words' and some form of the 'book of the covenant'. In that case, we should consider the so-called 'ritual decalogue' as simply another section of the 'book of the covenant' of Exodus 21–23. This would also explain the apparent ambiguity in Exodus 34:27,28 as to the actual terms of the renewed covenant. So much, then, for the known written sources of Exodus.

What are we to make of the rest of the book of Exodus? It is reasonable to suppose that the material was preserved orally, as doubtless the sayings and doing of Jesus were preserved, before our written Gospels came into existence. Oral preservation would see most likely in the case of racy anecdotal portions, like the story of the plagues, for instance (Ex. 7–11). The loving repetition of the details of the construction of the sacred Tent, which appear both in chapters 25–31 and in chapters 35–40, also suggest an oral Mosaic tradition rather than a written document. True, similar verbal repetition occurs frequently in the Ras Shamra epic poems: but such poems were probably transmitted orally long before they were written, and the contention here is that much of Exodus is in the same category. Such oral tradition was perhaps preserved by Levites in the various local sanctuaries of Israel, before the days of the one Temple at Jerusalem, and presumably told and retold at festivals by the local priests. This may well have led to slight verbal differences, such as we can see in the Gospels, without affecting the general reliability of the whole. There may even have been complementary circles of tradition, as one part of the Mosaic story was recounted in one centre and one part in another. No doubt every centre would cling to the parts already existing in writing, and to the central outline of the story of redemption, covenant-making and law-giving, for these are the 'bones' of the narrative. If any 'J' or 'E' ever existed separately (to use two symbols of Pentateuchal sources familiar to students of source-criticism), we should have to think of them in terms of this type of local formulations of essentially the same Mosaic tradition. If any 'G' ever existed (to use the symbol employed for the common basis of such sources), it would correspond to this common outline of oral tradition, plus the parts already written from the start, and so would be material held in common by all centres. We should, therefore, even if such a hypothesis were correct, only have in the law a position similar to that in the New Testament, where we have in the Gospels four independent, but similar and mutually supporting, accounts of the sayings and doings of Jesus.

At what stage all was combined or written down in our present form, we cannot say, nor is it likely that future discovery will help us to decide. It need hardly be said that, while the question is interesting, it is not of any theological significance. Some conservative scholars would put the final editorial activity in the time of Joshua; others would suggest the days of Samuel. At the other extreme, there are those who would prefer the time of Ezra; and almost every period in between has been suggested by some scholar or another. The important point to realize is that the age of the document is no guide to the age of its recorded material, which may well be far older. It is perfectly possible (if necessary) for oral tradition to preserve an account with just as much fixity as a written document, while normally one expects continual minor verbal changes in living tradition, especially in anecdote. We may quite well believe Exodus to be a genuine historic record of events of the Mosaic age, irrespective of whatever method God used to bring it into its present shape. Where certainty is impossible we do well to keep an open mind, with great reverence, being careful not to confuse traditional ideas of the composition of the books with what the Bible actually claims for itself. On the other hand, we must remember that we need not restrict the extent of written Mosaic material to those passages specifically mentioned in the Bible as being written: the bounds may well be far wider. Further, whether we accept oral or written sources or a combination of both, there are certain areas of Exodus (*e.g.* the various Mosaic experiences of God) that describe the religious experience of Moses in the same way as the Lord described His temptations in the wilderness. In either case, there was no human witness, so, if this was not a reliable tradition, it is hard to see what value it could have had as a later reconstruction. In addition, we must not forget that both the broad outline of the corpus of Mosaic law (whatever of later explanations or additions) and the institution of a 'tent' for worship in the desert, are ascribed in Exodus to Moses himself. Within these limits, we are free to seek whatever explanation best fits the evidence.

ANALYSIS

COMMENTARY

I. ISRAEL IN EGYPT (1:1 – 11:10)

a. Israel before Moses (1:1–22)

1:1–7. Background. 1. *And these are the names* . . . The initial 'and' found in the Hebrew makes clear that Exodus is not a new book, but simply the continuation of the Genesis story, and the fulfilment of the promises made to the patriarchs. But this is an appropriate place for a break: it is the last time in the Pentateuch that 'sons of Israel' is used to describe Jacob's immediate family. From now on, the phrase will be a collective patronymic, describing the whole people of God, formed like any Arabic tribal name.

2–4. There is a sonorous roll in the names of the twelve phylarchs, like the list of the twelve apostles in the New Testament. A new work of God is about to begin.

5. *Seventy* may be used as a round number, or as a sacred figure. It may however be obtained exactly by excluding Jacob's daughter Dinah from the total. The Greek text of Genesis 46 adds the five children of Ephraim and Manasseh, thus making the 'seventy-five' of Acts 7:14.[1] The theological point is the difference between the small number who entered Egypt and the large numbers who left.

7. The Hebrew deliberately repeats three verbs used in Genesis 1:21,22 which may be translated 'were fruitful . . . swarmed . . . became numerous'. This increase was interpreted as God's promised blessing on His creation. A considerable time had passed since Joseph's death: at the very shortest reckoning, Moses was the fourth generation after Levi (Nu. 26:58) and he may have been many hundred years later (Ex. 12:40). *The land was filled* is either the land of Goshen (probably the Wadi Tumilat, stretching from the Nile to the line of the present Suez Canal) or else, by a natural exaggeration, the whole territory of Egypt. This last interpretation, although statistically incorrect, expresses well the feelings of the native Egyptians, perhaps outnumbered in some parts by the unwelcome immigrants.

---

[1] One Hebrew manuscript from Qumran does contain the reading '75': see Cross, p. 137, for details.

1:8–14. Pharaoh's labour camps. 8. *A new king* need not necessarily mean the next pharaoh. Indeed, if Israel's stay in Egypt was a matter of centuries (Ex. 12:40), then it may have been a new dynasty. The XVIIth Dynasty had been Hyksos (Semitic and foreign); the XVIIIth was a native dynasty (1570–1310) and at once expelled the foreign overlords. On independent grounds, it is usually considered nowadays that the exodus took place in the early years of the XIXth Dynasty (1310–1200), *i.e.* the 13th century BC. In either case, this is the simple language of popular folk history, expressing a truth, but not concerned with exact dates.

10, 11. Forced labour was an old principle in highly-centralized Egypt, as in all the ancient world: neither pyramids nor Nile canals would have been possible without it. *Taskmasters* is a technical term, and would describe the hated Egyptian officials, under whom there were minor Israelite officials (Ex. 5:14); *mas* (translated 'task') was a technical term in Israel for 'forced labour' (usually Canaanite and therefore foreign, 1 Ki. 9:21). How such taskmasters were hated can be seen from the stoning of Adoram later (1 Ki. 12:18). *Pithom and Raamses.* This is a vivid touch of great value for dating the event, since the building of both cities is associated with Ramesses II (*c.* 1290–1225 BC), probably in connection with his Asiatic campaigns. Pithom is probably Tell er-Retabe ('Broomhill') in the Wadi Tumilat. Raamses may be modern Qantîr ('Bridge'), on the eastern arm of the Nile delta, but the exact location of both cities is disputed.

12. *The more they multiplied and ... spread abroad.* Such attempts to control the growth of the people of God are vain. Again, two Genesis verbs (Gn. 1:22 and 30:30) are used to describe their triumphant growth. But it was a life of bitter, unrelieved drudgery (14) and the rude animal health of this biologically superior people 'disgusted' the sophisticated Egyptians (*cf.* NEB). Others prefer the translation 'sick with worry', comparing Genesis 27:46.

1:15–22. Pharaoh's second plan: genocide. 15. *The Hebrew midwives.* 'Hebrew' seems to be a term of wide application in the early Old Testament, referring to all the semi-settled West Semitic peoples, in a cultural not genetic sense, and usually on the lips of a foreigner (as in verse 22). Here the term is appropriate, in the mouth of the pharaoh. In

Exodus 5:3 it is again properly used, as describing the God of Israel to Egyptian pharaoh. In the legal code 'Hebrew slave' (Ex. 21:2) has a much wider meaning than 'Israelite slave'. The word probably has a connotation something like modern 'gipsy', in a derogatory sense, combining the ideas of wandering and animal-trading. The 'Apiru, or unskilled labourers, of the Egyptian texts, and the Habiru of the Tell el-Amarna tablets are probably the same cultural group.[1] *Shiphrah* and *Puah* are two good Semitic names, of an archaic type (compare Gideon's servant Purah in Jdg. 7:10), meaning something like 'beauty' and 'splendour' respectively. For the first, compare the form Sapphira (Acts 5:1). Like the names Pithom and Raamses, these detailed memories assure us that we are dealing with genuine historical tradition. But why only two midwives? Either these were the only two, or they were the only two who disobeyed, or they were the only two whose names were remembered. The first alternative would, however, mean that the total number of Israelites was only a few thousand at most. Perhaps the third suggestion is the best, most congenial to folk history and to Semitic languages. In Hebrew 'the midwives' means 'those particularized by the following circumstances' (see Ex. 2:1).

16. *The birthstool*: literally 'the two stones' upon which the Israelite woman crouched while giving birth: there are other Semitic parallels. A less likely suggestion is that it is a reference to the distinguishing organs of the male children, who were alone to be killed.

19. *They are vigorous and are delivered before the midwife comes to them.* We are not told whether the midwives were lying, or whether the quick delivery of 'Hebrew' babies was a biological fact. Arabian parallels are quoted by Driver, but Rachel certainly had a hard delivery (Gn. 35:16). Even if they lied, it is not for their deceit that they are commended, but for their refusal to take infant lives, God's gift. Their reverence for life sprang from reverence for God, the life-giver (Ex. 20:12,13), and for this they were rewarded with families. The relevance of this to modern controversy about abortion should be carefully pondered.

22. The Hebrew for *river* (AV, RV) here is a loanword from Egyptian, and means '*the* river' *par excellence*, that is, *the Nile*

---

[1] For some of the technical literature dealing with the relationship between these groups, see Hyatt.

(RSV, NEB). (Other possible loan-words from Egyptian are 'reed' and 'frog'; and numerous Egyptian proper names occur, in the tribe of Levi especially.) To execute by drowning was an obvious method in a country such as Egypt and Babylonia, just as death by stoning was obvious in rocky Israel (Jos. 7:25). Whether Israel in general obeyed pharaoh's edict, we do not know: certainly the parents of Moses braved pharaoh's anger (Heb. 11:23). *Every daughter*. These presumably would become slave wives, and so could be absorbed by the Egyptians in a generation. The whole vain attempt to wipe out the people of God finds its parallel in the New Testament attempt by Herod to destroy a generation of babies at Bethlehem (Mt. 2:16). But, as in the New Testament, God's chosen agent is protected: neither pharaoh nor Herod can stand in the way of God's plan. Jewish expositors have seen parallels to pharaoh's action in the attempted genocide of Israel by Hitler and others: Christian expositors have sought such parallels in the bitter persecutions suffered by the church throughout her history.

b. Early life of Moses (2:1–25)

2:1–10. Birth and adoption. 1. *The house of Levi.* Amram (whose name is given in 6:20) was grandson of Levi, if the genealogies are complete, so that 'house' is quite literal, meaning 'family'. Levi had no priestly associations in the early days, as can be seen from Genesis 49:5–7 where, with Simeon, he comes under his father's curse for a bloodthirsty attack on Shechem (Gn. 34). The curse will be fulfilled: but in the case of Levi it will be turned into blessing, for Levi will be 'scattered' as the priestly tribe (Nu. 35:7,8). In view of the meaning of the root *lawah* 'to adhere', and the use of *lawi* in southern Arabic to mean 'a priest', some have suggested that the name Levi denoted an occupation, not a tribe. The Bible, however, while quite conscious of this meaning of the name, associates it not with priestly status, but with circumstances of birth (Gn. 29:34). For the choice of Levi as the priestly tribe, in reward for faithfulness, see Exodus 32. *A daughter of Levi.* The Hebrew text should probably be translated *the daughter*, as in Numbers 26:59. If Jochebed was Kohath's sister, then she would be literally 'the daughter of Levi' (6:20). However it is idiomatic in Hebrew to use the definite article to describe her as the particular descendant of Levi about whom the following anecdote will be told.

2. *Bore a son.* The story does not say that Moses was her first-born son. His sister, obviously several years older, appears in verse 4, and Aaron is three years older than Moses (Ex. 7:7). It is quite unnecessary to assume that they were Amram's children by another wife, although such plural marriages were common. Miriam is, however, usually described as 'Aaron's sister' (Ex. 15:20), never as Moses' sister: this has been used to support the above theory. But Old Testament narrative as a rule introduces facts only when relevant to the story: we cannot argue from silence.

3. *She could hide him no longer.* A healthy child cries too loudly to be hidden at three months old. His cries may later have attracted the attention of pharaoh's daughter (5). *A basket made of bulrushes.* The Hebrew would be better translated by 'papyrus basket'; the word is used elsewhere only of Noah's ark (Gn. 6) and may possibly be connected with Egyptian *tebet*, 'chest'. Any market in Asia is loaded with baskets of this sort, holding everything from pigs to fruit. It was coated with 'bitumen' (Gn. 11:3; 14:10) to make it watertight, and possibly to provide extra insulation against the hot sun. Isaiah 18:2 refers to papyrus skiffs as plying on the Nile, so that the 'basket' was a miniature Nile boat. *And placed it among the reeds.* These would be in shallow water, where the current could not carry the basket away, with less danger of crocodiles than on an open sandbank or beach. There would also be some protection from the heat of the sun, in the reeds. The *sûp*, 'reeds', whatever water plant it was, gave its name to the 'Reed Sea' or 'Reed Marsh' of 13:18. The writer remembers seeing a very thick growth of reeds (though not of any great height) roughly where the Sweet Water Canal joined the Suez Canal.

Jochebed's act, like Abram's claim to be the brother of Sarai in Genesis 12, is just within the law. She had indeed thrown her son into the river as ordered, but in a wicker basket. Some scholars have seen the story as parabolic or ideal, however, on the grounds of similar stories told of Sargon of Accad and others. But the existence of so many stories only shows that this was a favourite way of abandoning babies in the ancient world. It was in fact the ancient equivalent of leaving them on the steps of a hospital or orphanage today. The shallows of a river near any Asian village would be the ideal place today to expose a baby and ensure its being found by the women who came to wash clothes or prepare food. Discovery would be certain; there was a good wicker basket which could be salvaged, clearly visible.

5. *The daughter of Pharaoh.* The Apocrypha calls her Tharmuth (Jubilees 47:5); see Hyatt (p. 64) for 'Merris' and 'Bithiah' as other names for her. It is hard to see why the names should be invented, so that we may well have a fragment of reliable extra-biblical tradition here. Compare Jannes and Jambres, as the names of the magicians who opposed Moses (2 Tim. 3:8). If the pharaoh in question was Ramesses II, he had close on sixty daughters. He also had numerous 'hunting-lodges' scattered over the delta area, where duck and other game were plentiful, so there is no need to assume that Moses' parents lived near the royal capital Zoan.

6. *She took pity on him.* No eastern mother could bring herself to abandon a sturdy boy-baby like this. We may suspect that a girl-baby might not have fared so well, but they did not come under the pharaoh's decree of execution. In all this, God's providence was at work.

9. *Your wages.* It probably appealed to the robust Israelite sense of humour that Jochebed was 'spoiling the Egyptians' by receiving pay for nursing her own son: but there was also a deeper purpose in it. No doubt it was in these early years that Moses learnt of the 'God of the fathers' (Ex. 3:15) and realized that the Hebrews were his fellow countrymen (Ex. 2:11). Psychologists rightly stress the importance of impressions received during the earliest years. Without this ancestral background, God's later revelation to Moses would have been rootless, and the Sinaitic Covenant could not have been seen as a sequel to, and consequence of, the Abrahamic Covenant (Ex. 3:6).

10. *Moses, mōšeh,* would be the active participle of the Hebrew verb *māšâ,* 'pulling out'. A different vocalization could give the passive meaning 'pulled out', but there is no need to press this. As often in the Old Testament, this is not intended as a piece of exact philology, but a pun, based on assonance. Possibly pharaoh's daughter chose the Egyptian name which appears as the second half of Thuthmose, Ahmose, and many other similar forms. Whether the name 'Moses' was itself considered as a shortening of some such longer form, it is impossible to say, nor indeed is it important to know. The Bible also seems to mean not only that the name Moses is capable of supporting a pun of this sort (which to the Hebrew was rich in spiritual meaning), but that it was deliberately chosen because of this capacity. There is nothing impossible here: West Semitic dialects were widely understood, and even spoken, in the delta area. An Egyptian mistress might well understand and use the tongue of her domestic servants to give orders, like many a 'memsahib' in later days.

2:11-15. The rejection and flight of Moses. 11. *Grown up.* Acts 7:23 says he was forty years old at the time. Exodus merely says that he was eighty years old when he spoke to pharaoh (Ex. 7:7) and that he had spent many days in Midian (Ex. 2:23). It is possible that forty years is symbolic for a generation, which the Western world usually reckons at thirty years. When Acts 7:22 says that he had been 'instructed in all the wisdom of the Egyptians', this is doubtless correct, if he was reared with other princelings. All this was the other side of God's preparation. With the possible exceptions of Solomon, Daniel and Nehemiah, no Old Testament character had such a training (Dn. 1:4). Study of law would probably have been one aspect of any such education. Hammurabi's Code, for instance, was widely studied and annotated by Egyptian scribes, so that Moses may have been well acquainted with it.

And looked on their burdens. This phrase means more than 'to see'. It means 'to see with emotion', either satisfaction (Gn. 9:16) or, as here, with distress (Gn. 21:16). Moses is one who shares God's heart. God too has seen what the Egyptians are doing to the Israelites, and He will come to deliver (Ex. 3:7,8). It was not Moses' impulse to save Israel that was wrong, but the action that he took. *Beating*, 'killed' (12) and 'strike' (13) are all various forms of the same Hebrew verb. This gives the narrative a connectedness impossible to reproduce in English. It also gives the feeling of 'eye for eye, tooth for tooth' (Ex. 21:24). Perhaps the Egyptian was one of the hated taskmasters; and if *Hebrew* has the wider meaning suggested above, then *one of his people* is a necessary narrowing down, to mean an actual Israelite.

12. *Hid him in the sand.* This is a touch of local colour. There was no sand in most of Israel's rocky hills, and a body was not so easy to hide as in Egypt.

13. *The man who was in the wrong* (NEB). This is a lawcourt term. Compare the description of pharaoh himself as 'in the wrong' (Ex. 9:27) and of God as 'in the right'. It is true psychological understanding that makes the guilty party reject Moses, in terms that pharaoh himself might have used later (Ex. 5:2). No doubt the other Hebrew, the innocent party, accepted Moses gladly, as the publicans and sinners welcomed Christ later (Mt. 9:10).

15. *The land of Midian.* The location is quite uncertain, but clearly it was somewhere beyond the Egyptian frontierposts, and to the east. Somewhere in the Sinai peninsula, or the Arabah (the area south of the Dead Sea), or that part of Arabia east of the gulf of Aqaba, would suit. In Ptolemy's day the land of 'Modiana' was certainly to the east of the gulf. If, as in Genesis 37:25, the Midianites travelled widely, whether for trade or for pastoral reasons (Ex. 3:1) or for war (Jdg. 6:1), all these areas could be covered. As the later Israelites were bitter foes of the Midianites, it is unthinkable that the tradition of the Midianite sojourn of Moses could be invented. It is possible that 'Ishmaelites' (Gn. 37:25) and 'Kenites' (Jdg. 4:11) were clan names used within Midian. Alternatively, Judges 8:24 might possibly support the view that 'Ishmaelite' was a wider term than 'Midianite': but probably the terms are used loosely. *By a well.* Wherever there was a well in the desert, there would be a settlement: and for those who were there, it was always '*the* well'. The village well was a natural place in which to meet the stranger. Similar interviews are recorded of Jacob (Gn. 29:10) and Christ (Jn. 4:6,7); in each case help, whether material or spiritual, is given to the helpless, a picture of what God will do.

2:16–22. Moses in Midian. 16. *The priest of Midian.* Some scholars have seen support in this for the so-called 'Kenite hypothesis', which assumes that Mosaic religion stems from that of Midian, and in particular from Moses' father-in-law. The Midianites by tradition belonged to the same Abrahamic stock as Israel (Gn. 17:20) and it is most unlikely that Moses would have learnt from them anything that he did not know already of the 'common law' of the western Semites. Furthermore the biblical account is quite clear, both that the new revelation was made to Moses at 'God's Mountain' (Ex. 3:1) and that his father-in-law only subsequently accepted it, when validated by events (Ex. 18:11). *Seven daughters.* Again, the ideal or sacred number: but it may well be used here in a literal sense. Arab women (never men) still draw water in Israel and Jordan, while the flocks are usually attended by boys and girls.

18. *Reuel*: perhaps meaning 'friend of God' or 'shepherd of God', the latter very appropriate in a pastoral society. A less likely meaning would be 'God is a shepherd/friend'. Just as there is doubt as to the location of Midian and even Sinai itself, so there is doubt as to the exact name of Moses' father-in-law. This name Reuel is quite a possible form, and in Genesis 36:4 it actually appears as an Edomite name. In Exodus 3:1 the same man is called Jethro, the nominative form of a not uncommon South Arabic name. In Numbers 10:29 a Hobab appears, the son of Reuel of Midian: it is not certain from the text which of the two is father-in-law to Moses.[1] Hobab is again a good Semitic name, and Judges 4:11 certainly describes Moses' father-in-law as Hobab. All this means either that several variant traditions have survived as to the identity of Moses' father-in-law, or that he had at least two names. There is of course no problem in supposing him to have two (or more) names, since double names are known from South Arabic sources. In such cases the biblical editor sometimes specifies both names together, as in 'Jerubbaal (that is, Gideon)' (Jdg. 7:1): but sometimes both are used independently within a few verses (Jdg. 8:29f.). The matter is of no theological significance and it is best to assume that the name meant so little to Israel that such uncertainty was possible. Tradition however is unanimous that Moses married the daughter of a Semitic priest of the Eastern desert, and lived there for a considerable period.

21. *Zipporah*. We might translate as 'warbler' or, less kindly, 'twitterer'; it is the name of a small bird. Compare the equally simple names of Rachel, 'ewe' and Leah, 'heifer' (Gn. 29).

22. *Gershom*. This name contains a pun by assonance, for it is translated as though it were the Hebrew *gēr šām*, 'a resident alien there'. Philologically, it is probably an odd noun meaning 'expulsion', from the verb *gāraš*; the general sense is thus much the same. As often in the Old Testament, the remark is rather a commentary on the meaning of the name rather

[1] On the whole question, see Hyatt, who discusses the various possibilities at length: *ḥōṭēn* is a general word for 'relation by marriage', including 'brother-in-law'.

than an exact translation (*cf.* Ex. 2:10). See Hyatt for the suggestion that he is the ancestor of the Levitical clan of 'Gershon' (Nu. 3:21–26), with change of final consonant.

2:23–25. The frame of reference. 23. *The king of Egypt died.* It is uncertain which king of Egypt died; perhaps Seti I, or even Ramesses II, in which case *many days* would refer to his long reign. The passage stresses the length of Moses' stay in Midian, and also that it was now safe for him to return to Egypt (*cf.* Ex. 4:19).

24. *God remembered his covenant with Abraham.* Even before the vision of the burning bush, the narrator sets the deliverance from Egypt squarely in the context of the patriarchal promise. To Israel of old, the whole course of the history of salvation could be summed up as being 'promise and fulfilment': God promises, God remembers, God acts in salvation.

c. Meeting with God (3:1 – 4:31)

3:1–6. The vision of God. 1. Moses *was keeping* the flock. The Hebrew suggests that this was his habitual occupation. There is no hint in the Bible that Midian was a copper-mining group, or that the Kenites were travelling blacksmiths, although both these views are favourites with modern scholars, and tempting archaeologically. There were certainly copper-mines in the Arabah south of the Dead Sea, and Israel in the wilderness is credited with making numerous copper objects (Ex. 35ff.), but further than this biblical tradition does not go.

The west side of the wilderness: Hebrew *'aḥar*, 'back, behind'. This must be 'west' from the Midianite point of view, and therefore it may be a Midianite term. As usual in Semitic thought, one faces east when giving compass directions; 'behind' is therefore 'west'. *Horeb, the mountain of God*: or possibly 'Horeb, the great mountain', using a common Semitic idiom to describe great size or force (*cf.* Arabic usage). Those who use the conventional critical symbols to describe the presumed source of the Pentateuch claim that 'Horeb' is found in the Elohistic and Deuteronomistic material, while 'Sinai' is the name used in Yahwistic and Priestly material. We do not know why the two names are used, seemingly interchangeably. It has been suggested that Horeb is a part of Sinai, but this is pure guess-work. Horeb is demonstrably Semitic, probably meaning 'desert' or 'desolation'. It is conceivable that it was the Semitic name for the non-Semitic place-name Sinai. Sinai must be an old name, and is probably connected etymologically with the desert of Sin nearby. It is doubtful etymology, however, to link the name either with *sᵉneh* (Heb. 'thornbush'), or *Sin*, the Accadian moon god. More serious, apart from the question of its name, is the fact that we do not know where 'God's mountain' (the popular term, as used in this verse) was. Was it within the Sinai Peninsula? If so, was it in the south (the traditional area) or in the north east among the mountains of Seir, overlooking the oasis of Kadesh Barnea, where Israel made her tribal centre for so long? Or was it in the mountains of Arabia, to the north east of the Gulf of Aqaba? The general geographic details in the Bible seem to point to the southern area: and the traditional site of Ğebel Mûsa, 'Moses' mountain' (7,467 feet), has much to commend it, though others will prefer the higher peaks nearby. It is noteworthy that, as in the exile in Babylon, this most striking event of Israel's faith took place on foreign soil (*cf.* Abram's call) and that later Israel seems neither to have known, nor cared, exactly where it was. Neither is there any suggestion of later pilgrimage to it, with the possible exception of the journey of Elijah (1 Ki. 19). Israel, however, knew that 'God's mountain' lay somewhere to the south of Canaan. This is clear from the descriptions of God as coming to the help of His people from Paran or Seir or other vaguely-defined mountains to the south (Dt. 33:2). This is in marked contrast to the Canaanite view, by which the gods lived on a mountain in the far north.

There is no evidence in biblical thought that the Israelites even considered that God lived at Sinai. Rather Sinai was the place at which He had shown Himself to Moses (Ex. 3:2) and upon which He would later give the law to His people (Ex. 3:12). Sinai could therefore be said, in modern terminology, not so much to *be* God's mountain as to *become* God's mountain, because of what He did and said there: this is a dynamic not a static concept. God, in early days, might be worshipped at any place where He had appeared (Ex. 20:24), and Sinai is yet another example of this. True, there are numerous later Nabataean inscriptions in the area of Sinai, indicating that at least subsequently it was considered a holy mountain. On these grounds it has been claimed that it may already have been a holy place to the Midianites. This we can neither prove nor disprove, in view of the total lack of evidence. Moses at least did not come to the mountain with any religious intention, according to the text, but purely to pasture his flock.

2. *The angel of the Lord*: literally 'messenger of YHWH'.[1] As verse 4 speaks of God Himself calling to Moses out of the bush, 'angel' here is probably only a reverential synonym for God's own presence, as in the patriarchal stories (Gn. 18:1; 19:1). Driver has some wise comments on this verse, quoting Davidson. Advanced angelology does not occur until the apocalyptic books of the Old Testament (Ezekiel, Daniel, Zechariah). Throughout the whole of the earlier period, it would be better to translate the word 'angel' as 'messenger' and leave it to the context to decide whether this emissary is human, superhuman, or simply a reverential way of referring to God Himself, as apparently here. *In a flame of fire.* There may be a deliberate reminiscence of the Genesis story, where the angel beings that guard the tree of life have flaming swords (Gn. 3:24). Fire is a symbol of God's presence when He descends on Sinai too (Ex. 19:18), as often in the Bible. Exodus 13:21 speaks of God's guiding and protecting presence as a 'pillar of fire'. Perhaps the basis of this symbolism lies in the purificatory, as well as the destructive, properties of fire (Dt. 4:24); the metal refiner was a familiar sight in the ancient world (Mal. 3:2). Normally, however, fire seems to speak of God's holiness and, in particular, His anger in relation to sin (Ex. 19:18; 32:10).

A bush. This word appears also in Deuteronomy 33:16, which clearly derives from this passage. 'Who dwells in the bush' ought not therefore to be seen as independent belief that God lived in that bush or its immediately surrounding area, but simply as a reference to God's local Self-manifestation on this occasion. What exactly did Moses see? Was it a supernatural vision (as in the case of some prophets, *e.g.* Ezk. 1) or was it an actual physical phenomenon? If the latter, did he see a bramble bush literally blazing in the desert; or the shrub called 'burning bush', in brilliant flower; or the sunset light falling full on a thorn bush and producing the effect of flames? All have been suggested in turn. It does not matter: whatever it was, God used Moses' initial curiosity to attract

---

[1] See commentary on 3:15, below.

him to the place. The true revelation, however, was not the burning thorn bush, but God's word that came to Moses there.

4. *God called to him.* This is better than 'God called him'. The whole concept of Christian calling derives from the belief that God has communicated with us personally, and has called us by name. If we forget this, the doctrine of election can become unrelated to our obedience, and so impersonal, abstract and forbidding.

5. *Do not come near.* This should be translated 'stop coming near, as you are doing' (*cf.* Jn. 20:17). God does not ultimately forbid men to approach Him: but Moses is not yet ready, for he does not recognize the presence or nature of God. There will be times later when Moses will 'come near', to intercede for others (Ex. 32:30), and his greatest prayer will be to have this vision of God. *Take off your sandals.* This is still one of the Asian signs of worship. There are two possible origins of this mark of reverence. First, it may be the sign of acceptance of a servant's position, for a slave usually went barefoot (Lk. 15:22). Secondly, it may be a relic of very early days when men laid aside all covering and pretence to approach their god. Hence early Sumerian priests performed their duties naked, although the Israelite priest always wore a linen kilt, for modesty's sake (*cf.* Ex. 20:26). Bare feet, considered as a symbol, are not so appropriate for those who live in cold northern winters. *Holy ground*: made holy by the presence of God, and by the Self-revelation that He will make there. This is preferable, as stated above, to assuming that it was already a Midianite holy mountain, or even that it was a Midianite 'holy bush'. Had it been, the son-in-law of Midian's priest would surely have known all about it. 'Holy' bushes and trees are common throughout the world, from the old sacred trees of Canaan to the sacred banyans of India today, but this concept is not Israelite. Israel's concept of holiness was not only dynamic but moral: it was constituted not only by the active revelation of God, but by the nature of the One who so revealed Himself. This is the first occurrence of the word 'holy' in the Bible, and it is significant that the concept is linked with God.

6. *The God of your father.* The Samaritan text reads the plural 'fathers', referring to Abraham, Isaac and Jacob, as in the second half of the verse. This is certainly the general sense: the stress is not on Amram or even on Abraham, but on 'the

God of the fathers'.[1] This is a most important point and, if accepted, will affect exegesis of subsequent passages. Moses brings no new or unknown god to his people, but a fuller revelation of the One whom they have known. Not even Paul's words to the Athenians on the Areopagus are a fair parallel here (Acts 17:23). The only true parallel is the continuing Self-revelation made by God in later centuries, culminating in the coming of Christ. Yet in its day the Mosaic revelation, while a fulfilment of patriarchal promises, was as new and shattering to Israel as the coming of the Messiah was later to prove to be.

3:7-12. God's call and God's promise. 7. *Taskmasters*: almost 'oppressors'; *nōgēs* is an interesting Semitic word, which appears in modern form as the title for the Emperor of Ethiopia (the 'Negus').

8. *A land.* This was part of the great promise to Abraham (Gn. 13:15). God meets us initially where we are, at our recognized point of need, however shallow, and from this He leads us on to acknowledgment of needs at a deeper level. God promised a childless man a son; a landless nomad a country; an unknown man fame (Gn. 12:1-3). Nor were these unworthy promises, for, in laying hold of these, Abraham was, at a deeper level, longing for the things that only God can give to man: continuity, stability, identity, as we might put them in modern terms. *Flowing with milk and honey*: 'oozing' would be a better translation. This is a dairyman's metaphor: the drops of milk ooze from the animal's teats, so full of milk is she. This description of Canaan is a pastoralist's dream. Milk, curds, cheese and honey are not the produce of closely-settled arable country. *Cf.* Isaiah 7:22, where 'curds and honey' are the product of an area that has reverted from tilth to pasture, because of war. The phrase is a frequent and probably proverbial description in the Pentateuch of the hill country of Canaan, and is an accurate one, when Canaan is compared with the more arid country of Sinai or even with oases like Kadesh-barnea. The milk would be largely from sheep and goats. *Honey* (Heb. *dᵉḇaš*) seems always in the Bible to mean honey from bees. Honey in Arabic is *'asal*: *dibs* to the Arab is sweet grape syrup, boiled to the consistency of fruit squash,

[1] But see Hyatt for argument as to the appropriateness of the singular here, 'father'.

66

so some have suggested this as the meaning of the Hebrew here. But the grape belongs to the life of cultivation, not primitive pastoralism: hence its avoidance by the Nazirite (Nu. 6:3) and Rechabite.(Je. 35:6).Further, there is no evidence that Israel ever made such grape syrup.

The Canaanites. There follows a standard popular description of 'pre-war Canaan', not a scientific ethnography. The classic expression of the list is in Deuteronomy 7:1, where there are seven peoples mentioned, made up by the addition of the Girgashites. Since this is the sacred number of seven, it may signify the totality of peoples; but Genesis 15:19 gives the fullest list, with ten nations. Perhaps there is a reminiscence of the Egyptian way of describing their enemies in general as the 'nine bows', *i.e.* nine hostile nations. It is, however, important to realize that these 'nations' of Canaan are not mutually related to each other, as Israel's twelve tribes were. They may have shared a common cultural and religious pattern, but that is all. There is no evidence that they shared common historical traditions, in the way that Israel's tribes did: nor indeed have we evidence to show that they even lived in distinct and separate areas. *Canaanite* was the term still used long afterwards by the Phoenicians to describe themselves: it may mean 'traders'. *Hittites* probably means immigrant groups from the old Hittite empire in the north: it can hardly mean Hittites by blood (*cf.* Gn. 23). Sihon and Og, the semi-settled kings of east Jordan, are called *Amorite* (Nu. 21:21); so is the coalition of five kings in the Judaean hills (Jos. 10:5). By origin the word *amurru* means 'Westerner' and was given originally by the settled Mesopotamians to their nomadic neighbours to the west. *Perizzite* may be 'villager', perhaps used in a derogatory sense like modern 'pagan', but the suffix may be of Hurrian origin (*cf.* 'Kenizzite'). *Hivites* appear to be confused in the manuscripts with 'Horites'. If so, they would preserve the name, if not the blood, of the Hurrian conquerors of half a millennium before. The usual Egyptian name for Canaan (Khuru) seems derived from this group. The Gibeonite confederacy is described as Hivite (Jos. 9:7). *Jebusites* are the aboriginal inhabitants of Jebus or Jerusalem (also called Amorites, Jos. 10:5). It is hard to see why they should be singled out, unless it is because they remained unconquered till David's day (2 Sa. 5). The Jebusites at least cannot have been a distinct racial grouping. Ezekiel certainly regards them as a mixture of Amorite and Hittite elements (Ezk. 16:3) and this seems very likely, from their position. In Joshua's day, they form part of the southern Amorite confederacy. Normally the Canaanites are the inhabitants of the western plains and valleys, while the Amorites loosely occupy the central mountain range, and northern Transjordan.

10. *I will send you.* Davies points out that this is the apostolic commission of Moses. There is no contradiction between God's announced intention of working in person and His sending Moses: God normally works through the willing obedience of His servants, accomplishing His will. This passage may well have been in Christ's mind when He gave a similar apostolic commission to His disciples in New Testament days (Jn.20:21).

11. *Who am I?* This is not an existential question, but an expression of disbelief (*cf.* Jdg. 6:15). Moses, unlike his early days in Egypt, has learnt to distrust himself so thoroughly that he will incur God's anger (Ex. 4:14). Self-distrust is good, but only if it leads to trust in God. Otherwise it ends as spiritual paralysis, inability and unwillingness to undertake any course of action. Moses, like Elijah (1 Ki. 19), is a picture of a man who has had a 'nervous breakdown', and is now unwilling to work for God at all.

12. *I will be with you.* The phrase 'I will be' (Heb. *'ehyeh*) is almost certainly a play on YHWH, God's name, explained in verses 14 and 15. The only way to bring out the play on words in English would be to translate 'I, God, will be with you'. God answers Moses' objection as to his own inadequacy in two ways. First He promises His own presence; secondly He gives Moses a sign or proof that He is with him. After this Moses has no right to protest further. It is now no longer lack of self-reliance (which is good), but lack of faith (which is sin). *This shall be the sign for you.* In spite of various more sophisticated interpretations, the simplest explanation of the 'proof' seems best. The freed nation of ex-slaves will worship God one day at this very mountain of Sinai. The proof of the pudding will be in the eating, as we say. It will be the success of Moses' mission that will show beyond contradiction that God was indeed with him and had sent him. Such signs always follow faith. Meanwhile Moses must go forward in faith: this is typical of the whole biblical approach to signs. The great covenant and the law-giving at Sinai was thus the fulfilment of this sign (Ex. 19 onwards). This promise alone explains the

insistence of Moses to pharaoh that Israel must keep a
festival to YHWH in the desert (Ex. 5:1); only so can it be
fulfilled.

3:13–22. God tells His name. 13. *What is his name?* Some
commentators stress the use of *mâh*, 'What?' in this instance,
rather than the idiomatic *mî*, 'Who?' They regard it as a
question dealing more with God's nature than with His mere
title. We cannot assume that the Israelites were ignorant of
the titles of the God worshipped by their patriarchal ancestors,
and presumably also worshipped by them during their stay in
Egypt (but see Joshua's blunt words in Jos. 24:14). It is true
that the word translated *God* could also be translated as 'gods
of your fathers': but the singular possessive suffix in 'his name'
shows that only one God is in question. Exodus 6:3 shows that
Israel was quite aware that the patriarchs used the name El-
Shaddai (RSV 'God Almighty') for God (*cf.* the proper name
Ammi-shaddai in Numbers 1:12), along with many other titles.
So the question of the Israelites does not spring from ignorance,
nor is it a trick question framed to test Moses' knowledge of
the traditions of his own people. To ask the question, 'Under
what new title has God appeared to you?' is equivalent to
asking, 'What new revelation have you received from God?'
Normally, in patriarchal days, any new revelation of the
ancestral God will be summed up in a new title for Him
(Gn. 16:13) which will in future both record and recount a
deeper knowledge of God's saving activity. We may therefore
assume that, in asking this question, they were expecting a
new title for the patriarchal God.

14. *I am who I am* (Heb. *'ehyeh 'ăšer 'ehyeh*): possibly 'I will
be what I will be'. This pithy clause is clearly a reference to
the name YHWH. Probably 'Yahweh' is regarded as a
shortening of the whole phrase, and a running together of the
clause into one word. The clause certainly contains the
necessary vowels, and the consonants come close enough.
Indeed *'ehyeh* ('I am' or 'I will be') is given as a form of God's
name in the second half of this verse. But this is almost
certainly a Semitic punning assonance in explanation of the
name, rather than the name itself, which appears in verse 15.
'Ehyeh, for instance, is never used as part of a proper name in
the Old Testament. Davies rightly points out that since this
is the only place in the Old Testament where there is any

explanation of the meaning of the name YHWH, we ought therefore to take very seriously the association with 'being' which is clearly stated here. However Noth rightly remarks that this is not 'pure being' in a philosophical sense, but 'active being' in terms of revelation. Granted, however, the general connection with 'being', what is the exact meaning? Simplest of all, does it mean that God exists, as opposed to idols without being? Along these lines, Hyatt sees 'I am He who is' as a possible translation: he also sees Hosea 1:9 as a possible reference to this meaning (in a negative sense). Does it mean 'I am incomparable, inscrutable to human eyes' (Ex. 33:19)? This, though true, would hardly be a further revelation. Or does it mean 'I will only be understood by My own subsequent acts and words of revelation'? This would seem to fit the biblical pattern, for in all subsequent Israelite history God would be known as the One who brought Israel from Egypt (Ex. 20:2). The revelation of the name therefore is not merely a deep theological truth; it is a call to the response of faith by Moses and by Israel.

15. *The* LORD. Here the full form of the divine name is used, YHWH, usually represented as LORD (in capitals) in English versions. The pious Jew of later years was reluctant to pronounce God's name lest he incur the penalty for taking the name of YHWH in vain (Ex. 20:7). He therefore read the vowels of *'ªḏōnāy* 'my Lord', with the consonants of YHWH, so producing the hybrid 'Jehovah' in English.[1] This commentary follows one standard practice of writing God's name as YHWH, in capitals without the vowels. Readers may please themselves as to whether they pronounce it as Lord, Jehovah or Yahweh. Perhaps the easiest way to understand what the name YHWH meant to the Jews is to see what it came to mean, as their history of salvation slowly unrolled. It ultimately meant to them what the name Jesus has come to mean to Christians, a 'shorthand' for all God's dealings of grace.

16. *Elders.* This is the mention in Israel of what was a common institution in rural Semitic society. Thanks to the traditional advice of Jethro (Ex. 18:21), 'elders' were later to become an important part of Israel's judicial system. No doubt

[1] Broadly speaking, occurrence of this 'personal name' for God is thus held to belong to the J-source (not a Y-source). Passages which contain the 'general name' for God, *'ªlōhîm*, are credited to the E-source.

tribalized Midian was so ruled already. Numbers 11:16ff. contains the account of the sharing of the Spirit's gifts with this group. *I have surely visited you* (AV, RV). The meaning is *observed* (RSV), 'noted', but always with a view to action. Driver translates 'shown practical interest in'. The verb is often used in the Bible of God's saving activity towards His people. See Genesis 21:1; and Luke 1:68, where the Hebraic tinge has entered the Greek. 'Visit' gives a wrong impression in modern English, as though God paid a brief call and then departed. The same root appears in connection with the Israelite officials of 5:6.

18. *The God of the Hebrews.* The name YHWH would mean nothing to pharaoh: the 'gods of the Hebrews' (for he would probably so understand the 'plural of majesty') would be meaningful. Indeed, this very terminology occurs in treaties of the time, not of course with reference to Israel, but in the wider context of Habiru groups further north. *Met with us.* If correct, this almost suggests hostile confrontation. So pharaoh may have understood it, from his experiences of the vagaries of Egyptian gods: so Moses may have been content for him to understand it, in order to convey the necessity of the coming sacrifice. It could, however, simply mean sudden unexpected meeting (*cf.* Ex. 1:10, 'if war befall us').

A three days' journey into the wilderness. There are three possibilities here: either Sinai was regarded as a three-day march from Goshen by the direct road; or else Moses is using a ruse to escape from Egypt; or else 'three days' is used loosely of a vague period of time. The first would be impossible unless, with some scholars, Sinai be placed at Ğebel el-Halal, on the 'way of Shur', in a straight line between Goshen and Kadesh.[1] Even then, only unencumbered adults could make the journey in three days. The third is quite possible: 'yesterday and the third day back' is the usual Hebrew phrase for 'previously' (Ex. 5:7). It is the second that poses the moral problem: did Moses ever intend to return? Abraham and Jacob (Gn. 12 and 27) and many other biblical characters lied to attain their purposes, although they are never commended for it, and in these two cases the Bible makes plain the harvest of suffering that deceit brings. But there is no necessity to assume actual

---

[1] See Rothenberg for map and discussion: more recently, Hyatt seems to favour this view.

deceit by Moses. True, it is unlikely that he ever intended to return, else he would not have pressed for women and children, flocks and herds, to accompany the men on this journey (Ex. 10:9). That pharaoh never expected them to return is clear from his violent reaction. The whole process is in fact a complicated piece of Oriental bargaining, like Abraham's conversation with Ephron the Hittite (Gn. 23). Moses' demand for complete freedom, though couched in polite words, is there from the start. Pharaoh gradually raises his offers: sacrifice within Egypt (Ex. 8:25); not too far away (Ex. 8:28); adult males alone may go (Ex. 10:11); all but the flocks may go (Ex. 10:24). To make a moral issue of such bargaining, or to use it as an ethical yardstick, is to misunderstand Eastern customs. This is a gusty folk narrative, like that of Jacob and Laban (Gn. 30): we may pass moral judgments on it, but it is doubtful if the original narrator did. This was not the purpose of the story. Some commentators have felt that Moses deliberately made the demand as low as this in order to give pharaoh every chance of granting it. If he was so stubborn as to refuse even this, there was no hope: he was without excuse.

Sacrifice. Davies and others stress that Moses proclaims a *ḥaḡ*, 'a pilgrimage feast' to a holy site. But the Hebrew verb here is *zāḇaḥ*, the ordinary word for sacrifice, with no necessary location implied. Presumably the reference is to the covenant sacrifice at Sinai (Ex. 24). The whole event will be a vindication of Exodus 3:12, where 'serve' has probably a sacrificial nuance.

19. *Unless compelled*: so the LXX, reading *'im lō'* for *wᵉlō'*. But the older translation could stand, if the text is understood as 'no, not even when smitten heavily' referring to pharaoh's stubborness.

20. *Wonders*: *niplā'ôṯ* is perhaps the nearest Hebrew word etymologically to 'miracles', but its connotation is very different. We think of 'miracle' as a transcending, suspension or reversal of the natural order. The Hebrew thinks of it as a marvellous use of the natural order, by the God who created it and controls it. In one sense, therefore, the Hebrew did not distinguish between the 'natural' and 'supernatural', for all was God's work. The plagues of Egypt are the series of 'wonders' meant here, although the crossing of the sea and desert sustenance and guidance are other examples.

22. *Despoil the Egyptians.* Of course the ornaments were not 'borrowed' from the Egyptians (AV), but 'asked', so that moral indignation is again out of place. Daube, partly on the basis of this passage, sees the whole of the exodus story as told in language appropriate to the freeing of the Hebrew slave, described in Deuteronomy 15:12–18. He must not be sent out 'empty-handed' (verse 21): he must be compensated for his years of slavery. So Israel must be compensated for her trials in Egypt: so too, when Christ triumphs over death, He showers gifts on His freed people (Eph. 4:8). It is hard to say which came first. Either the process of manumission of a Hebrew slave affected the language here, or else Israel's foundation experience of salvation affected her formulation of the slave laws later. The first view is quite unexceptionable, provided that we do not say that the process of manumission actually created the facts of the exodus story.

4:1–9. The three signs. 1. *YHWH did not appear.* Moses accepted the reality of the revelation of God: but will his people do so? The promised sign of sacrifice at God's mountain will not be enough for them, for it demands initial faith (like the sign of Christ's resurrection, Mt. 12:39) and that very faith they will not have. He pleads for signs at a lower level, signs that may induce faith if not create it, and validate his call in the eyes of Israel. John the Baptist was never given the power to perform 'signs' of this sort (Jn. 10:41); Christ refused to do them (Mt. 12:39), but many Old Testament characters were granted such validating evidence (*e.g.* Is. 7:11). This passage does not necessarily imply that Israel already knew the name of YHWH. The narrator or Moses may simply be using the new name to denote the familiar patriarchal God (Ex. 6:3). As the sentence is a strong denial, we might paraphrase by saying 'our ancestral God never appeared to you'. Moses is still thinking of that bitter experience of Exodus 2:14, 'Who made you a prince and a judge?'

2. *A rod.* Probably the familiar shepherd's crook of Psalm 23:4. In verse 20 it is called God's rod, as being used in signs, and in Exodus 7:9 it is used by Aaron. Those who trace sources emphasize the point that in the J tradition, it is a shepherd's rod in Moses' hand; in the E stream, it is a miraculous 'God's rod' (verse 20), while in priestly material, it is a staff in Aaron's hands (Ex. 7:9). Such apparent 'inconsistencies' are however only verbal, natural to oral tradition, and only assure us that we have independent witnesses to the trustworthiness of the tradition.

3. A *snake* or *serpent*: *nāḥāš*, the usual Hebrew word. Numbers 21:9 uses this word as explanation of the 'seraph', or serpent, that attacked Israel in the wilderness, and of which an image was to be put on a pole, but the incident is not a true parallel. Exodus 4:30 refers to the actual performance of this (verse 3) and the other signs in the presence of the Israelites (apparently by Aaron rather than Moses). In Exodus 7:9,10 Aaron performs this sign again, this time before the unbelieving pharaoh. There, however, the Hebrew word used for snake is *tannîn*, which might well mean a lizard or even young crocodile (Driver), appropriate on the Nile bank.

9. *If they will not believe even these two signs*, then a third more impressive sign is given. These three may well be taken together, as of a similar type. They are all three signs of a more superficial nature, and designed to promote belief. Israel they convince (4:31); to pharaoh, they are unconvincing (7:13,23). There is no direct evidence of the use of the sign of leprosy before pharaoh, but see the story of Miriam's leprosy and healing in Numbers 12. What the exact nature of these signs was, we cannot now say. We can tell how they are described in Scripture, and how therefore they must have appeared: a rod turned into a snake, a leprous hand healed, water turned into blood. Some take them literally, as what we would call supernatural manifestations of God's power. Others seek to find God, the Lord of nature, working in what we would call natural ways. Others regard them as spiritual metaphors. The last we may rule out at once: metaphors would never convince oppressed slaves, let alone pharaoh. Some outward signs there must have been, whether the first or second explanation is correct, or whether indeed the truth lies in a combination of the two. Probably we do wrong to draw any such distinction between the two: it certainly would not have occurred to a Hebrew to do so. However God chooses to work, whether through His created world or independently of it, it is His work and, like Israel, we must bow our heads and worship (verse 31).

4:10–17. Aaron, Moses' mouth-piece. 10. *Or since thou hast spoken.* There is an implicit criticism of God here. Not even the meeting with God has given the lacking gift of eloquence.

Compare Exodus 5:23 for a similar rebuke. Such an attitude to God is culpable, but very natural and common, not least among the saints of the Old Testament covenant (Jeremiah, the psalmist and Job are noted instances). Like Peter's failings, these lovable faults bring them very close to us, since we see ourselves only too clearly in them. *I am slow of speech*: lit. 'heavy of mouth'. This vividly expresses the frustration of the man who knows that he cannot speak (*cf.* Paul in 2 Cor. 10:10 for a similar rueful admission). We are never told that Moses' self-estimate was incorrect. He is blamed for making excuses, not necessarily because the reasons given are untrue, but because they indicate lack of faith. Moses expresses the same sense of inadequacy by referring to his 'uncircumcised' lips in Exodus 6:12, which Driver explains as 'lips which speak with difficulty', although the idea may be rather 'unclean lips', as in Isaiah 6:5.

11. *Who has made man's mouth?* The phrase reads, if translated literally, 'who has set a mouth in man?' The thought behind the older translations 'who has created' is not wrong. God in sovereign power divides His gifts among men as He chooses. The step from this sovereignty to the thought of creation is very small indeed (although the Genesis verb 'create' is not actually used). The thought of creation is specially appropriate here, since it is God the Creator, the Lord of nature, who will give Moses the signs as credentials. *Or seeing.* Some want to correct the text so as to read 'lame' by altering two consonants (*pissēᵃḥ* instead of *piqqēᵃḥ*) on the grounds that the other three conditions are physical disabilities. But it is equally possible that the words are to be read as two pairs: 'sighted' and 'blind' would go well together and mean, by the Hebrew idiom, 'all men' (*cf.* 'good and evil' in Gn. 2:17).

13. *Send . . . some other person.* This is the true meaning of the polite Hebrew phrase, 'send now by the hand that you will send' (*cf.* AV, RV, NEB), and it is therefore not surprising that God's anger was aroused. The phrase in itself is typically Semitic, when further particularization is either impossible or undesirable (*cf.* note on Ex. 33:19).

14. *Aaron, your brother, the Levite*: 'brother' is in the literal sense here. Elsewhere it can be understood as 'fellow clansman' or even 'fellow Israelite' (*cf.* Lv. 19:17). 'The Levite' seems an odd way for one member of Levi's tribe to be described to another member of the same tribe, unless it was Aaron's common nickname to distinguish him from various other Aarons in Egypt. Perhaps it is a later title for Aaron unconsciously used by the story-teller here, just as Moses' later surname was 'the servant of YHWH' (Dt. 34:5) or 'the man of God' (title of Ps. 90). Driver suggests that 'Levite', if it had the technical priestly sense of 'teacher', might in itself convey the idea of the ability to speak, in this context. *He is coming out to meet you.* Exodus 4:27 refers to his. Possibly Aaron was bringing the good news of Exodus 2:23, that the older 'pharaoh of the oppression' was dead. Events were to show the new pharaoh to be no better: but at least Moses was no longer a 'wanted man'. Exodus 4:19 does not necessarily mean a direct revelation from God to Moses. It could refer to a message or visit from Aaron, bringing the news (*cf.* 4:27), though this is not the most natural explanation. The thought seems to be rather the 'timing' of God, by which Moses and Aaron were independently led to this meeting. *Cf.* the meeting of Philip with the Ethiopian eunuch in Acts 8:26,27.

15. *I . . . will teach you.* The Hebrew word for 'teach' contains the same root as *tôrâ*, 'instruction', especially used in later times as a title for the law of Moses. There may be a hint of the later meaning here.

16. *A mouth . . . as God.* 'Mouth' is for 'mouth-piece'. Elsewhere the relationship between Moses and Aaron is compared to that between God and prophet (Ex. 7:1): for the prophet, God must 'put the words in his mouth' (verse 15).

4:18–20. Moses leaves Midian. 18. Moses must first drive the flocks back to Jethro, wherever the Midianite settlement was (was it only a seasonal camp?). Then, unlike Jacob (Gn. 31), he obtains his father-in-law's permission to depart with wife and family, who seem, in patriarchal days, still to have been considered as under the father-in-law's authority (*cf.* the position of the wife of the married slave who wishes to leave his master, Ex. 21:4).

19. *All are dead.* God's word to Moses, however conveyed, is couched in language that is echoed in Matthew 2:20, with reference to Herod's death. As Moses is also God's chosen instrument, and has had a miraculous deliverance from death, the parallel is the more appropriate. Presumably *in Midian* is used loosely, to cover Sinai as well (as not being in Egypt).

20. *His sons.* By an easy correction (*bᵉnō* for *bānāyw*) some editors would read the singular 'son', since only Gershom has been mentioned as yet (Ex. 2:22). But, although unmentioned, Eleazer must have been already born (Ex. 18:4) and, if so, the plural is more appropriate. Here is an earlier 'holy family' going by donkey to Egypt (*cf.* Mt. 2:13).

4:21-23. Israel, God's first-born. 21. *I will harden his heart.* This sometimes appears to us as a moral problem, but unfairly, because the Bible uses, side by side, three different ways of describing the same situation, with no sense of internal contradiction. Three different Hebrew verbs are used, but there is no essential difference in their meaning. Sometimes it is said that God hardens pharaoh's heart, as here. Sometimes pharaoh is said to harden his own heart, as in Exodus 8:15. Sometimes the position is described neutrally, by saying that pharaoh's heart was hardened, as in Exodus 7:13. Even to the Western scholar, it is a problem of theological interpretation, not one of history and fact. No-one doubts that pharaoh was stubborn, that he had an iron will and purpose, that he found it impossible to change his pattern of thought and adjust to new ideas. These and more are all implied in the biblical 'hard-hearted', which does not refer to emotion, as in English, but to mind, will, intelligence and response. Often 'dull-witted' would be a good translation. Different theological schools have battled over this passage in past centuries. Paul (in Rom. 9:14-18) uses it as an example not only of the absolute power and inscrutable will of God, but also of His merciful dealing with men. Paul, at the last, must find refuge in the knowledge of the absolute justice of God, as all of us must. However, the Hebrew writer did not even see a problem here. To him, God was the first cause of everything, without in any sense denying the reality, and moral responsibility, of the human agent involved. To see this ambivalence as the mark of two conflicting sources is to come perilously close to ignoring Hebrew psychology. The same train of thought will allow the Hebrew to see the crossing of the Red Sea as due to God's sovereign action, and yet as due to a conjunction of tide and wind (Ex. 14). These are not mutually exclusive explanations, nor even equally valid alternative explanations. To the Hebrew they are essentially the same explanation, phrased differently. Driver says: 'The means by which God

77

hardens a man is not necessarily by any extraordinary intervention on His part; it may be by the ordinary experiences of life, operating through the principles and character of human nature, which are of His appointment.' This is thoroughly Hebraic. A similar example of Semitic thought-form is to be found in the Lord's stated reason for couching truth in parables (Mk. 4:12).

22, 23. *My first-born.* This is the first introduction of the 'first-born' theme in the book (*cf.* Gn. 22). Passover, unleavened bread and the redemption of Israelite first-born are inextricably linked with the events of Exodus (*cf.* Ex. 11:4 for reappearance) and therefore doubtless in Israel's religious thought afterwards. The connection is very simple and patterned on the 'lex talionis', a fundamental principle of Hebrew law (Ex. 21:23). Israel, considered collectively, is God's first-born,[1] presumably as being His chosen people and as 'first-fruits' of all the peoples (Je. 31:9; 2:3). If pharaoh will not give God's first-born up to God, to whom all first-born belong in any case, then pharaoh's own first-born must die instead. Since 'Israel' is collective here, it is reasonable to suppose that 'pharaoh' is also a collective term; thus 'your first-born' includes all the first-born in the land. Otherwise we should have to assume that the original reference was to pharaoh's son alone and no others. 'First-born' also conveys the thought of 'the choicest' in Egypt: this would again include a wider circle than pharaoh's immediate family.

4:24-26. Moses, the 'blood bridegroom'. This is an obscure passage, even to early Jewish commentators, yet its very obscurity and the problems that it raises show it to be a genuine piece of Mosaic tradition (*cf.* Gn. 6:1-4). It is connected with the necessity of circumcision, the 'covenant sign' given by God to Abraham and his descendants (Gn. 17:10), which Moses' son apparently did not yet bear, perhaps owing to his birth in Midian (but see Je. 9:25,26 for circumcision in these areas). At all events, its acceptance on this occasion is another forging of the link between the new revelation at Sinai and the 'God of the fathers', since circumcision was the patriarchal sign. Compare the ceremonial circumcision of the generation born in the desert, before embarkation on the

---

[1] Hyatt points out that only here in the Old Testament is Israel so described: Jeremiah uses the word of Ephraim.

'holy war' against Canaan (Jos. 5:7). Circumcision is a symbol of putting away all that is unpleasing to God, and of dedication to God for the task ahead. But this dedication to God is only man's response of obedience to God's prior grace and calling (Gn. 17:10). True circumcision is an inward, not an outward, matter (Je. 9:26; Rom. 2:29). It had of course, like much of the Mosaic law, great hygienic value, although this was presumably unknown to the original recipients. That circumcision was widely practised in other surrounding countries need not disturb us: not the nature of the sign, but the thing signified, is important.

24. *A lodging place*: a 'caravanserai' where travellers may camp for the night. Such an 'overnight camp' or 'halting place', always by water, is not an anachronism, provided that we rid our minds of the modern associations of the 'inn' of the older translations. The 'good Samaritan' found a more sophisticated version on the Jericho road (Lk. 10:34). A larger group would have pitched a 'caravan camp', but this is a lonely traveller, with his wife and child. *Sought to kill him.* 'Him' is ambiguous, and could refer to either Moses or Gershom; the natural presumption would, however, be Moses. On the other hand, if the 'him' refers to Gershom, then there is a closer link with the context (death of the first-born), as showing how Moses' first-born nearly died. Some have assumed that Moses, like his son, did not bear the sign of the covenant on his body, but this is unnecessary (Moses was a baby in a Hebrew home) and unlikely in view of the known Egyptian practice. In any case he was struck down by some dangerous sickness or other blow as the sign of God's displeasure.

25. *A flint.* This is the flint knife used in Joshua 5:2, showing the archaic nature of the custom. Such stones are common in the desert. Perhaps the stone knife, as a natural object, uncontaminated by human hand, is more fit for God's service. For the same reason YHWH's altar must be unhewn natural stones (Ex. 20:25). At best, men can only mar God's creation by their workmanship. *Touched Moses' feet with it*: see modern translations and footnotes. This is a better translation than the old 'cast it at his feet'. However, the Hebrew does not contain the word 'Moses', but simply says 'his feet', leaving the identity of the person unsolved.

26. *A bridegroom of blood.* The exact meaning of the phrase, in the original context, is now lost to us. Later the phrase was sometimes used of the circumciser: but this may be purely a late development, based on this text. Davies well says that the point here is the necessity of circumcision, and not the 'when' or 'upon whom' it is practised.

4:27-31. The mission begins. 27. *The wilderness*: better 'the grazing land'. Aaron now receives his revelation, ensuring that the two brothers meet halfway between Egypt and Midian at the holy mountain. This has suggested to some that Israel, even when in Egypt, was aware of this sacred place. Moses' experience at the lodging place must have taken place between Midian and the mountain: this certainly would support the eastward position of Midian, on whichever side of the gulf it was.

30. *Aaron spoke all the words.* Aaron, as promised, is Moses' spokesman and, presumably as such, does the 'signs' before Israel. It is assumed, but not stated, that Israel was unbelieving at first. They certainly showed unbelief later, on many occasions.

31. *They heard*: better, 'they rejoiced' (with the alteration of one letter in the unpointed text), following LXX. This makes better sense, as their response of joy to the 'gospel', now preached to them, and confirmed by such signs.

d. Confrontation of pharaoh (5:1 – 11:10)

5:1-5. The mission to pharaoh. 1. *Thus says YHWH* This is the typical form of utterance of a Hebrew prophet (*cf.* Am. 1:3); the analogy would be seen by later Israel. The phrase *the God of Israel* is not often used in the early days, when 'Israel' still means a man rather than a people. 'Sons of Israel' (RSV 'people of Israel'; AV 'children of Israel') is the usual early term (Ex. 5:14, *etc.*). *Hold a feast.* This is literally 'keep a pilgrimage festival'. It clearly seems to refer to the great religious occasion of Sinai. This is the root that gives 'Haggai' as a proper name, and 'Hadji' as an Islamic title, meaning 'one who has performed the pilgrimage'. Perhaps (as in the phrase 'God of the Hebrews', verse 3) the brothers are using terminology which would convey their meaning more readily to pharaoh. The Egyptians must have been well used to the sudden exodus of desert Arabs gone for a pilgrimage to some desert shrine. The editors quote such worship as the reason for absenteeism of workers in Egyptian records, and Genesis 50 is a good parallel, with the burial of Jacob.

2. *Who is YHWH?* This question may include ignorance of the very name of what pharaoh must have considered as some new god of the desert people. In the main, it expresses incredulity at the sheer audacity of the challenge to his absolute authority. Compare the amazed question of Moses, 'Who am I?' on receipt of God's call (Ex. 3:11).

3. *Lest he fall upon us with pestilence or with the sword.* Here the urgency of the desert festival is explained to pharaoh. Disobedience to the vision of God (presumably that at the burning bush) will bring punishment to the whole nation of Israel. The *three days' journey* has already been discussed (see commentary on 3:18, above): it is probably best to take it as a vague indication of distance.

4. *Get to your burdens.* Pharaoh's reaction to these agitators is quick and violent. Pharaoh is a picture of all totalitarian rulers, states or individuals, and he shows it clearly here. There are only two ways of dealing with unrest: either an increased unreasoning authoritarianism, or a careful consideration of the reasons. Pharaoh chooses the first: that was how he 'hardened his heart' (Ex. 4:21) and made collision (and therefore disaster) inevitable.

5. *The people of the land* usually means 'the common people', as opposed to the nobles. It also has the derogatory meaning of 'non-Israelites' as opposed to the returned exiles (Ezr. 4:4). Here, pharaoh is probably referring in both senses to the alien labouring class of Egypt, the state slaves, largely Semitic in origins and including Israel. *Are now many* echoes the old fear (Ex. 1:10) of the indigenous people who see themselves swamped and outnumbered by newcomers. Many modern immigration restrictions stem from this fear. Christians should carefully ponder their attitudes to such laws on the basis of Scripture, noting how readily fear leads to hatred and cruelty, as here.

5:6-19. Bricks without straw. The daily work quota is fixed, and pharaoh will not, or dare not, raise it. But by refusing the 'chopped straw' normally used for reinforcing the sun-dried brick, he can greatly increase the work-time needed to attain the target. Sun-dried mud brick is a cheap and favourite building material in Africa and Asia today: when reinforced, and where protected by overhanging eaves from direct rain, it lasts very well. Bricks of all sorts have been found in Egypt, some with regularly chopped straw, some with rough roots and oddments, some without straw at all. Perhaps pharaoh was not the first employer to use this method to quell labour troubles.

6. *The taskmasters . . . and their foremen.* The first are Egyptian, the second Israelite. For *šōt̤rîm* (Israelite 'gangers') the LXX has 'scribes, accountants', so must have read *sōp̤rîm*, which is possible.

7. *To make bricks.* The process interested the later Israelites, who normally built in stone (as in West Asia to this day), since stones lay everywhere and had to be cleared from the field in any case. For similar interest, see the account of the building of the Tower of Babel in Genesis 11:3.

8. *They are idle*: literally 'they are slack', a common complaint of employers about employees from that day to this.

9. *Lying words*: probably referring to God's promise that He would deliver Israel. Aaron had brought this news to Israel (Ex. 4:30) and pharaoh would have heard of it indirectly at least.

12. *Stubble for straw.* 'Stubble' suggests uneven, rough material, a poor substitute for the regular 'straw'. The use of the cognate verb along with the noun (both in verse 7 and here) underlines the contemptuous attitude. 'Stub themselves stubble' would be an attempt to reproduce the effect in English.

13. *The taskmasters were urgent.* These, of course, were the Egyptians. A sympathetic 'ganger' might have eased the difficulty, but not pharaoh's men. The whole purpose was to break Israel's hope of freedom.

14. *The foremen*, being Israelites, were beaten: not, of course, the Egyptian 'overseers' or 'taskmasters'.

15. *Cried* is the very verb already used of their cry to God, which God has heard and is answering (Ex. 2:23). Now they 'cry' in real earnest, to pharaoh himself: but he, unlike God, will neither hear nor answer. Doubtless his purpose (which he certainly achieved) was to set them against Moses and Aaron (Ex. 5:21).

16. *The fault is in your own people*: *i.e.* in the Egyptian overseers. The phrase is obscure, and could be also translated 'you

are at fault' or 'you are sinning against your own subjects'
(with the LXX and the Syriac), *i.e.* the Israelites. However
taken, the general sense of the protest is clear: the treatment
of Israel is not fair. But since the treatment is intended to be
unfair, such a protest is bound to fail from the start. See Hyatt
for a full discussion of possible meanings of the phrase.

5:20 – 6:1. The discouragement. 20. *They met.* This is
the same pregnant word as Moses and Aaron had used to
pharaoh to describe the encounter with YHWH (Ex. 5:3) at
God's mountain. *Waiting for them*: more than 'standing';
perhaps 'stationed' would be better. Were the two leaders full
of hope? or were they determined to bear the consequences of
failure?

21. (May) *YHWH look . . . and judge.* This is the traditional
prayer of the innocent sufferer (*cf.* Gn. 16:5). It must have
stung Moses to the quick, as we can see from verse 22. *Made
us offensive*: literally 'made us stink'. The Hebrew foremen may
be direct and crude, but they communicate their meaning
very plainly. Clearly, they look only for worse things to
follow.

22. *Why didst thou ever send me?* The protest of Moses is one
of the most human documents in the whole Bible. God has
not yet kept His promise: so far from being delivered, the
Israelites were worse off. All Moses' forebodings about his own
lack of success seem to be confirmed by events.

6:1. *Now you shall see.* Here comes a renewed promise of
God, which goes further than before. Not only will pharaoh
release them from his land, which he has so far refused to do.
He will actually 'expel' them. The verb seems a definite
reminiscence of Moses' 'expulsion' to Midian and probably
contains a play on the name of Gershom, his son (Ex. 2:22).

6:2–13. Renewed calling by God. Some scholars regard
this as a second account of Moses' initial calling: but certainly
in the present context it fits well as renewed encouragement
and reassurance of call, at a moment when Moses is most
conscious of failure.

2. *I am YHWH.* The speech begins and ends (verse 8) with
this sonorous declaration, which guarantees all the contents.
I appeared. This is to assert that the patriarchal experience of
God was just as valid as that of Moses. It also asserts, in spite

of some modern views, that Abraham, Isaac and Jacob all worshipped one and the same God. Further, it is to assert the identity of the God worshipped by the patriarchs with the God experienced by Moses at Sinai. This is fundamental to the understanding of the Mosaic revelation.

3. *God almighty* (Heb. *'ēl šadday*). The use of this name or title for God in patriarchal days can be proved independently, from the occurrence of archaic proper names like Ammishaddai (Nu. 1:12) alongside Ammiel (Nu. 13:12). The name was not used later, except in poetry as a conscious archaism, so its very meaning was forgotten. Later Hebrew orthodoxy translated it as 'the all-sufficient One', but this is impossible philologically. It appears to be an old Mesopotamian divine title, connected with the root 'mountain': compare the way in which 'rock' is often used as God's title in early days (Dt. 32:4), perhaps as a symbol of stability and as a place of safety. In view of patriarchal origins in Mesopotamia, such a linguistic 'fossil' is not surprising.

By my name YHWH I did not make myself known to them. This seems a very clear statement that the name YHWH had not been used by the patriarchs as a title for God. This is borne out by the fact that YAH or YO (in either case the shortened form of YHWH) does not appear as a formative element in Israel's personal names before the time of Moses (with the one possible exception of the name of Moses' mother, Jochebed, Ex. 6:20). In the generation after Moses, such names appear only slowly, but religious conservatism could account for the continued use of 'El'. An example is Hoshea, son of Nun, whose name was deliberately changed by Moses to Joshua, thus containing the new name YHWH (Nu. 13:16). From then onwards, such forms are increasingly common in the Old Testament, convincing proof of the date of introduction of the new title. But if this is so, how do we explain the use of YHWH as a divine name from Genesis 2:5 onwards, whether by itself or in connection with Elohim, the more general word for God? or what appears to be the specific statement of Genesis 4:26 that, in the primeval days of Enoch, the name YHWH was first used? The first is not a serious question: it would be natural to use the later name when telling the earlier story. Indeed, even had it been done consciously, it might be seen as an assertion of the identity of the God worshipped in early days with the God of the Mosaic revelation (see Hyatt, p. 80, for a possible explanation of the combination of the two names). The common critical division of the Pentateuchal material into the so-called 'sources' J and E derives from the belief that one recorder of tradition (J) prefers the later 'particularized' name, even when its use is strictly an anachronism, while the other (E) uses the 'generalized' and earlier name throughout. Even the most extreme critic would admit that both J and E knew the later name since, on his count, both lived well after Moses. Genesis 4:26 is a problem of more substance: it seems to say that, in the primeval days of Seth or Enosh, men began to 'call upon the name of YHWH'. Either it means that the name was known from a very early age, but not in Israel (only a tiny fraction of Enosh's descendants being reckoned as Israel), or the phrase 'call on the name of YHWH' must be used in its later and general sense (Ps. 116:17) meaning 'pray'. In that case, the reference might simply be to the origins of organized worship, known to be of vast age, here attributed to the time of Seth and Enosh. (See Hyatt, p. 79, for possible use of similar forms to the divine name among early Amorites, presumably related to Israel.)

4. *I established my covenant with them*: as in Genesis 17:1–8, where the land of Canaan is promised to Abraham. 'Established' probably refers back to this initial covenant made with Abraham. It could conceivably, however, refer to what God is doing now for Israel through Moses. Israel's occupation of Canaan is always seen in the Bible as a fulfilment of the promise made to Abraham (Gn. 15:18). On the other side the expulsion of the Canaanites is seen as God's punishment for their wrongdoing: compare Genesis 15:16.

5. *I have remembered my covenant.* Henceforward, every 'saving act' of God will be seen as 'remembering' this initial binding relationship which He had freely established. 'Remembered' does not mean that God had previously forgotten. Anthropomorphisms are freely used in Hebrew to describe God. Also, words which we should think of as describing emotional states are often used to describe actions, not emotions ('love' and 'hate' are a good pair of examples). Thus 'to remember the covenant' is to act in a way which can be seen by man to be a fulfilment of the promises of that covenant.

6. *I will redeem*: literally 'I will act the redeemer-kinsman' or *gō'ēl*. The best illustration of this is Boaz' actions directed towards Ruth (Ru. 4). For the legal formulation, see Leviticus

25:25. Driver suggests 'reclaim as a right' or 'vindicate' as possible translations on these grounds. Unlike the verb *pāḏâh*, *gā'al* suggests a close personal relationship between redeemer and redeemed: it is thus appropriate of the God of the covenant.

7. *I will take you for my people.* This is one of the clearest statements of the mutual relationships brought about by the covenant. For an amplification, see Exodus 19:5,6, at the actual covenant-making between God and Israel. *Who has brought you out.* This is the beginning of the great credal statement of Israel's faith, which can best be seen in the introduction to the ten commandments (Ex. 20:2). As Israel grew in her experience of God, fresh 'articles' would be added to this creed, but this basic 'article' would remain the same throughout her history.

9. *But they did not listen.* This is very true to life. Moses' confidence was apparently restored by this recommissioning, but Israel (once bitten, twice shy) will no longer listen to him. *Broken spirit*: better 'impatience', 'anger' over what they must have considered a betrayal of trust.

12. *How then shall Pharaoh listen to me?* Small wonder that Moses, conscious of inadequacy so great that even his own fellow countrymen will not listen to him, demurs at the thought of bearding pharaoh again, with his clumsy speech. Perhaps the 'uncircumcised lips' has a reference to Moses' mysterious experience at the caravanserai. His body may now be circumcised and dedicated to God, but can his lips be, if even his own people turn away from him?

6:14-27. Genealogical insertion. The main story will continue in verse 28. At this point the narrator breaks off, in order to identify and particularize Moses and Aaron more precisely. The Hebrew method of identification was to give a genealogy, in this case the genealogy of the founding fathers, beginning with Reuben, the senior tribe. It is repeated from the beginning up to the mention of Levi, the required tribe. No further tribes are then mentioned. Next within Levi, the family of Amram is singled out and his sons Aaron and Moses mentioned (in the correct order, according to the biblical tradition). The remainder of the genealogy has a priestly interest, dealing with Aaron's family, especially his third son Eleazer (Nadab and Abihu having died, Lv. 10:1-3), and the birth of Phinehas. This is the orthodox priestly line in Israel, as can be seen from Numbers 25:10–13. This passage is only an excerpt from a much larger document: see Numbers 26.

16. *Merari* may be an Egyptian name. Such names are very frequent in the tribe of Levi, whatever the explanation: Moses and Putiel (verse 25) are other examples. Clearest of all is Phinehas which means 'Ethopian, black man'. There may well have been much intermarriage in early days (Gn. 41:45).

20. *Amram* married his paternal aunt. This would be forbidden by Mosaic law (Lv. 18:12,13), so this detail would never be invented later. For other early 'transgressions', compare Abraham's marriage to his half-sister. *Jochebed.* Much argument has centred on whether the first syllable does or does not contain YHWH's name in the shortened form *Yō* (as in Joshua, for instance). If so, the argument is that the name YHWH may have been used and known in Moses' own family (as a 'family title' for God) before its wider use in the rest of Israel. This seems very unlikely. In spite of various false scents, there is no certain evidence for the use of the name outside Israel earlier. If it were known even to the descendants of Kohath alone, one would think that there would be more than one instance of its use. If the vocalization of the AV is correct, it would mean 'YHWH is glory' (compare Ichabod, 'there is no glory'). It is probably better to vocalize as *yakbīd*, 'may He (the unnamed God) glorify', a very common Israelite name pattern: it would then contain no reference to the name YHWH. Names formed from the third person singular of verbs are frequent: *cf.* Jacob and Ishmael. *Aaron and Moses.* In all genealogies, they are given as the fourth generation from the patriarchs. This may not be significant. Steps are often omitted in Hebrew family trees, either for symmetry (as apparently in the case of Christ's genealogy, Mt. 1) or for other reasons. If 'four generations' is understood literally, then the stay in Egypt cannot have been much over a century, and the 'four centuries' of Genesis 15:13 must be understood roundly as 'four generations'.

6:28 – 7:7. God's renewed calling. 29. *YHWH said to Moses.* After the interruption of the genealogy, the action continues. Once again, God's remarks are prefaced by the statement 'I am YHWH', which is not only used as authentication and guarantee of command or promise, but is also an explanation of its reason and nature (*e.g.* Lv. 19:18, 'You must love your neighbour as yourself: I am YHWH').

7:4. *My hosts, my people*: literally translated 'my armies' and, if so, compare the statement that the 'sons of Israel' went out from Egypt 'in full battle array' (if this is the correct translation of Ex. 13:18). The picture is not incorrect, so long as we do not interpret it in terms of a modern disciplined army. Every man was a soldier in an ancient 'horde' and no doubt every man in Israel had some weapon, even if only knife or sling. David, for instance, could describe YHWH to Goliath as 'the God of the armies of Israel' and 'YHWH of armies' (1 Sa. 17:45), while Exodus 15:3 says bluntly that 'YHWH is a man of war'. No doubt the thought passed readily from the 'armies of Israel' to the heavenly armies, equally at God's disposal. *Great acts of judgment. Cf.* Exodus 6:6, for Israel is 'in the right' and pharaoh is 'in the wrong', as he himself will admit in Exodus 9:27. This is another way of looking at the 'signs' of verse 3, for every plague is also a judicial activity of God, at once righteous Judge and Saviour.

7. *Eighty years old.* This age is consistent with the '120 years' given as Moses' age at death (Dt. 34:7), allowing for forty years in the desert. 120 years of lifespan is unusual but possible, in the literal sense of the words. But 120 years was also the 'ideal' lifespan allowed by God to man in primeval days (Gn. 6:3), so that the number may well be used here in a symbolic sense. Three generations (to 'see one's children's children', Ps. 128:6) were also symbolic of completeness. Three generations of forty years each are 120 years.

7:8-13. The signs before pharaoh. Of the three signs given to Moses, while all may have been performed before Israel, only one (the rod becoming a snake) is here mentioned as performed before pharaoh. A second (water turned into blood) becomes a plague (Ex. 7:20). Possibly the third sign has some relation to Exodus 9:10, the skin plague. As predicted, the sign has no effect on pharaoh, the more so as his own 'scientists' are able to reproduce it. They are able to produce 'blood' and 'frogs' later, but not apparently any further plagues.

9. *Serpent*: not the word of Exodus 4:3, but *tannîn*, which might be, as suggested above, a young crocodile; possibly a large lizard or water-monitor. The Hebrews did not always make fine distinctions in natural history.

11. *The sorcerers*: *ḥarṭummîm*, probably an Egyptian word. Certainly it is used only of this Egyptian group (except in Dn. 1:20, *etc.*, which seems to be quoting the Pentateuch). It is explained in the context as 'wise men' and 'spell-mutterers'. The names Jannes and Jambres, traditionally given to these sorcerers (2 Tim. 3:8), occur independently as early as the Jerusalem Targum (2nd century AD). Magic was very prevalent in Egypt, and a number of papyri deal with the subject.

12. *Swallowed up their rods*: a good translation would be 'gulped down'. Any snake-keeper despairs of the cannibal ways of his charges, even today: these were real snakes all right. It hardly seems possible for 'swallowed' to be taken in anything but a literal sense, though some would like to understand it figuratively. We are still left with the question as to what actually happened and even more puzzling questions as to how pharaoh's magicians were able to copy Moses. Undoubtedly these magicians were adepts at sleight of hand, jugglery and perhaps even hypnotism: but we can hardly say that Moses used these, even if Acts 7:22 says that he was instructed in all the wisdom of Egypt.

7:14–25. The first disaster. The 'plagues' are described by cognate Hebrew words, all meaning 'blow' or 'stroke', as well as by the three words already used for 'signs'. This underlines their twofold nature, both as proofs of God's activity and as exhibitions of the nature of that activity, in judgment and salvation. Some find a moral problem here, not in the actual occurrence of the disasters, nor in the subsequent escape of Israel from the shattered land, but in the biblical interpretation of these disasters as the wrath of God. But, if God is in control of all things, is not everything His work? Unless this was the wrath of God to Egypt, how could it be the salvation of God for Israel? Either both interpretations were correct, or neither was. It is typical of the difference between faith and unbelief that the same series of events may be interpreted in either way. So the Christian interprets every event in terms of the loving purpose of God towards his life (Rom. 8:28). Since no event can shake this faith, it is ultimately the victory that overcomes the world (1 Jn. 5:4). (For an interesting and full discussion of the various plagues, see the appendix in Hyatt, pp. 336ff.).

17. *Turned to blood.* Any thick red fluid would answer, for the thought is not one of clinical analysis but of outward resemblance. We must reject, however, the suggestion that what is meant is the light of the setting sun, reflected on water. While it might alter the appearance of the flood waters temporarily, it would not affect the taste or smell. Either the red clay washed down from Ethiopia (which causes the annual phenomenon still called the 'red Nile' by the Arabs) or the multiplication of red plancton (as at times off the Queensland coast) would seem to be the best explanation. The 'stretching out' of the rod, occurring simultaneously with the change in the water, would then be an example of God's perfect timing, as at the crossing of the Sea of Reeds (Ex. 14:21) or of Jordan (Jos. 3:15).

19. *Waters . . . rivers . . . canals . . . ponds . . . pools.* The reiterated nouns are to emphasize the extent of the blow, lest we should think from verse 17 that only the main Nile stream itself was affected. As ultimately the Nile is the source of almost all ponds and irrigation canals in Egypt, this extension is not surprising. In South East Asia today, in the floods of rainy season, the foul river water spreads over the plains and contaminates pure wells miles from the bank. As the Nile was worshipped as a god, and as its water was the life-blood of Egypt, while fish was a most important food, this blow was devastating. *In vessels of wood and in vessels of stone.* Although the Hebrew actually says 'in trees and stones', Davies is probably incorrect in seeing it as a reference to sap in the trees, and to underground springs: this is not called for by the narrative. The RSV translation makes the best sense: but see Hyatt for references to a similar disaster in Mesopotamia, where even the groves and gardens were filled with blood.

22. *The magicians of Egypt did the same*: or, at least, they appeared to produce the same results. One would have thought to reverse the effect would have been more helpful: but doubtless that lay beyond their powers (*cf.* the plague of frogs). The difference therefore did not lie so much in the phenomenon, as in the method by which it was produced. They achieved their results by their 'spells': Israel's results were obtained by reliance on God alone, and therein lay the difference.

24. *Dug round about the Nile*: a vivid eye-witness touch. A 'well' dug in sandy soil near a river bank will serve the purpose of a 'water filter'. Incidentally this shows that the water had not become literal blood (which could never be filtered), but some thick reddish fluid of a disgusting nature (verse 18 states only that it was unpalatable to man, not that it was poisonous, as AV suggests).

25. *Seven days*. One of the very few notes of time in connection with the plagues, and valuable if it is to be taken in a literal and not symbolical sense. A quick reading of the text would suggest that the plagues followed one another in very close succession: but this may not necessarily be so. The terminal date is set by the exodus itself, which took place at passover (the spring full moon). If the Nile flood is the beginning of the series of plagues, this is normally between June and October, after the melting of the Ethiopian snows and the heavy spring rains on the highlands. The hailstorm of Exodus 9, to judge from the plants affected, seems to have occurred in January. Therefore the total period involved for all the plagues can hardly have been less than six months. For similar lengthy periods compressed in tense biblical narrative, compare Exodus 1:8, the new king 'who did not know Joseph'.

8:1–15. The second blow. 2. The word *frogs* may be onomatopoeic, meaning 'croakers', and is found in several other Semitic languages. Frogs are not mentioned in the Old Testament outside this narrative and two Psalms that refer to it (Pss. 78:45 and 105:30). It is doubtful if they were as much a feature of Canaanite life as Egyptian. If the turning of the water into blood was connected in some way with the Nile flooding, 'frogs' would be a very understandable sequence. Bull frogs in rainy season are deafening, sounding like herds of cattle in the distance. Frogs in Egypt were associated both with the god Hapi, and also with the goddess Heqt, who assisted at childbirth, and thus were a fertility symbol: see Hyatt.

7. *The magicians* again did likewise. One wonders if this is not told with a touch of conscious humour, for it only increases the problem, as with the water turned into blood. The plague is, after all, brought about by the extraordinary number of frogs this year: to increase their numbers still more will hardly help pharaoh.

8. *Entreat*: an unusual word, meaning 'intercede'. This is the first occasion on which pharaoh has been really moved, and on which he makes a promise to let Israel go, a promise which he does not keep. Later, this becomes a familiar pattern: when he did not keep it the first time, no doubt it became easier and easier to do the same again.

9. *Be pleased to command me*: literally 'glorify yourself'. This might be construed as a polite gesture to the ruler. It will also be a clear sign that the plague was both sent and removed by God. The thought of the 'timing of God' is thus emphasized even more: He can cause the plague to depart at any time He wills.

14. *The land stank.* The man who first wrote and told this story had smelt dead frogs in tropical sunshine. This is modern 'realism', millennia old, on the part of someone who had been an eye-witness of the events and who knew Egypt well.

8:16-19. The third blow. There are nine plagues listed before the great disaster (the death of the first-born, that ushers in Israel's redemption in chapter 12). There may be a deliberate correspondence to the 'nine bows' of Egypt's traditional enemies (see note on Ex. 3:8). Alternatively the 'ten' may be seen as a perfect number, as in the case of the ten commandments (Ex. 20), symbolizing the completeness of God's judgment on Egypt. If this is so, it is probably because ten is the sum of seven and three, two numbers used in Scripture for their significance. Those who divide the Pentateuch into sources see no one source as presenting accounts of all the plagues (see Driver for details). Following this, some have seen 8:16-19 as repeated in 8:20-32, and as referring to the same plague. Nevertheless, especially since the Hebrew words used for the small flying insects are not the same in either case, this seems unnecessary: they may be considered as separate plagues.

16. *Gnats*: the word occurs only here and in passages based on this context, and its exact meaning is conjectural. 'Fleas' or 'sandflies' are other suggestions: but 'mosquitoes' may be the best translation.

17. *All the dust of the earth became gnats.* This phraseology seems purely to be a reference to the numbers of the mosquitoes, not to their origin. If it is late autumn in Egypt, the fields are still flooded. Mosquitoes will breed in unbelievable numbers; when disturbed they rise in a black cloud, and the air is full of their shrill buzz. So far, therefore, there is strict sequence in the plagues. To say 'all the dust' is the exaggeration proper to a folk-story, as in Exodus 9:6 where 'all the cattle' die (yet in Exodus 9:21 there are still cattle). It would be carping and pettifogging to criticize this; it conveys the desired impression.

18. *They could not.* Here, for the first time, the sorcerers fail. At last they know that Moses and Aaron are not producing conjuring tricks, by sleight of hand, as presumably they themselves have been doing all along. They admit that this is God at work. Henceforth they cease to compete; but their rout is not complete until in Exodus 9:11 the plague of boils strikes them too.

19. *The finger of God*: literally translated. This is a natural metaphor, which reappears in Exodus 31:18 (*cf.* also Lk. 11:20) for God's activity. Elsewhere the same metaphor in essence appears either as 'God's hand' (1 Sa. 5:11) or 'God's arm' (Jb. 40:9). In every case, it would be plainly wrong to understand the phrase in a strictly literal sense: and in every case, it is the clear-eyed interpretation of faith, as applied to an event which is opaque to the unbeliever. Whether God brings about this event by what we call 'natural causes' or not, is quite immaterial to this interpretation. Hyatt quotes Couroyer as claiming that 'finger of God' is an 'Egyptianism' for Aaron's rod: but this does not seem very likely.

8:20–32. The fourth blow. 20. *Rise up early*: a common verb of this meaning in Hebrew. It seems to be, in origin, a nomad's word, and means 'load your beast', or perhaps even 'shoulder your pack'. It is an illustration of the way that Israel's early life left its linguistic imprint on later generations (*cf.* 'tents' in 1 Ki. 12:16) and incidentally confirms the historicity of the accounts of the nature of that early life. To stress the 'early' aspect is, however, probably incorrect: 'get up' would be a sufficient translation. *Wait*: the same Hebrew word as in Exodus 5:20. There Moses and Aaron 'took up position' to meet the frustrated Israelite delegation, returning from the court of pharaoh.

21. *Swarms of flies*: 'mixture' would be a literal translation. The Hebrew is a collective, and there is no accompanying noun to tell of what insects the 'mixture' or 'swarm' consisted.

Perhaps it was not one definite species, but simply swarms of all sorts of flying creatures, attracted by the decaying frogs. Like several other roots, the word is used only in Exodus (and in the Psalter when referring to Exodus). However, Exodus 12:38 has a closely related word to describe the 'swarm of people' that accompanied Israel on the exodus, the 'mixed multitude' of English translations. Flies are a curse in every tropical country, especially after a flood, when filth and carcases of drowned animals litter the land. No doubt the Nile floods are now beginning to abate. The LXX translates the word by *kynomuia*, literally 'dog-fly'. This, to judge from the description, corresponds to the modern gadfly or Marchfly, with a painful bite. If any one species is meant, this is a reasonable suggestion and, since the LXX was produced in Egypt, it is based on local knowledge as well as Jewish tradition. Isaiah 7:18 uses a fly (presumably of similar type) as a symbol of the Egyptian army.

22. *I will set apart the land of Goshen.* Here is the first mention of 'preferential treatment' or special providence for Israel, in connection with the plagues, and also a deliberate justification of such preferential treatment. The purpose is to show by this setting-apart that the plague is no mere accident, but instead God's judgment upon Egypt. RSV is undoubtedly correct in reading 'division' for 'redemption' in verse 23: it only requires a change of one Hebrew letter, to make the sense agree with verse 22. In either case, the sense is the same. Note, however, that God does not always deliver His people from suffering (Heb. 11:35), but through suffering.

Goshen. This is the first mention of the area in Exodus. From Genesis, it is already familiar as the home of the Israelites (Gn. 45:10). It was perhaps *Kesem*, the 20th 'nome' or 'department' of lower Egypt. It is usually sited in the Wadi Tumilat, a fertile strip of country along a freshwater canal, running from the Nile to the centre of the old Suez Canal. Some also include part of the delta to the north west, which is good pasture land. If, as is probable, the capital was then at Tanis, it was nearby; and both Pithom and Raamses, the store-cities built by Hebrew labour, would also be in the vicinity, on any reckoning. In itself, this area could hardly have supported more than a few tens of thousands of people. But arguments as to the Israelite population, based on the size of Goshen, are dangerous. We know neither the exact limits of Goshen,

nor its density of population, nor do we know how many
Hebrews were living scattered elsewhere in Egypt, for reasons
of work. Like the Ibo folk in Nigeria, one small area of
Egypt was their actual homeland, however widely spread. If
however Israel still lived mainly in one compact area, we can
see how God could have preserved them from the flies and
other Egyptian plagues. Certainly if they had observed any of
the hygienic regulations of the later law of Moses, there would
have been no flies to bother them.

25. *Within the land.* This is pharaoh's first offer. Moses
refuses on the grounds that to sacrifice in Egypt would be like
killing a pig in a Muslim mosque, or slaughtering a cow in a
Hindu temple. Racial rioting would break out at once. Here
again sensitive Christian consciences have often blamed Moses
for telling a half-lie, at the least, on the grounds that this was
sheer pretext. But it was a genuine enough excuse, as far as it
went. The little Jewish colony at Yeb/Elephantine, on the
Upper Nile, endured a pogrom at the hands of the Egyptians
in the fifth century, for this very reason of animal sacrifice.

26. *Abominable to the Egyptians*: in the sense that the Egyptians would consider the sacrifice of a sacred animal as blasphemous. Animal sacrifice, as such, was not unknown in Egypt:
see Hyatt for details. A bull with certain marks was sacred to
Apis, cows to Isis, rams to Amon, and so forth, covering nearly
every possible sacrificial animal. The Persians unfairly won a
battle against the Egyptians in the days of Cambyses by driving
a 'screen' of sacred animals ahead of them, at which no
Egyptian bowman would shoot, just as ruthless modern man
will use women, children, or prisoners of war as a 'screen'.

27. *Three days' journey*: familiar from Exodus 3:18. Pharaoh
apparently now consents to their sacrifice in the desert, but is
doubtful about the elastic 'three days' journey'. However, as
he does not keep his promise to release Israel, the extent of
the agreement is immaterial.

9:1–7. The fifth blow. 3. *Cattle*: ironically, after the
discussion of the Egyptian horror of animal sacrifice. The next
plague deals particularly with 'beasts' (better than 'cattle').
Like the turning of the Nile waters to blood, this is a direct
blow at Egypt's gods. The list of animals given here is probably
purely explanatory, and reads like a later stock list of domestic
beasts. *Camels* were not widely domesticated and used till

Gideon's time, though in sporadic use much earlier. The plague in question may have been anthrax. With piles of dead frogs rotting in the fields, and with flies spreading the germs, it would be very likely, and deadly in its effects.

4. *A distinction.* As before, Israel is spared the blow that falls on Egypt. As a pastoral people, if her cattle had died, she would have been utterly ruined. But the agriculture of Egypt was many-sided; it was not until after the destruction of the crops as well (Ex. 9:31; 10:7) that the situation was really serious. If Israel's cattle were all in one location, the anthrax must have halted short of this area, so that they were not affected.

5. *Tomorrow.* There was a set time, as before, lest the blow should appear haphazard. Otherwise the Hebrew could be translated vaguely 'in the future' just as fairly as 'tomorrow'. But pharaoh remained stubborn, even after ascertaining for himself that Israel's cattle had actually escaped (verse 7). So apparently had some of Egypt's: for they were yet to die in the hailstorm (Ex. 9:20). As mentioned (on Ex. 8:17), 'all' in verse 6 must not be pressed, unless it merely refers to the cattle 'in the fields' and not those in sheds, as the custom still is at certain times of the year. It certainly denotes a disaster of unparalleled magnitude.

9:8–12. The sixth blow. 8. The *ashes from the kiln* would be black and fine. Perhaps 'soot' would be the best English rendering, for it is described as very fine 'dust' blowing in the wind. Soot flying in the wind may be a symbol of the rapid spread of the disease, or else the skin of the sufferer may have been covered with black spots, when the eruption broke out. This time, the sorcerers were completely discomfited; there is robust humour in the description of their affliction (see verse 11).

9. *Boils breaking out in sores.* The first word is better translated 'inflamed areas', a term common in the medical sections of the law of Moses (Lv. 13:18). This then breaks out in various 'heads' or 'open sores'. The older commentators think of 'Nile scab', still common at the time of the rising of the Nile, a persistent skin irritation. Another possible meaning is areas of infected 'prickly-heat', an eruptive skin rash common to all tropical countries.

12. *YHWH hardened the heart of Pharaoh.* Davies points out that, while it has already been said that God will harden pharaoh's heart (Ex. 4:21), this is the first occasion on which this form of words is used after an actual plague. Previously, the position has always been put from the other side: pharaoh has hardened his own heart. The moral would be that God hardens those who harden themselves.

9:13–35. The seventh blow. This plague, perhaps as the seventh, is prefaced by a theological introduction, beginning with the familiar idea that pharaoh must acknowledge God's power. *Let my people go, that they may serve me* gives both the grounds for redemption (in the relationship between YHWH and Israel) and the ultimate goal (for 'serve', while it may refer immediately to the pilgrimage festival at Sinai, and its accompanying sacrifices, undoubtedly signifies much more).

14. The secondary goal is again given, as being that pharaoh should realize the uniqueness of YHWH. Now, however, a new theological point is stated. Pharaoh has been treated mercifully so far: his life has been prolonged so that YHWH's name and power should be exalted (verse 16; *cf*. Rom. 9:17). This brings, as corollary, the further thought that all the plagues came in mercy, rather than judgment; for each one was an opportunity for pharaoh to repent. Instead, he hardened his heart, making his final judgment both certain and inexcusable.

16. *Let you live*: 'maintained you alive' is the sense of the Hebrew verb, rather than 'raised you up' in the sense of 'created you'. The point in the context is God's patience and forbearance. Paul stresses this note too in Romans 9:16–18. Otherwise, God would have wiped them all out with the plagues (verse 15). It is interesting that Paul seems to quote this verse, in Romans, from the LXX, not from our MT: see Hyatt.

17. *Exalting yourself*. This unusual form is found only here. 'Being obstructionist' would seem a better translation in view of the derivation of the word, which also gives meanings like 'pile up a siege-mound'.

18. *Very heavy hail*. Sudden storms like this are not unusual in Western Asia and can be very destructive, but this was of devastating magnitude. Stones ranging in size from marbles to golf-balls have been seen. On 18 November 1969, there was a hailstorm of this nature in Sydney NSW. The writer personally measured some hailstones that were $1\frac{1}{4}$ inches in diameter;

cars were dented, and some windscreens broken by the stones. *Such as never has been.* There are recorded instances of such destructive storms later (Jos. 10:11), but the violence of this particular storm was unique even in an area prone to hail (the Nile valley, in between deserts, acting as an air funnel).

19. *Get your cattle . . . into safe shelter.* This is the first instance in which it was possible for pharaoh and his men to avoid the actual blow by faith and obedience to God. As always, when any 'gospel' is preached, some availed themselves of the opportunity and some did not. Cattle are usually out of doors in Egypt from January to April; after that, they are kept indoors, for protection from the heat (Driver).

23. *Thunder and hail.* The hail appears to have been accompanied at the same time by a violent thunderstorm, not unusual in sultry weather, marked by the electrical discharges popularly called 'fire balls' (verse 24; *cf.* Ezk. 1:4). As on Sinai, thunder and lightning are signs of God's presence (Ex. 19:16). Hyatt maintains that hailstorms are much rarer in Egypt than Palestine: if so, this heightens the miracle.

25. *Everything.* This must again be taken in a poetical rather than a mathematical sense. Nevertheless the extent of the disaster is seen from Exodus 10:7, where the Egyptians themselves beg pharaoh to release the Israelites before any more plagues follow. The economy of the country has been ruined.

26. *Only in Goshen . . . there was no hail.* If the thunderstorm was moving up the funnel of the narrow Nile valley, with hot desert and hills on either side, it is understandable that an area to the east escaped damage, where the air currents would be completely different. If so, Israel rightly saw in this, not a geographical peculiarity, but the very hand of God delivering His people.

27. *I have sinned.* For the third time, pharaoh promises amends. The terminology is that of the lawcourt: YHWH is the innocent party, and pharaoh and his people are the guilty parties. Our understanding of the meaning of the biblical term 'justification' derives largely from this Old Testament background: God as it were 'put us in the right', guilty though we are.

28. *Thunder*: the Hebrew reads literally voices of 'God', which, by a common Semitic idiom, may only mean 'mighty thunderings'. But from Sinai to the Gospels (Ex. 19:19; Jn. 12:29) 'thunder' is seen as a symbol of God's voice. So particularly here, the phrase ought to be given its full sense: God is speaking in judgment.

30. *I know*: an example of the 'theological realism' of the Bible. Moses does not believe that pharaoh will keep his word, yet he grants the request so that pharaoh may be without excuse (*cf*. Rom. 1:20). For another example of such realism, see Joshua's blunt reply to the protestations of the Israelite tribes (Jos. 24:19).

31. *The flax and the barley were ruined*: a vivid detail, typical of oral tradition, explaining why the disaster was not complete until the locust hordes devoured the wheat and the spelt later. Such details guarantee, by their artlessness, the integrity of the tradition-stream in which they occur. In this case, the details have added importance as, if accepted, they date the hail to January, at latest, when barley ripens and flax blossoms. Wheat ripens a month or two later (see Driver). Flax was of great importance in Egypt, for linen making: but right down to Roman times, wheat was the main export crop (*cf*. the 'Asiatics' of Genesis 42, who came down to Egypt to buy grain, as often reported in Egyptian records).

10:1–20. The eighth blow. Once again, there is a theological framework and background to this plague.

2. *Tell . . . your son*: *cf*. Exodus 12:26,27 for this insistence on 'theology as recital'. Faith is kindled by recounting the great 'triumphs of God' (Jdg. 5:10,11), in this case His *signs*, and by telling how He *made sport of* Egypt. This last concept, as usual, represents not an emotion but the effect produced. It is an anthropomorphism, an expression of divine activity in human terms, like God's laughter in the Psalms (Ps. 2:4), and must not be unfairly pressed as a theological point.

4. *Locusts* are still one of the most dreaded pests of areas bordering the desert, despite every effort of international locust control. In November 1969, huge swarms began to cross the mountains from the area of Gilgandra, in inland NSW, towards the rich Hunter Valley, covering the very ground where they landed. In Western Asia, the position has always been serious: witness the prophets from Amos (7:1–3) to Joel (1:1–7), where the dreaded locust has become an eschatological figure of doom and a picture of God's judgment.

8. *Who are to go?* In answer to the pleas of his people, pharaoh makes another very half-hearted offer: adult males may go, but no-one else. This Moses refuses, demanding complete liberation of people and stock alike. As a result, the brothers are driven helter-skelter from the enraged pharaoh's court (verse 11). Now the doom must come: pharaoh's action has made it certain. No doubt, from pharaoh's viewpoint, it was a reasonable suggestion to make. From the practical point of view, he had wives, children and flocks as hostages for Israel's return. From the religious viewpoint, only adult males took a full part in any ancient worship: even later in Israel, it was only the men who must appear before YHWH three times a year (Ex. 23:17). It was a man's world, but there were good reasons for it. The men, thus gathered, were the fighting force of the nation (*cf.* the biblical references to the 'armies of Israel' and 'YHWH of armies'). They were also the heads of the families: they therefore fitly represented the whole nation at worship before God.

13. *An east wind.* This makes clear how God the Creator uses His natural world, and ordinary locusts are the divine scourge. They are brought by an east wind from the Arabian steppes, and ultimately blown into the sea by a west wind (verse 19). The crossing of the Red Sea is another example of God's use of wind and wave (Ex. 14), with which compare the testimony borne to Christ in Matthew 8:27. Perhaps this is the origin of the later thought that 'winds' are 'God's messengers'. It is helped forward by the fact that the Hebrew *rûaḥ*, 'wind, breath', can also mean 'spirit', whether God's Holy Spirit or the spirit of men.

16. *I have sinned.* Once again comes the easy confession of sin, and the shallow repentance that springs only from a desire to avert the consequences (Heb. 12:17). In all this pharaoh is not a monster of depravity; he is, like Esau, a recognizable picture of ourselves as 'natural man', and thus a warning to us.

10:21-29. The ninth blow. 21. *A darkness to be felt*: presumably brought by the wind called today '*ḥamsīn*' (literally 'the fifty', like the English sailor's 'roaring forties'). It is so called because it blows intermittently for fifty days in spring, and often brings sandstorms from the desert. Near Jericho at this period, at the height of the storm, the visibility drops to almost nil, and the air seems thick and solid with sand. This is probably the meaning of the Hebrew *yāmeš*, translated 'to be felt' in RSV, very appropriate if describing the oppressive palpable blackness and heat of a sandstorm.

22. *Thick darkness.* The darkness is described in the strongest possible way by the combination of the two words, each meaning in itself 'darkness'.

23. The period of *three days* may be symbolic, or it may be another vivid folk memory, preserved in tradition. Presumably Israel had 'light' because the sandstorm did not cover this area. Sandstorms are apt to be 'streaky' in their coverage in any case, even in the area affected. If Goshen was well to the side of the delta and Nile valley, the likelihood would be greater.

24. *Your flocks and your herds.* Whether these are held as hostages for the Israelite return, or whether pharaoh is now resigned to the loss of his slaves and merely wants to salvage their stock (and understandably so, if there has been heavy mortality among his own), we are not told. Moses of course refuses; he sees through the plan. Pharaoh's angry reaction is instant and final.

25. *Sacrifices.* This does not necessarily mean (with Davies) that pharaoh himself must also give a sacrifice gift, a sort of trespass-offering to YHWH. It means that he must allow Israel the means to sacrifice to YHWH by allowing them to take all their flocks and herds; otherwise it is a hollow permission. Whether either Moses or pharaoh took this elaborate Eastern bargaining seriously is quite another question.

29. *I will not see your face again*: but what of Exodus 12:31? If we are sticklers we can say that, after the death of the first-born, pharaoh merely sent a message to Moses and Aaron without a personal interview. But it would be unfair to hold either Moses or pharaoh to words spoken in the heat of anger. Moses is but accepting the fact that pharaoh's impatience, expressed by his words here, has made the final judgment inevitable; there will be no more of this sort of interview or parleying.

11:1–3. Egyptian jewelry. It is clear from the start that this is to be the last plague: so from now on preparation for Israel's departure will be made. Apparently this 'spoiling of the Egyptians' will not actually take effect till passover night (12:35).

2. *Jewelry*: the Hebrew word is as vague as English 'things'.

It takes on something of the meaning of 'jewelry' only because of the precious materials mentioned (*silver* and *gold*). To introduce the question of dishonesty is out of place. Egypt is glad to see the last of them (12:33), and gladly gives whatever is asked as the price of departure. Not until after the episode of the golden calf (Ex. 33:6) will it be 'taboo' for Israel's men to wear such ornaments.

3. *Moses was very great.* Moses' influence may have been because of the performance of these 'signs', or because of the memory of his royal upbringing. He himself is described in Numbers 12:3 as 'meek' or 'humble': that is to say, without ambition for himself. It does not mean that he was not of great stature; indeed, by the New Testament rule, it proves it (Lk. 9:48).

11:4-10. Prediction of the last blow. The form of these words suggests that they were a final warning delivered to pharaoh, perhaps before the final breach recorded in 10:29. Chapter 12, on the other hand, contains the instructions given to Israel herself for keeping the passover.

4. *About midnight.* Passover was the only night festival known to Israel (*cf.* Ps. 134:1). For the thought, see Daniel 5:30, where Belshazzar dies at night. 'About' in modern English suggests vagueness of time; but there is no vagueness in the Hebrew, so translate 'at midnight'.

5. *All the first-born.* The Bible certainly stresses both the universality of this plague and its indiscriminate nature ('duke's son, cook's son', as the English proverb says). To sit 'behind the two mill stones' (so the Hebrew reads literally) is to do the work of the lowest woman slave in the household, grinding corn (Is. 47:2). Is 'all' meant literally, or is it to be understood in a general sense here, as in 9:6 and elsewhere? Or should we translate Hebrew *bᵉkōr*, 'first-born', in a metaphorical sense as 'the flower of the youth' or 'the cream of the land'? Normally, however, this would be expressed by some form of the different root *bāḥar*. It was some blow by which the very choicest of Egypt's youth were suddenly laid low, including the heir to the throne himself (the first-born of pharaoh). Nothing less than this would explain pharaoh's reaction. Perhaps God used some such plague as that by which he punished David (2 Sa. 24). At one and the same time, this too can be described as a pestilence and as the activity of the 'angel of YHWH'. Egypt and Philistia were famous as regions where plague was endemic (Ex. 15:26). Both bubonic plague and poliomyelitis (the latter as attacking the young) have been suggested as possibilities.

6. *A great cry.* This is another motif of the book. Israel had 'cried' to YHWH for deliverance (2:23), they had 'cried' in vain to pharaoh in their anguish (5:15). Now it is the Egyptians who will 'cry' in anguish at God's judgment.

7. *Not a dog shall growl*: the Hebrew has the obscure 'sharpen its tongue', perhaps implying the lolling tongue of a panting dog, or else the similarity between deep growls in the throat and the noise made by sharpening a blade on a stone wheel. Compare Joshua 10:21, where the same phrase is used of men, not dogs. NEB has the rather curious translation 'not a dog's tongue shall be so much as scratched'. However, though the exact meaning of the words may be still obscure, the general sense is plain: not the slightest harm will be done to Israel.

II. EXODUS TO SINAI (12:1 – 18:27)

a. Passover and escape (12:1 – 13:22)

12:1-13. Preparation for the passover. This passage tells of the preparation for the passover, which must begin four days before the actual sacrifice, with the choice of the sacrificial victim; 12:21-27 will describe in detail some of the ritual to be used during the ceremony itself.

1. *In the land of Egypt.* The rest of Israel's law was given at Sinai, but it emphasized here that passover and the feast of unleavened bread were instituted in Egypt, before Sinai. Sometimes in recent years the question has been asked whether the passover was not itself the 'pilgrimage feast' which Moses had wanted to keep originally either at Mount Sinai or at 'three days' journey in the desert' (3:18), if these are indeed two separate destinations. Owing to pharaoh's intransigence (they say), Moses finally kept the feast in Egypt. Those who hold this view feel that the date (the spring moon) was already fixed, and that this accounts for the increasing urgency of Moses' demands for Israel's release. In their view, Moses feared that, unless they kept the festival, God might attack them with some plague (5:3). This is exactly what He does to the Egyptians, and would presumably have done to Israel had they not been 'covered' by the blood of the sacrifice (12:13). This is ingenious, but does not seem to accord altogether with biblical evidence. It also involves the view, held by some scholars, that passover was kept by Israel's ancestors long before the exodus, and only later associated with that event as a memorial (unless the desert festival, contemplated in 3:18, was to be something totally different from the passover —perhaps the covenant sacrifice at Sinai).

Israel possibly did have 'new moon sacrifices' long before Sinai, for, although they are commanded in the law of Moses (Nu. 28:11), there is no suggestion that this is a new observance, and the custom was widespread in the ancient world. There is no theological objection to such a view: circumcision (Gn. 17:10) and apparently sabbath (Gn. 2:3) were also part of Israel's religious tradition long before the law. But, while there may well also have been regular sacrifice of a lamb at the full moon, Israel's 'passover' was a special instance and had a special significance (*cf.* verses 11–14). The question of the origin of these Israelite festivals is just as irrelevant as is the question of the origin of circumcision, which certainly existed as a rite widely used for countless ages before Abraham. The real question is what this festival meant to Israel, and what historical act of God it commemorated in later days; and of this there is no doubt.

2. *The first month of the year.* The month is called here by its Canaanite name *'ābîb*, 'newly ripened corn' (Ex. 13:4) and later by the Babylonian name Nisan (Ne. 2:1). It corresponded to March–April of the western calendar. Passover was thus both a spring festival and a new year festival, although there is no need to read into either of these feasts the innuendoes of some scholars of comparative religion. In the Bible, passover is a spring festival only because Israel actually escaped from Egypt in the spring (Ex. 13:4). It was therefore purely a matter of commemoration of a historical event. Exodus also states bluntly that the new year was henceforth counted from this month simply because the exodus (which took place then) was the beginning of Israel's life as a nation. Like all of Israel's festivals, its observance was thus firmly grounded in Israel's history and God's saving acts. Exodus 23:16 and 34:22 probably preserve the memory of an earlier Semitic tradition by which the agricultural year ended (and therefore presumably began) in the autumn, *i.e.* October. If the 'dead' winter months were not counted at all, either autumn or spring could be considered as the beginning of the year: but this seems unlikely, although similar instances are known from other agricultural countries.

3. *All the congregation of Israel.* This is the first occurrence in the Pentateuch of what was to become a technical term, describing Israel in its religious sense (*'ēdāh* occurs very frequently in this sense: Deuteronomy, with later books, prefers *qāhāl*) and which underlies the New Testament use of *ekklēsia*, 'church'. The word 'congregation' is not an abstraction: it implies the physical meeting together of Israel, usually for a religious purpose. *On the tenth day.* It is probable that the early Hebrews, like the Chinese, divided the month into three sections of ten days each, the first being 'entering' and the last 'departing'. The old English concept of 'waxing' and 'waning' moons is similar, but based on a twofold division of the month. The Day of Atonement fell likewise on the tenth of a month (Lv. 23:26,27). This explanation seems preferable to the assumption here of any specific sacredness in the number ten. The evening of the fourteenth day (when the lamb was to be killed, verse 6) would thus be exactly halfway through the month, when presumably the moon would be full.

A lamb. The Hebrew *śeh* is quite a neutral word and should be translated 'head of (small) stock', applying equally to sheep and goats of any age. The Hebrews, like the Chinese, seem to have regarded any distinction between sheep and goats as a minor subdivision. Probably because of this, to 'separate the sheep from the goats' is proverbial of God's discernment in New Testament times (Mt. 25:32). Those who know the small black or brown sheep of Asia, with short curly fleeces, will appreciate the difficulty of distinguishing them, except by their tails. Also the *śeh* may be of any age: verse 5 says it is to be 'son of a year', which may mean 'of the first year', *i.e.* 'born within the year'. So the Rabbis understood it at all events. Modern translators, with 'one year old', are probably pushing European ideas of chronology on to an Asian text. But, in either case, it is only this description of its age that shows us that the sacrifice is a 'lamb' and not a full-grown 'sheep'. *For a household.* Passover was a domestic and family festival, and thus shows its early origin. It has here no temple, no meeting-tent, no altar and no priest: but representation, if not substitution, is clearly implied.

4. *Make your count.* In later days, the minimum 'count' of persons for eating one lamb was ten adults: but this figure was reached by artificial exegesis. In early days, it seems to have been a question either of appetite, or the size of the sheep, rather than of theology.

5. *A male a year old.* It was to be a young unblemished male, as usual in sacrifices, presumably as representing the perfection of the species. If it was already *a yearling* (NEB), then it was fully grown as well.

6. *In the evening*: literally 'between the two evenings'. Jewish scholars are not agreed as to the exact meaning. The phrase is also used of the time for the regular evening sacrifice (Ex. 29:39) and of the time for lighting the lamps in the meeting-tent (Ex. 30:8). The orthodox piety of Pharisaic Judaism understood the meaning as being between the time in the afternoon when the heat of the sun lessens (say 3 or 4 p.m.) and sunset. Other groups preferred the time between sunset and dark, or other similar explanations.

7. *The blood.* Passover was scarcely a sacrifice in the later sense of the word. It was not directly connected with sin, although it was 'apotropaic' in the sense of averting God's 'stroke', and a blood ritual was therefore associated with it. The fact that there is a blood ritual is not remarkable: what is remarkable is that there is no association of priests with a rite of a type later strictly limited to them. Therefore it is clear that this festival arose before the establishment of 'professional' priesthood in Israel. As presumably in patriarchal times, the head of the family is to act as its priest. But, in spite of this patriarchal relic, the *doorposts and the lintel* suggest settled life, such as Israel had in Goshen. Although, strictly speaking, there is no thought of 'atonement' here, the rationale of the blood ritual is the same: it represents a life laid down (Lv. 17:11).

8, 9. *Roasted*: 'barbecued', roasted over an open fire in a pit. That the sheep was eaten at all shows that it was not thought of as a sin-offering (Ex. 29:14). The 'roasting' is probably another archaic feature of nomadic life (see Hyatt, p. 26). It has also been suggested that roasting would deal with both blood and fat, forbidden to Israel (Gn. 9:4; Ex. 29:13). Presumably the prohibition against eating it *raw* would either refer to earlier customs still, or perhaps to magical practices of the Canaanites. *Boiled* would represent more sophisticated later cooking methods (1 Sa. 2:15). Roasting the animal whole, with head and intestines, was also very archaic. In modern Jewish observance of passover, a shank of lamb can represent the whole beast. The accompanying *unleavened bread* (Australian 'dampers') will be considered below (see commentary on 12:14-20). The *bitter herbs* (variety unspecified, so probably general: wild lettuce could be meant) were probably a primitive condiment, though later Jews saw them as symbolizing the bitterness of Israel's bondage. The Evangelist may have seen in this the key to the bitter 'myrrh' mixed with Christ's drink at the cross (Mk. 15:23), especially since He was seen as the passover victim (1 Cor. 5:7).

10. *Let none of it remain.* As well as being 'apotropaic' in averting God's stroke, the passover was also a communion meal. As such, it was to be eaten ceremonially in God's presence: nothing might remain over, nor be taken away (Ex. 23:18). This was either to prevent profanation, or to discourage magical practices.

11. *In this manner.* Uniquely among Israel's communion sacrifices, they are to eat it fully prepared for instant departure. Some scholars explain this as the usual custom of nomads: but that would not account for the *haste* (literally, perhaps, 'anxious haste') with which they are to eat it (*cf.* Is. 52:12, where the 'new exodus' from the Babylonian captivity will not be in this 'anxious haste'). This can be explained only in terms of the mingled dread and anticipation of God's visitation on this first passover night.

It is YHWH's passover. Probably the word *pesaḥ*, 'passover', in itself referred primarily to the victim, and secondarily to the feast in which the victim was the central feature. Literally we should translate 'it is a passover victim for YHWH'. The meaning of the word itself is explained in verse 13. Others, however, feel that the addition of 'YHWH' means that the word *pesaḥ* could be used originally to describe a wider range of festivals; this feast however is peculiarly YHWH's, and is so described.

12. *I will smite all the first-born.* 'Smite' usually means 'kill' in Hebrew, and here the context makes it clear. Ramesses II had a very long reign, and Merneptah, who succeeded him, was not his eldest son. Perhaps then it was Merneptah's elder brother who died on this night. As we shall see below (see commentary on 14:18), there is no biblical reason to assume that a pharaoh died at the crossing of the Sea of Reeds.

All the gods of Egypt, like the Egyptians, will be the object of God's acts of righteous judgment. This may refer to the way in which the plagues affected the Nile and the various animal symbols of the gods of the Egyptians, or it may refer to the defeat of the spiritual powers that stand behind these symbols. No doubt the Egyptians used to pray to their gods for the safety of their first-born.

13. *I will pass over you.* The cognate verb is used here to explain the noun that gives its name to the festival. The verb itself is in turn partially explained by the second half of the verse: no *plague* or 'blow' will fall on them. In 1 Kings 18:21 this verb means 'to limp', and the cognate adjective means 'lame' frequently in the Old Testament. Because of this, editors have made wild guesses that the original meaning was a 'limping dance'. But this verse is the only explanation of the name of this festival given in the whole of the Old Testament (*cf.* what was said of the meaning of the YHWH, above) and must therefore be taken seriously. Whether it was correct etymology or a pun, *pesaḥ* to Israel meant 'a passing-over' or 'a leaping over' and was applied to God's act in history on this occasion, in sparing Israel.

12:14–20. Preparation for unleavened bread. The connection between the redemption of the first-born and passover has been seen. The connection between passover and the feast of 'unleavened bread' is equally close, so that they are normally considered one festival, not two (Ex. 23:15) and apparently called together 'unleavened bread'. Many scholars have seen this feast as originating in the settled agricultural life of Canaan, as they have seen passover originating in the pastoral life of Israel's nomadic ancestors. They therefore see the final united festival as an amalgamation of the two, after settlement in Canaan. There is no need to remind the reader that this runs counter to biblical evidence. Earlier eating of 'unleavened bread' there may well have been, either in the desert (where 'dampers' are usually cooked and eaten) or in Canaan: but this would simply be the outer form of the festival. In Israel this feast, like all others, commemorated God's saving acts, and had a historical not agricultural significance.

14. *This day*: that is, the evening of the 14th day (verse 18), remembering that the Hebrews counted from sunset to sunset (see NEB, 'from the evening which begins the fourteenth day'). This marked also the beginning of the 'week' of unleavened bread. We have seen from verse 8 above that the eating of 'unleavened bread' formed a part of the passover ritual itself: this eating is now extended to cover the following week.

15. *Seven days* is the holy number, symbolizing completeness. It was therefore quite common for sacred periods to last for a week. *Leaven* seems to be a biblical symbol of corruption, as well as of pervasive spread (by fermentation), though the equations are not specifically made until the New Testament (Mt. 16:6; 1 Cor. 5:6–8). Another symbol was fermentation of wine, which presumably accounts for its avoidance by Nazirites (Am. 2:12) and Rechabites (Je. 35:6), unless this is a pure archaism, dating from desert days, when the vine was unknown. Usually the 'leaven' was a pinch of the old fermented dough, kept beside the oven to 'raise' a new batch of bread by mixture with new dough. Some scholars have seen this rule as a hygienic principle, the starting of the process again from zero once a year, and the scraping out of the old kneading troughs, which, if made of wood, must have become stale and offensive, if not dangerous to health. Others have seen it as a nomad's need to bake such unleavened 'biscuits' in large numbers before a desert march, rather like the 'ship's biscuits' of a later age of travellers. Today such 'unleavened bread' may be bought in packets in any Jewish shop at passover time (usually called 'Matzos' in English). But the biblical explanation is simple: Israel left in such haste that their dough had no time to rise. Of course, the later feast was a memorial of this historical happening, not an exact copy of the happening itself. For instance, the Israelites, in hurried exodus, could not possibly have observed the virtual 'sabbath' on the first or seventh day (verse 16).

Cut off from Israel refers to the expulsion from the physical community of God's people, which might well be fatal if, in the desert, a man were driven out of Israel's camp. In itself, it is not necessarily a death penalty, but there may be an accompanying expectation of God's judgment. The attitude of the Essene community towards offenders, as depicted in the Dead Sea scrolls, is exactly the same, involving physical expulsion. For the early Christian attitude, see 1 Corinthians 4:4,5.

16. *What every one must eat.* This 'sabbath', with which the feast of unleavened bread begins and ends, is not as sacred as weekly sabbath, or atonement day. Cooking may still be done, unlike stricter 'sabbaths'.

19. *A sojourner or a native.* This, like the moral law, was as binding on 'resident alien' as true-born Israelite. As the price of their settlement, aliens were expected to keep the law of the land, while they were never compelled to worship YHWH. This is an important theological principle.

20. *Nothing leavened.* In later Judaism, the hunt for leaven all through the house has become a symbolic ritual. Here it is simply a practical exclusion.

12:21–28. Ritual of the passover. This adds a few details not included in the account above, but in the main it is repetition.

22. *Hyssop*: the herb 'marjoram', by ancient tradition, although this will hardly suit the reference in John 19:29. Its use is purely utilitarian: it is a common Palestinian herb which, when fastened in a bunch, would make a good sprinkler. Perhaps nomads already used it for sprinkling or dusting their tents. It was used for purificatory rites under the law (see Nu. 19:6). Some, however, see another reason for its use as being the strongly aromatic nature of the herb. *Basin.* Most modern commentators translate thus, rather than 'threshold', which would not make such good sense (unless the lamb has been slaughtered on the threshold, but, if so, there has been no reference to this). The Hebrew word *sap̄* has both meanings: LXX supports 'threshold', but the Syriac prefers 'basin'.

None of you shall go out. The Israelites must not leave the protection of the blood till morning, just as the fugitive must not leave the 'refuge-city' (Nu. 35:28). This detail must have been intended to be part of the later, not the contemporary, ritual: for during passover night Israel left their houses and fled from Egypt, although admittedly it was after God's 'stroke' had fallen.

23. *The destroyer*: *i.e.* the destroying angel sent by God, or else the angel of death (*cf.* David's vision in 2 Sa. 24). Israel knows no dualism; this 'destroyer' is no demonic power uncontrolled by God. Death is part of His judgment on Egypt, as death is the universal judgment on sin (Gn. 2:17).

26. *When your children say.* This question has nowadays become a deliberate and conscious part of the passover ritual: but it does not follow (with some scholars) that therefore the whole story was written and the ritual composed to answer a typical child's question. The child could only question the meaning of a ritual that was already in existence: otherwise, there would be nothing to question. It does not need a very deep knowledge of child psychology to recognize that, given any such symbolic ritual, children's questions are inevitable.

27. *You shall say.* Many scholars today see the passover, and the historical recital which accompanies and enshrines it, as the core of the book of Exodus, and indeed of the whole Pentateuch. Nobody would deny that the deliverance of Israel from Egypt is central to the Torah. However, in the action of the book, the passover is certainly not the only climax. Passover itself is not the redemption, but only the dawn of redemption. Either the crossing of the Red Sea or the making of the covenant at Sinai might justly be seen as the true climax of Exodus. Nevertheless, as passover was one of the three great festivals to be observed at the central sanctuary (Ex. 23:14), it is possible that the observance of the festival was a powerful aid to the preservation of the traditions of Israel's deliverance from Egypt, and an opportunity for proclamation of the saving acts of God.

12:29–51. The midnight exodus. This passage describes the actual happening of the first passover night, already foreshadowed. It also includes the reason for observance of 'unleavened bread', various statistics and further ritual regulations about the passover.

29. *The captive who was in the dungeon*: literally, the 'pit-house'. Pits were a common prison. Here the opposite pole to pharaoh is not the 'mill girl' (11:5), but the prisoner of war in the dungeon. It may have been that the story of Joseph was in the narrator's mind (Gn. 37:24).

31. *Go forth.* When it is now too late to save pharaoh from judgment, there comes the full permission awaited so long in vain. *As you have said* must include women, children, flocks, herds, and journey to the desert. The next verse amplifies this.

32. *Bless me also!* Driver sees this as referring to the coming festival. Surely, however, the desire is for a farewell blessing, instead of the curse which has been clinging to Egypt. In the

Bible 'curse' and 'bless' are used primarily with reference to the practical results which they produce.

34. *The people took their dough before it was leavened.* It had not yet 'risen', as a housewife would say. If leaven was in it, it would of course continue to ferment; but not if wrapped up in wet cloth where no air could get to it, as here. The thought seems to be that they had not as yet added the pinch of old dough to it.

36. *Thus they despoiled the Egyptians* describes the practical result. They left Egypt like a victorious army, loaded with enemy spoils (see verse 41 for the army metaphor again). The very wording is designed to recall the promise of 3:22 (see especially the last clause). Exodus is full of such internal echoes.

37. *Succoth*: probably Egyptian *ṯkw*, which is just a transliteration of what is a Semitic name meaning 'cattle sheds' (*cf.* Gn. 33:17, not of course the same place). It seems to be at or near the ruin Tell el-Maskhuta, near Lake Timsah, at the eastern end of the Wadi Tumilat. The Israelites would then have marched the length of Goshen eastwards, if identifications are correct. *Six hundred thousand.* Numbers 11:21 gives the same figure, which seems very high, as it would imply a total of at least two or three million with women and children. Some modern scholars understand these figures as being those of the census of David's day (2 Sa. 24) or later, when they would be quite possible, but where we already have a completely different set of figures given in the text. We may assume, if we like, that the figures have been wrongly preserved in the manuscripts (perhaps in earlier days having been written in cipher, not in full), or we may follow Petrie in his belief that *'eleṗ*, 'thousand,' really meant 'clan' in early days. In either case, we really have no idea of the exact number involved. It was great enough to terrify the Moabites (Nu. 22:3), yet small enough to be based on the oases around Kadesh-barnea (Dt. 1:46). No theological point depends on the exact numbers, and so the question is unimportant. Whether there were six thousand or six hundred thousand, their deliverance was a miracle. By the time they reached Canaan they were certainly a sizable horde (to use the historian's term), to judge from the archaeological impact on Canaanite civilization.

38. *A mixed multitude.* The Hebrew says 'swarm', from the same root as that used in 8:21 to describe the plague of gadflies. These people would either be the result of inter-marriage, or else kindred Semitic groups who seized the opportunity to escape. Numbers 11:4 uses a different derogatory word to describe the same people. On various occasions in the Pentateuch (as in this instance from Numbers) this group is seen as the occasion of various sins within Israel. If they have no real roots in Israel's religious traditions, this would not be surprising.

41. *On that very day* may not mean '430 years to the day'. It may only stress the end of the period, and the reality of the exodus on that particular day. Alternatively it might mean 'on the very day of the festival' which had just taken place. The length of Israel's stay in Egypt has already been discussed; possibilities range from 430 years (as here) through 400 years (Gn. 15:13) to 215 years (LXX and Syriac, which make the 430 years cover the patriarchal as well as the Egyptian period).[1] The 'four generations' of Genesis 15:16 is probably only a rough equivalent of 400 years. Again, the exact length of the stay is immaterial: what is important is that God delivered Israel at the end of it. That the above figures all remain open possibilities shows how little stress Israel laid on the actual number: if we wish to harmonize, we may put it as 'four generations', reckoned as of different lengths. (For discussion, see Hyatt *ad loc.*, and also in his Introduction.)

42. *A night of watching.* At once a play on words and an attempt to explain why passover was uniquely a night festival. Paraphrase as 'it is a watchnight service, for YHWH watched that night . . .'.

43. *No foreigner.* No 'stranger's son' can join in the passover meal, nor can the hired servant. But a *gēr*, 'protected resident alien', may eat the passover, if he and all his are circumcised (verse 48). A slave born in the house would naturally be circumcised, and thus eligible. Even a slave 'bought for money' may eat it if circumcised, because, as a possession, he is part of the family. This at one and the same time reiterates the essential 'family' nature of the passover, and is part of the Israelite concept of 'symbiosis', which allowed a lamb from a man's own flock to represent him as a sacrifice, and

[1] G. I. Davies has suggested that the LXX figure is connected with its misunderstanding of *ḥᵃmušîm* in 13:18 as 'in the fifth generation' rather than 'armed'. Alternatively it could be a deduction from the family tree of 6:14–26.

also demanded the stoning of his household, slaves and animals, if he himself had sinned (Jos. 7:24,25).

46. *In one house.* Driver, perhaps rightly, sees the three regulations of this verse as emphasizing the unity of the passover. One lamb is to be eaten in one house, and no bone is to be broken (presumably to prevent part of the lamb being carried out). John 19:36 sees this last as fulfilled at the cross: the same unity aspect is stressed in John 17:11.

13:1–16. Consecration of the first-born. In this passage, verses 1–2 and 11–16 deal directly with the question of the consecration of the first-born to God. Verses 3–10 appear at first sight to be unconnected, but closer examination will show the link with the 'first-born' theme. They deal with the feast of unleavened bread, which is virtually the same as the passover. This in turn is linked in thought with the death of Egypt's first-born and the preservation of Israel's first-born sons. There is a possible further link, mentioned below.

2. *Consecrate* could mean either 'sacrifice' or merely 'consider as belonging to God'. Instances of both meanings could be found in the Pentateuch, although not all referring to humans. The 'first-born' is explained here as the 'womb-opener', which is a technical word: when so defined, 'first-born' certainly cannot be translated 'flower' or 'cream' of the population, as suggested above (see commentary on 11:5).

3. *YHWH brought you out.* This associates the feast of the unleavened bread with the deliverance from Egypt. Not only so but (verse 8), like passover, it is to be associated with instruction given by father to son, presumably the first-born son. As he is the one peculiarly concerned, there is a double link with the context.

9. *A sign on your hand.* Later Jews interpreted this, like the phrase *a memorial between your eyes*, quite literally, as applied to the law of Moses. They wrote short sections of the law and bound them with thongs on the arm and forehead (the so-called phylacteries). But the very fact that language like this can be used of the feast of unleavened bread shows it to be pure metaphor. Over-literalism has always been one danger of the Christian, as of the Jewish, church.

12. *That are males.* Only the male first-born animals are involved in the law as to the offering of the first-born. Usually males alone were eligible for sacrifice on the altar. For *set* *apart* translate 'make them pass over' (*i.e.* by fire) and understand the meaning as 'offer up as a whole burnt offering'.[1] This is the sinister phrase which is used in 2 Kings 16:3 of Ahaz sacrificing his own son 'to Molech', or 'to the King' or 'as a burnt offering', whatever the phrase may mean in detail. In Canaan this might be done to first-born sons: in Israel it might only be done to first-born animals, sacrificed to YHWH.

13. *Redeem.* The above is the basic principle, but it is modified in two important ways. The offspring of beasts that are ceremonially unclean cannot be sacrificed to God, and the offspring of a human being must not be so sacrificed. The latter had been made clear to Israel's ancestors long before (Gn. 22). The donkey is mentioned as being the one unclean beast that was both common and domestic in Israel: thus it was a recurring problem. Pigs were an object of sacrifice elsewhere, but were regarded as 'unclean' in Israel, and so presumably not kept, as among Muslims, while dogs were mere scavengers, like kites and ravens. The donkey appears to have been a sacrificial animal in Amorite culture (*e.g.* Mari); so that there could also have been a religious reason for its exclusion from YHWH's altars. In extreme emergency, as 2 Kings 6:25 shows in time of siege, donkey meat was eaten and there seem to be references to donkey's milk in places (Gn. 49:12). If this was never drunk, it is hard to see why such large herds of she-asses were kept, unless for breeding purposes (Jb. 1:3). Perhaps the odour of the milk and meat was considered offensive; perhaps it was because of the sacred nature of the beast in other cultures; or perhaps because of the symbolism of the ass in fertility cults. Though such an animal could not be sacrificed, it still must be 'devoted' to God by being destroyed, unless it is redeemed by a sheep, which might be sacrificed in its place. The verb *pāḏāh*, 'redeem', is used, either of the donkey foal which may be redeemed by the substitution of another victim, or of the baby boy, who must be redeemed. *Pāḏāh* seems to mean 'to buy back for a price': Deuteronomy 9:26 shows its application God's redemption of Israel from Egypt.

15. *The first-born of cattle.* Israel's 'devotion' of first-born animals to YHWH is seen as analogous to the death of the

---

[1] Many modern versions follow BDB, and translate *heʿĕḇîr*, as 'set apart', unless there is a specific reference to sacrifice in the context. But 'setting apart' normally involved sacrifice, to Israel.

first-born (animal and human) in Egypt. Likewise the 'redemption' of the first-born son is seen as the memorial of Israel's 'redemption' from Egypt. Like all of Israel's religious customs, it is interwoven with the history of salvation: henceforth, it will commemorate a historical event. In origin, no doubt, the offering of the first-born to God was the equivalent of the offering of any other 'first-fruits' (Ex. 23:19). This latter harmless custom was always allowed, and even enjoined, in Israel. Perhaps the idea was similar to that which seems to have underlain the offering of the 'tithe': the whole is consecrated to God by the offering of the part.

All the first-born of my sons I redeem. The sacrifice of first-born sons as burnt offerings to God ceased to be after the time of Abraham (if it had ever existed among Israel's ancestors: archaeology can prove the existence of the custom only in Canaan). That is clearly the point of Genesis 22, with the substitution of the ram for Isaac. Henceforth, if child-sacrifice occurred in Israel, as at times it certainly did, it was due to ignorance (as in the case of Jephthah, Jdg. 11:39) or wilful apostasy (as in the case of Ahaz, 2 Ki. 16:3). For the rest, Numbers 3:11-13 says that YHWH chose the Levites for Himself in place of all Israel's first-born: they represent all the first-born of Israel, as a lamb might represent one particular first-born son.

13:17–22. The Egyptian desert. 17. *By way of the land of the Philistines*: better 'by the Philistia road', *i.e.* 'by the road that leads to Philistia'. This was the direct route, but was heavily guarded by Egypt: the commentators give instances of the careful lists, kept by the Egyptian guards, of arrivals and departures at the frontier. The Israelites would certainly have 'seen war' (Hebraic for 'experienced war') along that route. The later geographical and ethnological name for the area is used quite naturally. The Philistines themselves did not settle there *en masse* until the twelfth century, after Israel's occupation of Canaan. However there were certainly isolated Minoan-style trading settlements along the coast from much earlier times (see G. E. Wright, quoted by Hyatt, for the archaeological evidence). If therefore we object to colloquial anachronisms, we can argue along these lines. The area was in any case heavily garrisoned by Egypt long before the arrival of the Philistines.

18. *The way of the wilderness*: 'the road to the steppes' would be a better translation, for grazing country is meant. The exact location is uncertain, but it is clearly to the east of the Nile delta. If it is to the north-east of Goshen, then somewhere near Lake Sirbonis (a brackish lagoon on the Mediterranean coast) might be meant. If it is to the south-east of Goshen, then somewhere in the region of the Bitter Lakes would be indicated. As the ancient seabed was not the same as today, exact identification is probably impossible, in spite of the persuasive efforts of local guides, nor indeed is it necessary for faith.

The Red Sea: 'sea of reeds' would be an exact translation. The Hebrew *sûp* is probably the Egyptian *ṯwf*, 'papyrus', but it seems to be used of many types of water weed and even of seaweed. Any brackish shallow water would seem to suit the description. The Greeks later used the term 'Red Sea' to cover the Persian Gulf and both arms of our Red Sea, but this has nothing to do with the text before us, except that it is highly likely on other grounds that Israel crossed a northern extension of one of these two 'arms'. Broadly speaking, there are only three possible routes for the exodus, either near the Mediterranean coast (which is unlikely, because of the proximity of the Egyptian outposts) or directly across the Sinai peninsula to Kadesh (which not only seems to conflict with the biblical evidence, but would be very difficult from the point of view of the water supplies), or south to Sinai, and then north to Kadesh (which seems most likely on any score). In either of the latter two cases, a crossing of one of the northern extensions of our Red Sea would be necessary, and that would fit the indication of direction given here. (See Excursus 2: The Site of the 'Red Sea', pp. 44ff.)

19. *The bones of Joseph*: this links with Genesis 50:25, and the promise made there. Like Jacob his father (Gn. 49:29), Joseph never looked on Egypt as home, and showed it by his demand for a Canaanite burial (Heb. 11:22). A generation ago, old-fashioned Chinese of South East Asia were still unwilling to be buried anywhere but in China. The meaning of 'bones' is, more properly, Joseph's mummified body, as can be seen from Genesis 50:1–3. For the fulfilment of Joseph's wish, see Joshua 24:32 and the tomb at Shechem. But this was more than mere sentiment; this was a last exhibition of faith in the promises of God.

20. *Succoth . . . Etham.* The exact locations of these places are unknown, though, as above, we can make a fair guess at Succoth. They are usually marked on biblical atlases, but in totally different places, according to whether a 'northern route' or a 'southern route' for the exodus is favoured. Driver's discussion of location is fullest, but lacks much newer geographical information. In any case the text makes plain that the Israelites were still only on the edge of the steppe country.

21. *A pillar of cloud.* The Hebrew means properly 'something standing', and therefore is more 'column' than 'pillar'. It is arguable that a continual presence of God is intended by the 'standing' concept. This symbol of God's presence may either guide and illuminate the way (as here) or protect from enemies (Ex. 14:19,20). Sometimes the cloud is described as descending on the meeting-tent, when God speaks to Moses (Ex. 33:9). Sometimes the cloud is seen as brooding continually over the tent, until it is time for Israel to move on, when it lifts (Ex. 40:34–38). Cloud and fire are often associated with God as symbols: and so God speaks to Moses from Mount Sinai out of the cloud and fire (Ex. 19:18; *cf.* Mt. 17:5 and Acts 1:9 for New Testament parallels). The symbolism of fire is plain: the cloud probably symbolizes God's mystery, like darkness. If we ask ourselves what method God used to produce this effect, we can only hazard guesses, which may be incorrect, without in any way rejecting the interpretation of faith. Either, therefore, this was some purely supernatural manifestation, a vision produced in the minds of men, or it was a natural object used by God as a symbol of His presence. If the latter, it may have been some kind of desert whirlwind (*cf.* the 'willy-willy' of the Australian desert), which can produce rotating columns of fine sand which halt and move over the desert: or perhaps it may have been the column of smoke that arose in the clear desert air from incense or sacrifice before the meeting-tent, shot through by night with the reflection of the sacrificial fire. Whatever it was, God used it to symbolize His very presence in their midst.

b. Crossing the Sea of Reeds (14:1-31)

14:1–9. The location of the crossing. 2. *By the sea*: the original tellers and hearers of the story knew very well where the 'Sea of Reeds' was: to them it was pinpointed by these place names. Some are sites unknown to us (*e.g.* the good Egyptian name *Pi-ha-hiroth*, 'region of salt marshes') while others are ambiguous (several places called *Migdol* or 'watchtower' are known). *Baal-zephon*, 'Baal of the north' is interesting evidence for the influence of Canaanite religion on Egypt, for it is clearly the temple of a Canaanite god. *Turn back* should mean a reversal of direction. Perhaps it means a sudden swing to the south, instead of a direct march eastwards. In any case, the Egyptians would interpret it as failure to find the direct route to Canaan.

3. *Entangled*: 'confused' or 'lost' (*cf.* Est. 3:15). Israel seemed to have taken a 'dead-end' road, since the sea or salt marshes now barred their way ahead and the desert was a barrier round them on all other sides.

5. *Fled*: better 'given him the slip'. This does not run counter to pharaoh's earlier permission to Israel to depart; he now realized what this permission meant. In a system dependent on manual labour by one class or group in the community, the loss of that group is paralysing.

6. *He made ready his chariot.* This is not merely his personal chariot. The meaning is probably 'his chariotry', a collective, explained by the next verse.

7. *Six hundred picked chariots.* Such a number was of course more than possible for Egypt. But if we think the number far too large for a mere slave-chase, then we may take it in a symbolic sense, as corresponding to Israel's 'six hundred thousand' of Exodus 12:37. Alternatively the figure 'six hundred' may be used loosely for 'a detachment'. Six hundred appears to have been a common size for a battalion (2 Sa. 15:18). *All the other chariots*: there is no 'other' in Hebrew. The phrase is to be understood in the general sense of Exodus 9:6 (*cf.* 'all the king's horses and all the king's men') rather than in any strictly mathematical sense which would be foreign to the Hebrew mind. That a detachment of charioteers was lost in the Sea of Reeds is clear from the Bible; but there is no necessity to assume the loss of the entire Egyptian army. *With officers.* This term etymologically should mean 'third men', perhaps in the chariot. See Davies for a discussion of the obscure word. 'Knights' would be a good if old-fashioned translation (*cf.* 2 Ki. 7:2). Only the Hittites actually used three-man chariots in war, to our knowledge.

9. *Horsemen*: perhaps used as a loose poetic equivalent for 'chariots'. Chariots were an early Egyptian military weapon: cavalry was not used by Egypt in war until much later (Is. 31:1). However this was not war so much as a police operation, so perhaps the cavalry were used to scour the desert as scouts, in advance of the chariot column. In later days, the cavalry and chariots of Egypt were proverbial (Is. 31:3).

14:10–20. Israel's cry of terror. 10. Israel may indeed have *cried out* to YHWH for help, but their next reaction (as often in the steppe country; *cf*. Ex. 16:3, *etc*.) was to blame Moses. This was very wrong but very human: we recognize ourselves again and again in Israel.

11. *No graves*: a bitter irony, in view of the abnormal pre-occupation of the Egyptians with tombs (compare the similar obsession of the Nabataeans of Petra, and the Etruscans of Italy) but it is not likely that Israel meant it so. The situation was too tense for that.

12. *Is not this what we said?* It is futile to argue whether or not the Israelites had actually used these words to Moses in Egypt. They were not in the mood for niceties, and certainly these words express the attitude of Exodus 5:21. 'Said' in Hebrew often has the same sense as 'thought' (*cf*. Ps. 14:1, 'says in his heart').

13. *Salvation* is used here in its literal sense of saving life, or of victory instead of defeat in war (*cf*. 1 Sa. 14:45). As the Old Testament moves on, 'salvation' will gain a more spiritual and less material sense (Ps. 51:12), although the Hebrew was not conscious of any sharp contrast between the two.

16. *Divide it*: properly 'cleave it' or 'make a valley in it'. This is not a different view from that of verses 21 and 22; we must not press the metaphor too far in either case, since both metaphors are describing the same event.

18. *Glory over Pharaoh*. This would be obtained by defeating his forces. The Bible does not state that pharaoh himself died in this 'border skirmish', as the drowning of the Egyptians must have seemed to Egypt. It is therefore futile to try to date the exodus by searching for some pharaoh in history whose 'mummy' has not been preserved intact. To Israel, however, this was salvation and redemption and the judgment of God, all in one. She could not overemphasize its importance, and therefore neither can we.

19. *The angel of God*. The general name is used for God, not the peculiarly Israelite name of YHWH. Possibly therefore we should translate the phrase as 'divine messenger', in general terms, referring to the column of cloud and fire. This seems to be the sense of the second half of the verse. See Exodus 23:20–23 for another use of the word 'angel', almost as a personal representative of God.

20. *The night passed*: the Hebrew says 'it lit up the night', but the construction is strange, so most modern commentators follow the Greek rendering as above. See Noth for a full discussion. The main sense is clear: Israel now needs not guidance but protection, and this God gives to them. Hyatt, perhaps correctly, emends the first clause too, so that the verse reads 'The cloud grew dark, and they passed the night . . . '.

14:21–31. Crossing the sea. 21. *Moses stretched out his hand.* There is no contradiction between this statement, seen as the cause of the sea drying up, and the second statement below, that God sent *a strong east wind.* The action of Moses in stretching out his hand was necessary to show that this 'ebb' was no chance accident, but an act of God, working in might to save His people. Again, we might see the wonder as being the creator God controlling the natural world that He has made, and which He upholds, making wind and wave serve His purpose (Mt. 8:27). *East wind.* The same 'natural' force had already been used by God in connection with the locusts (10:13) and also appears in the Jonah story (Jon. 4:8). From the point of view of Egypt and Canaan, the east wind blows from the desert. Winds and fire are often described poetically in the Bible as almost personified messengers of the God who controls them (Ps. 104:4).

22. *On dry ground.* If these were reedy salt-marshes, with a soft bottom, connected with the main gulf (of which they would be the northerly extension), then a culmination of ebb tide and strong wind could dry them temporarily, long enough for a light-armed group to scamper across. *The waters being a wall.* This metaphor is no more to be taken literally than when Ezra 9:9 says that God has given him a 'wall' (the same word) in Israel. It is a poetic metaphor to explain why the Egyptian chariots could not sweep in to right and left, and cut Israel off; they had to cross by the same ford, directly behind the Israelites.

24. *In the morning watch.* 1 Samuel 11:11 also mentions this, the last of the three watches, from 2 a.m. to dawn, about 6 a.m. This, the darkest hour before the dawn, was traditionally the time for attack, when men's spirits are at their lowest. *Discomfited*: better 'confused, made to panic'. How, we are not told: Psalm 77:16–20 suggests a thunderstorm, and this may be the meaning of YHWH 'looking down' from the cloud.

25. *Clogging* is the reading of the versions for the difficult 'took off' of the Hebrew text. The sand or mud that allowed free passage to the lightly-armed Israelites would 'bog down' the heavy chariots, as the second half of the verse makes plain. This too may be the cause of the confusion mentioned in verse 24. However, broken axles would tend to follow rapidly, as the frightened horses plunged, so the Hebrew text may be correct, since the wheels would then certainly fall off.

27. *Its wonted flow.* Parallels in other Semitic languages (where the word means 'a stream that never dries up') shows this to be a correct translation, rather than the AV rendering 'strength'. The word stresses the unique nature of the occurrence: this crossing-place was not a ford that was regularly dry, but one that was usually under water. *Routed.* The marginal 'shook off' is the literal meaning, of which 'overthrow' is a free translation (*cf.* Ps. 136:15 and Ne. 5:13). To the later Hebrew commentators, this verb suggested the 'overthrow' of the builders of Babel's tower in Genesis 11:1–9. The popular etymology of the name Shinar (Babylonia) was from this same verb. The overthrow of pharaoh is implicitly linked, not only with the Babel story, but also with the flood story, by God's use of water in judgment.

30. *Dead upon the sea shore.* This is a very graphic touch, an eye-witness account. The drowned Egyptian soldiers stand for an old way of life in slavery, now gone for ever. Somehow the sight of those dead bodies was the concrete sign that salvation and a new life for Israel were now assured. Perhaps something of this enters into the Christian thought of baptism as symbolizing death as well as life (Rom. 6:1–4). No doubt it is this aspect of finality that gave to the miracle at the Sea of Reeds its position as prime symbol of salvation in the Old Testament (Is. 51:9–11).

c. The song of triumph (15:1-21)

This may be further subdivided: 1–18 is the 'song of Moses and the people of Israel', while verse 21 is specifically described as the song sung by 'Miriam . . . and all the women'. Verses 19 and 20 are a prose summary of the events. But, with the exception of a change to the imperative from the first person of the indicative, Miriam's brief 'song' is the same as the opening lines of Moses' song. So it is not clear whether Miriam and her women's choir in fact went on to dance and chant the whole of Moses' song, or whether Moses' song is a theological expansion on the theme of Miriam's song. Further, there is a division within Moses' song itself. Verses 1–12 deal with the exodus, while 13–18 deal with the future conquest of Canaan.

15:1-12. Crossing the sea. 1. *I will sing to YHWH, for he has triumphed gloriously.* The metre is bold and strong, and the thought simple, yet deep, while the language is full of archaisms. All this suggests an early date. Davies points out the importance of the 'for' in this verse. Normally in Israel's psalms 'for' introduces the reason for which God is praised (*e.g.* Ps. 9:4). The exact nature of God's act is explained in the prose adjunct of verse 19 below. *Triumphed gloriously*: better 'has risen up' (like a wave). The word is used both of pride (in a bad sense) and triumph (in a good sense) as here. Ezekiel 47:5 uses the verb of a river rising in flood.

2. *The Lord.* Here the Hebrew uses the shorter form YH, not the longer YHWH, as in verses 1 and 3. It is this shorter form of the divine name which appears in proper names, and in the common exclamation 'hallelujah' or 'praise YH'. For the thought, compare Psalm 118:14. *My song.* Cross and Freedman translate *zimrāṯ* as 'defence' or 'defender' rather than as 'song'. This would suit the context better, has LXX support, and is based on a cognate word in Arabic. If true, the same translation would go for Psalm 118:14, *etc. I will praise him.* This word does not occur elsewhere in Hebrew. The translation is a guess, from the parallelism, and from similar words in other Semitic languages. This is one of the many archaisms of the song.

3. *A man of war*: 'warrior' would be a better translation in modern English. Compare the title YHWH Sabaoth, YHWH of armies or 'Lord of hosts'.

5. *The depths* is a rare word, perhaps describing by its sound the gurgle and eddy of a returning tide-race. For the simile, see Jeremiah 51:63,64: so Babylon, God's enemy, will sink like a stone.

8. *At the blast of thy nostrils.* This is the theological interpretation of the 'east wind' which God had sent to dry the sea (*cf.* Ps. 18:15). The anthropomorphisms are part of all poetry: and the poetic nature of the whole passage warns us not to take literally the word *heap* (of the floods).

9. *I will pursue, I will overtake.* The heavy threefold beat of this verse is both impressive and primitive in its simplicity; compare Deborah's song in Judges 5 (verse 27 shows the beat even in the English). *Destroy them.* The heavy Hebrew verb, with its archaic ending, is properly 'dispossess them', and is often used later of Israel's expulsion of the Canaanites and occupation of their land. In the mouth of the Egyptians, it has poetic irony when applied to Israel.

10. *They sank*: better, 'went gurgling down' into the 'whirlpools' mentioned above (verse 5). *Lead* takes the place here of 'stone' in the simile above as a natural symbol of weight.

11. *Who is like thee . . . ?* This is the 'monolatry' of early days (the insistence on the service of YHWH alone) which will later lead to full dogmatic monotheism (the denial of the existence of any other God, apart from YHWH), as in Isaiah 45:5. YHWH is in a different class from these other *gods* or 'mighty ones', whose existence is neither affirmed nor denied, but ignored, for practical purposes. Psalm 97:7 makes all such beings, if they exist, bow down in worship to YHWH: in later days they were usually regarded as mere angelic powers, subservient to Him.

12. *Swallowed them*: 'gulped down', again with the archaic verbal suffix. As the crevasse in the desert swallowed Korah, Dathan and Abiram (Nu. 16:31) so the sea swallowed up the Egyptian army. Perhaps *'ereṣ*, 'earth', has its Ugaritic sense of 'underworld': see Hyatt.

15:13–18. The march to Canaan. Some scholars feel that the second part of Moses' song must have been written after the occupation of Canaan, with which it deals. In particular, some see references in verses 13 and 17 to Mount Zion and Solomon's Temple, but this is not necessary. Both phrases are archaic, and have parallels long before, in the

Ras Shamra tablets. The past tenses throughout may be 'prophetic perfects': future events are described as if they had already taken place. This is common in early days, and particularly familiar in the prophetic books of the Old Testament.

13. *Steadfast love*, often translated 'mercy', is (along with 'truth') the great covenant word of the Old Testament, to describe God's unfailing attitude of love towards His people (Ex. 34:7). In turn, this love is what God demands of His people (Ho. 6:6). *Redeemed.* God is seen as the *gō'ēl*, the 'redeemer kinsman' of His covenant people, Israel. See also on 6:6, above. *By thy strength.* Because of the phraseology, many editors have seen in this a reference to the ark, the symbol of God's presence and guidance, carried before Israel when on the march (Nu. 10:33). This is possible, but unnecessary: the same word for 'strength' is used of YHWH in verse 2, where the context makes impossible any reference to the ark. If *thy holy abode* referred to Jerusalem and the Temple, of course it would show a late date; but the reference may be purely general. True, in 2 Samuel 15:25 the word refers to the sanctuary, but in Jeremiah 25:30 it is general. The Hebrew *nᵉweh* means 'pasture': then perhaps 'sheep station' (in the Australian sense); then, more generally and poetically, any home. Here it could refer to the whole land of Canaan, to which Israel is moving.

14. *The inhabitants of Philistia.* The country cannot have taken this name until after the arrival of the Philistines in 1188 BC, so this phrase at least must date from after the conquest. The list of the nations here is given roughly in order, travelling north-east from Egypt.

15. *The chiefs of Edom.* '*allûpîm*, 'clan-chiefs' (see Ex. 12:37 for the possible meaning 'clan' as well as 'thousand' for '*elep*) is a technical term for Edomite rulers (*cf.* Gn. 36:15-19). They seem to have occupied a position somewhat lower than a king. It is fair therefore to assume that the *leaders* of Moab ('*ēlîm*, literally 'rams') is also a local technical term. Others have seen a reference to the great sheep-stations of Moab (2 Ki. 3:4).

16. *Pass by*: or 'cross over'. The reference may be to Israel's 'passage' by the territories of Edom and Moab (Dt. 2) or, more likely, a reference to the 'crossing' of the Jordan (Jos. 3) which would lead more directly to the occupation of

Canaan. *Whom thou hast purchased.* The word means 'to acquire', usually by money. It is an archaic word, used in participial form in Genesis 14:22 as a title of God, translated there as 'maker' in most English versions. Hyatt, on these grounds, would prefer to translate 'created' here.

17. *Thy own mountain*: literally 'the mountain of thine inheritance', but the translation gives the sense. It could mean 'the mountain country belonging to Israel, your inheritance' (for Israel as God's inheritance, see Ex. 34:9), but in view of Ugaritic parallels the existing translation is to be preferred. Because of the parallels, there is no need to assume a direct reference to Mount Zion or Solomon's Temple: the date therefore could be as early as Moses. *The place . . . for thy abode.* 1 Kings 8:13 uses this of the Temple: it could also refer to Shiloh, or any other early centre of Israelite worship. *The sanctuary.* This word is neutral and only means 'holy place', although in late days it was used of the Temple (as the one great holy place).

18. *The Lord will reign.* This thought is characteristic of the psalter later (*e.g.* Ps. 10:16) and so some scholars have seen it as argument for a late date. But there are also at least two references in the Pentateuch to the kingship of YHWH in Israel (Nu. 23:21; Dt. 33:5) and indeed the whole concept of covenant probably demands kingship as a necessary corollary.[1] Unless Israel from the start believed in the kingship of YHWH, it is hard to explain the violence with which the old-fashioned Israelites opposed the attribution of this title to mortal man a century later (Gideon in Jdg. 8:23 and Samuel in 1 Sa. 8:6).

15:19–21. Prose summary and Miriam's song. As mentioned above, the little couplet of Miriam's song is undoubtedly archaic: it may be compared with Deborah's song in Judges 5. However, it adds nothing to the Song of Moses.

20. *The prophetess*: like Deborah (Jdg. 4:4). The word is much less common than the masculine form. Moses is of course regarded in the Pentateuch as a prophet (indeed as the yardstick of all prophethood, Dt. 34:10); but what is

---

[1] Even in the case of God's covenant with Abraham, the title given by Abraham to 'God most high' (El Elyon) as 'possessor/creator of heaven and earth' (Gn. 14:22) probably involves the concept of kingship.

meant by 'prophetess' in this context is not clear. In Numbers 12:2 Miriam makes claim to have spoken YHWH's word just as Moses has: in Numbers 12:6 a prophet is defined as one who had visions or dreams (although Moses is specifically put into a different class). Because Miriam (the name that appears as 'Mary' in New Testament days) is here described as 'Aaron's sister' and not 'Moses' sister', some have concluded that Moses was only her half-brother. There is no other evidence for this, apart from the negative evidence of the Mosaic birth narrative; but the 'sister' mentioned there is not specifically named as Miriam. Hebrew 'āḥôṯ could mean 'half-sister' just as well as 'sister'.

A timbrel. This was like a Salvation Army tambourine, or a sort of small hand drum, as its onomatopoeic name ('thump!') suggests. Women usually danced and sang on occasions of victory rather than on liturgical occasions. See 1 Samuel 18:6 for a victory song: but Judges 21:21 seems to be dancing by women at the autumn festival, therefore liturgical. It seems spontaneous rather than organized music here, but that was probably true of much music in early days. Women singers had a particular role as mourners in later days (Am. 8:3; 2 Ch. 35:25) and later temple-singers included women (Ezr. 2:65; Ne. 7:67) and women singers formed part of the tribute demanded from Hezekiah by the Assyrians. Some of these singers may of course have been secular rather than sacred: but such a distinction was unlikely to exist in Israel in early days at least.

d. A desert journal (15:22 – 18:27)

15:22–27. Bitter waters. Israel is now clearly to the east of the salt marshes and inlets of the gulf; but how far south she was we do not know. The position of wells and oases is not likely to have changed since Mosaic times, and we can guess the general route (roughly, down the west coast of the Sinai Peninsula) until they turn due east at some point or other, dependent on the location of Mount Sinai. But the exact identification of the halts is not easy, since we do not know how many miles Israel could or would cover in a day. For nomads with flocks and herds today, ten to fifteen miles is good going, although of course men on a raid can cover much more. It has often been pointed out that Israel, if nomads at all, were 'donkey nomads', not 'camel nomads'. They could not cut across the desert, but must drive their flocks where there was pasture and water. This could be almost anywhere in et-Tih, the 'desert of the wanderers' as it is still called in Arabic.

22. *The wilderness of Shur* (Gn. 25:18) is generally taken as the north-west corner of the peninsula, in contrast to the 'wilderness of Paran' in the south-east (Nu. 13:3)[1] and the 'wilderness of Sin' in the south-west (Ex. 16:1). Whether the later Israelites themselves knew the exact location of all these places is doubtful, but they most certainly knew a list of 'halts' in the wilderness, with names and distances of water-holes. Either they or their ancestors may well have worked at the turquoise mines of Sarabit-el-Khadem, halfway down the west coast of the peninsula of Sinai.

23. *Marah.* Unlike many Old Testament etymologies, this is not a mere pun based on similarity of sound, for 'marah' could actually mean 'bitter' or 'bitterness', if it is a Semitic root. The word 'myrrh' seems to be from the same root, referring to the sharp flavour of the myrrh. Many desert oases are named from wells, springs and pools, since water is their essential common feature. The spring in question is probably the modern 'Ain Hawarah. *It was named.* The vague third person singular (literally 'he called its name . . .') need not necessarily refer to Moses, but could be taken (as RSV) impersonally, following the Semitic idiom. That means that the name may have existed long before Israel's passage. Most artesian wells are bitter and unpleasant because of mineral salts.

24. *The people murmured*: 'grumbled', explicitly against Moses, whom God had appointed as their leader, and thus implicitly against God Himself (Ex. 16:8). In so doing, they are typical of all humanity: that is why they can become both a lesson and a warning to us (1 Cor. 10:11). There are over a dozen passages in the Pentateuch where such 'murmuring' is mentioned; it was characteristic of Israel.

25. *YHWH showed him a tree.* The verb *showed* is the root from which the word 'Torah', 'instruction', is derived. This in itself shows how much richer the Hebrew concept 'Torah'

---

[1] It is only fair to say, however, that the exact location of this wilderness (if indeed it had an exact location) is uncertain: Numbers 13:26 places even Kadesh in the wilderness of Paran. Aharoni, quoted in Rothenberg, considers it to cover the whole Sinaitic peninsula.

was than the English concept of 'law'. Here, knowledge of a way to blessing and salvation is called a 'torah'. What the tree was, and how it sweetened the water, it is probably vain to ask. De Lesseps, quoted in Driver, mentions a barberry bush as so used by modern Arabs, and various parallels are quoted from other lands. No doubt the need was to find some pungent or aromatic shrub, whose flavour would cover the mineral taste and make the water palatable. Medieval commentators delighted to see here a reference to the cross, by which the bitterest of life's waters is sweetened. So long as we claim this only as an illustration of a great biblical truth, and not as an exegesis of the passage before us, this is fair enough. It has sometimes been suggested that God may have shown Moses this shrub not at that moment, but during his long stay in Midian previously. But the text seems clear that it was in response to Moses' cry of despair on this occasion. If God had showed it in Midianite days, it would have been another instance of His preparation of Moses. For a similar story of 'healing' of bitter water, see 2 Kings 2:21.

Made for them a statute and an ordinance occurs again in Joshua 24:25, with reference to the law-giving at Shechem: it sounds like a set phrase. *There he proved them.* The meaning is 'God tested Israel', the same root as is used in 'Massah' (Ex. 17:7). But there is no need to assume that this sentence really refers to the later happening. In the present incident of the bitter water, God was testing Israel just as truly as He did at Massah later. By their grumbling reaction, Israel showed only too clearly their true nature when under test. It is possible however that the 'testing' refers to the conditional nature of the promise in verse 26, which is also typical of the teaching of the book of Deuteronomy. God's blessing is always dependent on the obedience of His children to His revealed will.

26. *I will put none of these diseases upon you*: presumably the diseases 'put upon' the Egyptians refer in the first place to the plagues in general, but in particular to the turning of the water into blood, which made it undrinkable. Israel will never find the water that God supplies unpalatable: He is YHWH their healer.

27. *Elim*: the name 'terebinth-trees' seems taken from the most prominent natural feature. If Marah was 'Ain Hawarah, then Elim must be the lush Wadi Gharandel, seven miles

south, with its jujube trees and wells. There is no need to
spiritualize either the *twelve springs* or *seventy palm trees*. The
numbers may be strictly literal or round numbers, since both
figures, to the Hebrew mind, give the idea of perfection.

16:1–36. Bread from heaven. 1. *The fifteenth day* would
be a month after leaving Egypt, if the departure was on the
fifteenth day of the first month (Ex. 12:6,31). *The wilderness
of Sin.* There may be a linguistic connection between Sin and
Sinai, the sacred mountain. However, the present context
makes clear that they are not the same place. The wilderness
of Zin (a different Hebrew consonant) should not be
confused; it lay two hundred miles away to the north.

3. *In the land of Egypt.* They had forgotten the slavery of
Egypt, and now idealized its good points, as men will do.
Slaves do not eat much meat, yet here the 'meat cauldron'
looms large in their memories. Elsewhere, they remember
the pungent garlics and sweet melons of the Nile delta (Nu.
11:5). Their present complaint seems twofold: there is not
enough food and, in particular, there is no meat. Like all
pastoralists, they were very loath to slaughter their own
beasts (*cf.* Nu. 11:22), which was the only alternative to a
diet of milk and cheese in the desert. Note how they are
quick to impute the worst motives to Moses; he has done this
deliberately, so they say.

4. *Bread from heaven.* If *bread* is to be taken in its old sense of
'food' (as *leḥem* seems to have meant originally), then this
promise could cover both the quails and the manna. *A day's
portion every day.* God's daily provision of Israel's need may be
the source of the petition in the Lord's prayer dealing with
'daily bread' (Mt. 6:11). *That I may prove them* is presumably
either to do with the need for daily dependence on God for
food, or with the command not to gather food on the sabbath
day. On the Friday, a double amount must be gathered, as
outlined below (verses 25,26).

6. *You shall know that it was YHWH.* This provision of food
will confirm God's saving purpose to Israel; it will show clearly
that the exodus was no chance historical event.

7. Israel will see God's *glory* in His saving acts. Elsewhere
God's 'glory' is regarded as being physically manifested at
the meeting-tent, or in the cloud (Ex. 16:10).

8. *Flesh . . . bread.* Two distinct provisions are mentioned.

together here: bread (manna) and meat (quails), although little stress is laid on the quails here. See Numbers 11:31 for an account of a feeding by quails, which seems to have taken place after the law-giving at Sinai (not before, as here), and was followed by a plague.

10. *The cloud*: often the sign of God's presence, as in Psalm 104:3 where YHWH rides on the clouds. Usually the awful darkness of the thundercloud seems meant, a fitting symbol of God's majesty, wrath and inscrutability, but here it may mean the column of cloud (Ex. 13:22). The Old Testament knew the other side of God's nature also; but the full revelation of God could come only with Christ, where no cloud was needed (Mt. 17:1–8).

13. *Quails* (in Hebrew, a collective noun, like 'sheep' in English) migrate regularly between south Europe and Arabia across the Sinai Peninsula. They are small, bullet-headed birds, with a strong but low flight, usually roosting on the ground or in the low bushes at nightfall. When exhausted, they would be unable to rise above the low black tents of nomads, and too weary to take off again. A quail running on the ground is easy quarry for a nimble boy. The birds are good eating, and were a favourite delicacy of the Egyptians (Herodotus ii. 77) when dried in the sun. In Numbers 11, the quails became a 'plague' by which God punishes Israel. Here however there is only a passing mention of the quails, as the main interest is in the manna. Numbers tells us that it was the east wind that brought the quails: that fits with the known fact that quails fly north in March–April, roughly in the time following passover, presumably the date of the incident.

14. *A fine, flake-like thing.* The early Jewish commentators understood the word as meaning 'globule', something circular, but the early versions and the Targum of Onkelos favour 'scales' as the meaning. Since the Hebrew word does not occur elsewhere, there is no certainty, but cognate languages also suggest 'scales'. The simile of *hoarfrost* does not settle the shape, but only the colour.[1]

15. *What is it?*: *mān hû'?*, explaining the name *manna* (Hebrew *mān*) as though meaning 'the what's-its-name'.

---

[1] G. I. Davies, in a forthcoming article which he has kindly made available, argues for 'powdery' (with JB) on the basis of cognate languages, the Vulgate, and the LXX. This may well be correct.

This is often dismissed as mere assonance or popular etymology based on Aramaic, since the pure Hebrew form should be *mâh-hû*. But this is certainly how the Israelites understood the word, possibly thus giving a popular etymology in Hebrew to a non-Israelite word. We may perhaps compare the punning name 'Moses'.[1]

16. *An omer apiece.* In later days, this measure would be nearly a gallon; but in Arabia *ghumar* could mean 'a cupful' (see Driver). Perhaps this was also the early Hebrew meaning, although there is no evidence, owing to the scanty use of the term. A gallon per head would seem too much for food, as a daily ration.

18. *Nothing over . . . no lack.* Nothing miraculous may be intended, but merely that they pooled the manna collected, and each kept the agreed ration of an omer per head. Paul certainly seems to understand it in this way in 2 Corinthians 8:14,15.

20. *They did not listen to Moses.* In spite of the command, some tried to make God's loving provision for today last until tomorrow. Such obstinacy and lack of faith is only too typical of mankind. It is not surprising that the manna would not keep, for it disappeared when the sun rose (verse 21).

23. *A holy sabbath.* This is the first actual occurrence of the word in Scripture, although the idea of the institution is present in Genesis 2:2,3. Here the stronger word '*šabbaṭôn*' is used, alongside the usual word *šabbaṭ*. Elsewhere this is used only of New Year's Day and other particularly holy festivals.

24. *It did not become foul.* The miracle lay in the fact that, when kept overnight on this occasion, it neither melted nor went bad. A lower temperature would serve this purpose, but it is idle to speculate what method God may have used. Lower temperature would also account for the absence of manna on the next day, if it was indeed a precipitate of the type suggested below.

29. *ỲHWH has given you the sabbath.* On the basis of this, and the breach of the sabbath reported, some suggest that the Israelites had not kept the sabbath while in Egypt, but that it was by way of being a novel observance. Perhaps their

[1] Again, G. I. Davies points out, with numerous instances, that *mān* was used for 'what?' in Canaanite dialects. The form *mān-hû* need therefore be regarded neither as late nor as Aramaizing.

condition as slaves would account for this failure to observe it, even if some such custom had been known (in embryo at least) to their patriarchal ancestors.

31. *Like coriander seed.* The *manna* was white, round and sweet. It was obviously unknown to later Israelites: hence the careful characterization. This description, and its quality of disappearing in the heat of the sun (when collected by ants), prove almost conclusively that it was the Arabic *man*, a globular exudation of two types of scale insects, living on twigs of tamarisk. This substance is chemically composed of natural sugars and pectin, and is found today only in the south-western part of the Sinai Peninsula after the rains of spring. It is most plentiful in June, which would roughly be the time of year, if the Bible dating is followed. Whatever its actual nature, this was God's provision for His people all the days of the desert wandering: see Driver for full discussion. More recently, Bodenheimer (quoted in Hyatt) has given an interesting chemical explanation of the process.

33. *A jar*, made of gold, and at least initially filled with manna, was henceforth among the relics stored in the ark (Heb. 9:4), along with the two stone tablets of the commandments and Aaron's rod that budded.

17:1–7. Water at Horeb. 1. *Rephidim.* If this is Wadi Refayid (as both the name, and also the stage-list in Numbers 33:12–14 suggest), then the anxiety of the Amalekites is understandable. They want to drive Israel from the fertile oasis of Wadi Feiran, the best land in the peninsula, lying nearby. For the suggestion that Rephidim is the ridge of er-Rafid, on the east coast of Aqaba, see Noth. It is a puzzle, however, to see how Israel could have been short of water in such a place as Rephidim unless, as Driver suggests, they were camped in the desert, short of the oasis itself, or, with other editors, they were camped past the oasis, and between it and Sinai. But this puzzle is only one part of a wider problem associated with this passage. Briefly, Israel is short of water and grumbles (verse 1): to prove God's presence, Moses strikes the rock, and water flows out (verse 6). Because the Israelites contended with Moses, the place is called Meribah, 'contention' (verse 7): because they 'put God to the test', it is also called Massah, 'testing' (verse 7). It would be unusual, but not impossible, for a place to have two such 'nicknames' derived from the same incident, as this would imply. Also, in the present context, there is no hint that Moses is held to be blameworthy for his action. But in Numbers 20:13 a very similar incident is described. Again the name Meribah, 'strife' is give to the place, but, instead of the name Massah, 'testing', there is a play on the word Kadesh, 'holy place' (Nu. 20:1,13) on the grounds that YHWH there showed Himself to be holy. This occasion was clearly after Sinai, not before, and Moses was punished for some aspect of his action on this occasion by exclusion from Canaan (Dt. 1:37). Is this the same incident as in our text? If so, it would be an example of a slightly different account (as in the Synoptic Gospels) of the same story appearing in two different places. It is unnecessary to assume this, however, if we accept that the place name Massah alone belongs to the first incident, and Meribah alone to the second. Thirst was apt to be a continual experience in the desert, and there is no reason why such an event might not have happened twice. Since the events were so similar, it would be very easy to forget which place-name applied to which event, especially since both places were outside the normal range of the later Israelite. Of course, if the same event happened twice, there is no reason why the same name should not be used twice. In Psalm 95:8 the two names Massah and Meribah are linked, as examples of Israel's lack of faith and rejection of God: this may be parallelism and not identification, referring to two distinct happenings.

2. *The people found fault*: 'argued' with Moses. This verb is the key word of the passage, explaining why the name 'Meribah' ('argument' or 'strife') is used for the place afterwards. Some editors have brought forward alternate explanations, based on the view that the name arose from the 'judicial decisions' given beside the springs there, as at 'En-Mishpat' (Kadesh), 'Well of Judgment' (Gn. 14:7) or because shepherds 'contended' for the water (*cf.* Gn. 26:16–22). No doubt both were common occurrences, but they are not mentioned in this particular context as reasons for the giving of the name. Moses echoes the 'argued' in his reply and joins it with the second root that lies behind the name Massah ('test', 'put to the test').

3. *And our cattle*. With the usual imputation of ridiculous motives to Moses, there is a touch of characterization here.

Who but a cattleman would have worried about his stock
dying of thirst, if he were already dying of thirst himself?
Here speaks the true Israelite farmer.

4. *Almost ready to stone me.* This is the last stage of rejection
of a leader in Israel. See the case of David at Ziklag (1 Sa.
30:6) or Adoram at Shechem (1 Ki. 12:18). It must have
reminded Moses of the initial Israelite reaction to his coming
(Ex. 5:21). Christ (Jn. 10:31), Stephen (Acts 7:58) and Paul
(Acts 14:19) all faced stoning at the hands of God's people,
the very ones to whom they had been sent.

6. *At Horeb.* This is another puzzle, for 'Horeb' seems to be
used interchangeably with 'Sinai' as the site of the law-giving,
whatever the reason (some seeing it as denoting different early
collections of Mosaic material). Unless therefore Horeb covers
a far larger area than Sinai, it must be assumed from this
reference that Rephidim was so close to Sinai that the slopes
of the mountain actually reached Rephidim. Otherwise we
should have to assume that the geographical reference here
is vague and general only. But, apart from other considerations, the geographical knowledge shown elsewhere would
seem to rule this out as a possible explanation. *You shall
strike the rock.* As usual in Semitic idiom, it becomes 'the rock',
where English would say 'a rock', because it is the one in
question. Driver however prefers to take it of the whole rocky
mass, not any one crag. The Hebrew word used for 'rock'
here is not the same as that used in Numbers 20. *In the sight
of the elders.* It seems as if they alone were privileged to see this
sign, although all would drink of the water that gushed out.
Compare Exodus 24:11, where the elders alone share in
the divine banquet.

7. *Massah.* In the context, the 'testing' is explained as a
'testing' of whether God was with them or not. As Driver
points out, 'test' is a neutral word in Hebrew. Translations
like 'tempt' or nouns like 'temptation' are misleading in
modern English, though etymologically they are correct
renderings.

17:8-16. The war with Amalek. For the reason for
Amalek's challenge of Israel at this particular spot, see note
on 17:1 above. Napier points out that the last three episodes
in the story have dealt with the basic needs of Israel, provision
of food and drink in the desert. Now comes the fourth,

dealing with the last fundamental necessity of survival, delivery from enemies. Having proved Himself triumphant in all of these, God has abundantly shown that He can save His people.

8. The tribe of *Amalek* is regarded as of Edomite origin (Gn. 36:12). Like many other nomads, they ranged over a wide area, roughly described as 'the Negeb' or 'south land' (Nu. 13:29). They certainly camped in the oasis of Kadesh (Gn. 14:7) and therefore may have camped in the oasis of Wadi Feiran as well. In any case, the grazing in the peninsula would not support both Israel and Amalek at the same time, so it was natural that they should attack sooner or later. What their numbers were, we cannot guess: modern bedouin of the same area could raise a force of a few thousand men only. Perhaps this accounts for their typical method of attack (mentioned with indignation in Dt. 25:18): they hung about Israel's rear and flanks, and cut off the stragglers. No doubt this accounted for the later bitterness felt towards Amalek (1 Sa. 15:2).

9. *Joshua* first appears here. Usually he is described as Moses' 'junior assistant' (Ex. 24:13). Technically, his name was still at this date 'Hoshea', the older form. The new form 'Joshua', containing the name of YHWH, was apparently given to him at Kadesh (Nu. 13:16). When the spies were sent out, Joshua was tribal chieftain of Ephraim (Nu. 13:8): he and Caleb alone were faithful.

10. *Hur* is mentioned only once elsewhere (Ex. 24:14). Bezalel's grandfather (Ex. 31:2) is a different man. Later Jewish tradition is imaginative but valueless in making him out to be Miriam's husband. It is unlikely that his name means 'the Horite' or 'the Hurrian' (Davies). Even if it did, it proves no more about racial origins than does the name Phinehas, 'negro', in the tribe of Levi or 'Norman' when used as an English name.

11. *Held up his hand*: usually a military signal for beginning battle or for the advance. Presumably 'lowered his hand' could then be a signal for retreat. Otherwise the uplifted hand may be the sign of an oath (*cf.* Gn. 14:22, and this chapter, verse 16) to put Amalek under the sacred 'ban' or 'curse', that meant utter destruction. However, the usual explanation (that it refers to prayer) may well be correct. In this case, to lower the hands would be to cease to pray, and thus to cease to depend on God for help. See Psalm 63:4 for lifting up of hands in prayer.

13. *Mowed down Amalek*: 'prostrated' or 'disabled' might be a better rendering. The Hebrew form is rare, but the general meaning is clear from Aramaic.

14. *Write this.* One of the few passages in Exodus itself (others occur in Numbers and Deuteronomy) where there is clear reference to contemporary written records of material (*cf.* Ex. 24:4; 34:27). It is interesting that the 'writing' is paired with oral recitation here: no doubt this corresponds to the two great streams of sacred tradition, written and oral. It is also interesting that the oral is here seen to be in dependence upon the written document. The purpose in this instance was to record the 'sacred war' or 'ban' against Amalek, finally executed in Saul's day (1 Sa. 15), after which we scarcely hear of Amalek again. Perhaps the 'book' mentioned was the lost 'Book of the Wars of YHWH', to which reference is made elsewhere (Nu. 21:14).

15. *YHWH is my banner* seems a possible enough name for an altar (for the naming of altars, see Gn. 33:20), though it is more properly a title of God Himself, to whom the altar is dedicated.

16. *A hand upon the banner of YHWH.* This emendation is better than the MT 'a hand upon the throne of YHWH'. Presumably the idea in either case is an oath of perpetual war, taken with the right hand on YHWH's altar or on some tribal 'banner' symbolizing His presence. If 'throne' were read, it would refer to the ark, and this does not seem to have been yet in existence. The emendation is only one letter, *nēs* for *kēs*. See Hyatt for the various possibilities.

18:1–12. Jethro's visit. 1. *Jethro* (Reuel, in Ex. 2:18) is described as *the priest of Midian* or 'Midian's priest'. To judge by later Hebrew usage, that would mean the chief priest of Midian (1 Sa. 1:9), and thus denote high position. *Heard.* Every nomad in the peninsula would have heard by now of the Israelite breakaway from Egypt and her clash with Amalek. If Sinai was in the territory regularly grazed by Midian, then Israel was already on Midian's borders, while Amalek must have been Midian's immediate neighbour.

2. *Sent her away.* In later Hebrew this verb would refer to divorce, but here it seems to refer to some event not otherwise recorded in Scripture. Zipporah and her sons had perhaps been sent back to Midian by Moses for safety. The phrase is a necessary addition, in order to explain how it was that Jethro was able to bring Moses' family with him on this occasion when, in Exodus 4:20, we read that Moses had already taken them back with him to Egypt.

4. *Eliezer.* This is the first, and only, mention of Moses' second son, whose very name suggests a rekindling of faith in Moses' heart, compared with the despair shown in the name 'Gershom'. Since he plays no part in later tradition, not even the most captious of critics could claim him as an invention. The very fact that both his existence, and this coming to Moses, pose a problem is the strongest argument that this is trustworthy tradition. Manufactured tradition contains no problems. The form of the name is interesting: not even in the names of Moses' own children does the name of YHWH appear. This piece of evidence supports the view that the name was unknown in Israel until Moses' vision at Sinai, and was not, as Hyatt suggests, the name of the 'patron deity' of Moses' immediate family or clan.

5. *The mountain of God.* If this is Sinai, then Israel must be already well to the east of Rephidim. It is possible that the Israelites have already moved to the area mentioned in Exodus 19:2, immediately below the slopes of the mountain. Jethro must have known that this mountain was the goal of Israel's pilgrimage (Ex. 5:1) and that worship there was to be the sign of God's fulfilment of His promise (Ex. 3:12). If the mountain was already sacred to Jethro and his people, the rendezvous would be even more obvious to him.

6. *See, your father in law is coming.* 'See' is the reading of the versions; the Hebrew text has 'I', which does not make such good sense, unless it is a message sent in advance. RSV *Lo* is therefore probably correct.

7. *Did obeisance.* The whole scene is typical of eastern courtesy. Both men are now great chiefs in their own right, and behave accordingly. For the respect shown by Moses to his father-in-law, compare his readiness to accept Jethro's advice about judicial structures (verse 24). Such humility and respect for age is commended in the Scriptures (Lv. 19:32), if not popular today.

11. *Now I know.* Jethro confesses the supremacy of YHWH over all other gods, as demonstrated in His saving activity towards Israel. This may not be true monotheism (the belief that there is only one god), but it certainly leads to monolatry (the worship of one god to the exclusion of others) as a logical sequence. See Jonah 1:16 for a similar form of confession by non-Israelites. *Dealt arrogantly*. The RSV transfers this clause from verse 10 to the end of verse 11, where it makes better sense. If we want to keep the clause as part of verse 10, we must assume an omission, perhaps either 'YHWH destroyed them' or 'YHWH saved his people'. Alternatively, the *kî*, 'for', could be omitted: the sentence, although clumsy, could then be translated as it stands in the AV.

12. *Offered a burnt offering.* Was Jethro 'caught up' into the worship of YHWH, a 'new convert', as doubtless others were later? Or had he already known and worshipped YHWH previously? Jethro's own words here seem to favour the view that YHWH was a new god, as far as he was concerned. Those who hold to the 'Midianite hypothesis' (or 'Kenite hypothesis') think otherwise: they think that Moses learned not only the name of God, but also much of His ways of worship, from his Midianite kinsmen. They thus easily explain the puzzling fact that Jethro leads the worship on this occasion— not as a 'new convert' but as a recognized priest and teacher. However, this explanation is not necessary. Jethro's status as priest, and his senior relationship to Moses, would seem to be adequate grounds. Priesthood as such did not yet exist in Israel: it was a function of the 'elder' of the clan. *Burnt offering* is usually expressive of thanksgiving, or of the fulfilment of a vow: both would be appropriate here. This is probably the 'whole burnt offering', in which everything is devoted to God and nothing eaten. The general term *sacrifices* would cover the 'communion meal', feasting in the presence of God, as here and in Exodus 24:11, where the 'elders' again appear, possibly in a primitive priestly capacity.

18:13–27. Appointment of judges. The clear tradition of the Bible is that this institution in Israel was along the lines of Midianite practice, as a result of a suggestion by Jethro. The function of the officials is clear, while the technical word *šōp̄ēṭ*, 'judge', is not used here. In patriarchal days, family justice was dispensed by the clan chieftain. As slaves in Egypt, the Israelites could hardly have had an independent judicial system of their own. True, they had

Egyptian 'supervisors' and their own 'gangers' under them, but this was an organization for labour. When Moses tried to act as a ruler or 'judge' they resented it (Ex. 2:14). In addition, Israel appears to have preserved the old tribal structure to some extent: there was still a *nāśî'* or 'chief' for each tribe (Nu. 7:11) and these in primitive times may have had judicial functions as well. Deuteronomy 1:15 is an interesting sidelight on the whole question. Elders have also been mentioned already (Ex. 18:12) as sharing in sacrifices, and having some kind of representative function, possibly with primitive judicial duties as well. The title and position of *šōp̄ēṭ*, 'judge', was an old Canaanite one (the Phoenicians preserved the title even in their overseas colonies), but seemingly more in the sense of 'champion, leader', as in the book of Judges, rather than in a legal sense. The organization outlined below is primarily a military one, based on the *śar*, or commander of a certain number of men (*cf.* verse 21). Such a structure is very suited to a nomadic group in the desert. Like any ancient nation, Israel is always considered primarily as a fighting force, and organized accordingly. To see the anecdote as a separation of 'sacred' cases judged by Moses, and 'civic' cases judged by elders, seems mistaken: all justice was sacred to Israel. The administration of justice, of whatever kind, is here set in the context of sacrifice and sacred meal. The distinction is therefore not between sacred and secular but between difficult and simple matters, those already covered by tradition and revelation as against those requiring a fresh word from God, mediated through His agent, Moses.

13. *Sat . . . stood* are technical terms of Semitic law, denoting 'judge' and 'litigant' respectively.

14. *Why do you sit alone?* The wise question of an old chieftain who has learnt the great lesson of how to devolve authority. Like many a Christian leader, Moses was wearing himself out unnecessarily (verse 18) by trying to do everything single-handed. This is not always a mark of ambition: it is sometimes the mark of the over-conscientious and over-anxious. More, it was wearing out the people (verse 18 again), an aspect usually overlooked. Delay in justice, arising from similar reasons, was one of the causes of Absalom's revolt in later centuries (2 Sa. 15:1-6).

15. *To inquire of God.* This verb is often translated, in later devotional passages, 'to seek after God' in prayer. Here however it means to seek God's decision in a disputed matter, whether a legal quarrel or a need for guidance. In later days, the 'ephod' was used on such occasions, apparently containing 'Urim and Thummim' or the oracular lot stones (1 Sa. 23:9; 28:6): but this system probably did not exist till later (Ex. 28:30).

16. *I make them know the statutes of God.* Moses obviously regarded his judicial task as a teaching ministry, telling the Israelites of God's 'statutes', 'set laws', and 'decisions' or 'instructions', given on specific occasions to deal with particular cases. Perhaps we have here the method by which the law of Moses came into being, a combination of great principles of revelation and their application to day-by-day living in the desert.

19. *And God be with you!* The thought seems to be 'so that God is with you', *i.e.* 'blesses you'. However, the thought may correspond to the polite phrasing of verse 23 ('and if God so commands you'). Like any polite easterner, Jethro will not compel his son-in-law to take his advice, wise though it is. *Represent . . . before God*: 'towards God' or 'Godwards' would be a better translation. The thought is that the ordinary Israelites dare not approach God directly (Ex. 19:24).

20. *The way in which they must walk.* The word 'way' may be quite literal in Israel's case, referring to the journey through the wilderness. It is also very commonly used in a metaphorical sense (*cf.* Gn. 6:12), which seems to be the meaning here. The use of such a metaphor may be conscious memory of the original Hebrew meaning of the word translated 'decision', *tôrâ*, almost 'signpost'. Seen in this light, there is nothing hard or forbidding about the Hebrew concept of law: it is God's signpost to His road through life.

21. *Choose*: 'look out' is a possible meaning of this verb, so that 'choose' is a fair approximation. *Able men.* The Hebrew may have originally meant 'soldierly' men. It had however come to mean 'good men and true', in the English sense. We may compare the use of a similar phrase in Proverbs 12:4 of the ideal housewife. Driver points out that moral, rather than intellectual, qualities are demanded for such a position: this is proved by the explanatory clauses that follow. Much the same qualities are demanded of Christian workers in New Testament days (see Acts 6:3 and 1 Tim. 3:1-3).

24. *Moses gave heed*: 'obeyed' is the literal meaning, and it should be so translated. Moses was humble enough (and wise enough) to learn from his father-in-law. Compare the pregnant verse in Exodus 2:21, 'and Moses was content to dwell with the man': that too was true humility. Meekness (with faithfulness, Heb. 3:2) was the great distinguishing quality of Moses (Nu. 12:3).

27. *Let (him) depart*: the same root as in verse 2, where it is used of Moses' despatch of his wife back to Midian. This verse thus confirms the neutral sense of the word in the earlier instance. In Numbers 10:29–32 Moses appeals to his Midianite kinsman (whether father-in-law or brother-in-law is not clear) to remain with Israel as a guide in the wilderness, an area doubtless well known to Midianites. The Kenite clan was later found, either living among Canaanites in the northern plain (Jdg. 4:17) or among Amalekites in the Negeb (1 Sa. 15:6): in either case, outside their presumed homeland and allied to Israel. Numbers may refer to a different incident. Indeed Hobab/Raguel may not have granted Moses' request, as recorded in Numbers, although in this case it is hard to explain the later presence of Kenites among the Israelites in Canaan.

III. COVENANT AND LAW (19:1 – 31:18)

a. Preparation for covenant (19:1-25)

19:1-15. The instructions 1. *On the third new moon* is a possible translation and preferable to the vague 'in the third month', in view of the phrase 'on that day', immediately below. See Hyatt for the possible connection between the law-giving and the Feast of Weeks.

2. *The wilderness of Sinai*. The word conventionally translated 'wilderness' is not a sandy desert, but grazing country, not settled by man. Clearly, from this verse, the steppe of Sinai is directly facing Mount Sinai and some little distance from Rephidim, with the 'steppe of Sin' now well behind (Ex. 17:1). Sinai itself may be Ğebel Mûsa, Ğebel Serbāl or Ğebel Katarina, three striking peaks in the immediate vicinity. Detailed interpretation of the topography will depend upon which mountain is chosen. Here the view is taken that the traditional Ğebel Mûsa is the mountain in question: but no theological point depends on the exact identification, which may not have been clear to the later Israelites.

More far-reaching is the question as to whether Sinai was in the south of the Sinai peninsula at all. Some scholars place it, either near Kadesh-barnea in the north east, or somewhere in modern Arabia, to the east of the gulf of Aqaba. Those who place it near Kadesh do so because they consider that the stories in Exodus told at this point belong to the general Kadesh area (water from the rock; quails; advice of Jethro). Certainly similar incidents are told in Numbers of the Kadesh area. Rothenberg mentions the possibility of Ğebel-el-Halal, a lower mountain on the 'way of Shur', a well-used road between Egypt and Kadesh. Others suggest some peak in the mountains of Edom (Seir) to the east of Kadesh, in the area of the steppe of Paran. They quote in support later poetic references, where God is seen as coming to the help of His people from Paran or Edom (Hab. 3:3). Of course, the 'Paran' mentioned here could be the 'Pharan' of Eusebius, the modern Feiran oasis near Rephidim, in which case Mount Sinai would be meant. Edom lies in a straight line between Ğebel Mûsa and Judah, so that God would have been pictured as crossing over Edom in any case. More serious is the objection that this northern location of Sinai would make nonsense of the detailed itineraries of both Exodus and Numbers, where Kadesh is clearly reached after Sinai, and is at a considerable distance from it. Deuteronomy 1:2 clearly states that 'Horeb' and Kadesh are eleven days' journey apart. Also, none of these northern mountains has the striking isolation of any of the three southern peaks already suggested in the Sinai area.

The siting of Sinai to the east of the gulf of Aqaba depends on the twofold belief that the Sinai of the revelation must have been an active volcano at the time (perhaps near Tebuk, as Noth suggests), to judge from the description of the manifestations accompanying the theophany, and secondly that it was in the heart of the Midianite homeland, which certainly seems to have been in this area. Editors have, however, pointed out that it is most unlikely that such a nomadic group could have been persuaded to remain so near a volcano in eruption. In any case, the description of the theophany on Sinai does not necessarily refer to an active volcano (while details may have been borrowed from this, in a symbolic sense) and Exodus 18:5 implies that Jethro had made a considerable journey from his home to reach Sinai. Further, once again, a placing of Sinai east of the gulf would make nonsense of the careful itinerary (although not so completely as the northern siting of Sinai would do). On these grounds, then, the traditional site of Sinai has been accepted as being at least approximately correct. (See further the Excursus in Hyatt, pp. 203ff.)

3. *YHWH called to him.* This is the beginning of a great block of teaching (combined with some narrative background) that stretches from here, through Leviticus, up to Numbers 10. All is represented as being given at Sinai, and within a comparatively short time. From then on, the story deals with the journey to Kadesh Barnea, incidents on the way, and incidents happening there and thereafter. Curiously, little detail is preserved of the long 'wilderness period' (which, in biblical chronology, would have been some thirty-eight years: *cf.* Dt. 2:14), but such is the way of biblical history. Long periods are passed over in silence if felt to be spiritually insignificant, while short periods often receive detailed treatment.

4. *I bore you on eagles' wings*: see Deuteronomy 32:11. The *eagle* in question was probably the Palestinian vulture, circling tirelessly at great heights, and frequently mentioned in Canaanite texts (from Ras Shamra). Even more reminiscent of Deuteronomy is the thought of the conditional nature of God's covenant – conditional, that is to say, as regards enjoyment, for the bestowal is unconditional. Obedience alone will bring blessing, and assure status and privilege (verses 5,6; *cf.* Dt. 13:4,18). All that Israel needed initially for salvation from Egypt was acceptance of God's deliverance. Now the thought is introduced that obedience is needed as well as faith. This is not a contradiction: it is a fuller explanation of the nature of faith as response. Such teaching is not restricted to Deuteronomy: it is the heart of the book of the covenant (Ex. 20–23) and underlies the whole of the law of Moses.

5. *My own possession*: the word means 'special treasure' belonging privately to a king (*e.g.* 1 Ch. 29:3). This implies special value as well as special relationship. Deuteronomy 7:6 adds the word 'people' to it, to make the meaning still clearer. The word also implies choice or selection, in view of the second half of the verse ('all the earth is mine'), which is virtually full monotheism in its claim (*cf.* Gn. 14:22).

6. *A kingdom of priests.* The phrase does not occur elsewhere in the Old Testament (Hyatt), although Isaiah 61:6 is similar. Such a phrase certainly implies a king, and this king can only be YHWH. (For possible references to the kingship of YHWH in Mosaic days, see Nu. 23:21 and Dt. 33:5.) By the time of the judges it was axiomatic that, since YHWH ruled over His people, no mortal man might use the title of 'king' (Jdg. 8:22). But the true stress does not lie here; since kingship was virtually the only type of state known in the ancient world, 'kingdom' could well be translated today as 'state'. It is the universal priestly status of Israel to which attention is called. This is all the more understandable in view of the fact that there does not as yet seem to have been any priestly caste within Israel itself. Presumably the basic thought is of a group set apart peculiarly for God's possession and service, with free access to His presence. The thought of acting as God's representative for, and to, the other nations of the world cannot be ruled out. Whether realized at the time or not, this was to be the mission of Israel (*cf.* the ultimate promise to Abraham in Gn. 12:3). God's 'particularist' choice of Israel has a wider 'universalist' purpose.

A holy nation means primarily a nation 'set apart' from the other nations to belong to God. Normally, in later days, the word *gôy*, 'nation', means a non-Jewish (Gentile) nation, as in modern Hebrew: a different word is used to describe Israel, the chosen people of God. Till now, all peoples stand four square: the 'chosen people' will be an entity only after Sinai. At first, no doubt 'holy' merely meant 'dedicated' to God without any particular moral connotations. Such 'holiness' was contagious (Ex. 19:12) and might be dangerous, if not fatal. Then, because of the revealed nature of YHWH, such 'holiness', as descriptive of God, took on a strong moral meaning. Ultimately God's holiness became a compelling moral demand on His people (see Lv. 20:7). This holiness of the people of God, along with the priesthood of the chosen people, is emphasized again in the terms of the new covenant (1 Pet. 2:9).

These are the words. This almost sounds as if it were intended for an introduction to the ten commandments (*cf.* Ex. 20:1). But it is more likely to refer here to the promises that precede, rather than to the commands that follow.

8. *All that YHWH has spoken we will do.* This is necessary ratification of the covenant by the agreement of the people to keep the conditions (*cf.* Ex. 24:3). It is not unfair to see man's typical naivety in Israel's eager assertion. Her belief that she could keep such conditions is all the more ironic in view of her total failure so soon afterwards (Ex. 32). So Simon Peter (and indeed all the other apostles) would eagerly refute the charge that they would deny their Lord (Mt. 26:35). Like Israel, they did not know their own weakness as yet. By Joshua's day, though Israel would still make such easy assertions, their leaders would be slower to accept them at face value (Jos. 24:19). But, by then, they had learned a deeper lesson, that God could forgive and use even failures (Ex. 32:14). The deepest lesson of all is that God must change man's very nature, else he cannot serve God (Ps. 51:10).

9. *A thick cloud*: the Hebrew might be translated idiomatically 'thickest part of the cloud'. Cloud and darkness were a frequent symbol of God's presence. The reason for the manifestation on this occasion seems to have been so that the people should believe in the reality of God's communication to Moses, and thus believe in Moses as well as in God. If, as is possible, the dark cloud was a thunder-cloud, then the *hear* could be quite literal, describing the sound of thunder, which is often used in the Old Testament as a symbol of God's voice.

11. *The third day*: probably to denote the completeness of the process of purification. The necessary process of ritual purification, or setting apart for God, included the washing of garments (Nu. 8:21) and temporary abstention from sexual intercourse (verse 15, below). This was not because the latter was considered as wrong in any way, but because, by Mosaic law, it required ceremonial bathing for religious purification as an aftermath (Lv. 15:18). Nevertheless we may compare Paul's words, allowing temporary abstention that Christians may devote themselves to prayer (1 Cor. 7:5). *YHWH will come down.* The third person is a little awkward when put into God's mouth. Perhaps we should read, by an easy correction of the Hebrew text, 'I will come down' for 'he will come down'.' As Davies points out, there is significance in the verb: Israel never thought of YHWH as living on Sinai (as the Greeks thought that their gods lived on the snowy peak of

Olympus), but only as appearing there. Many other places were equally associated with divine manifestations in patriarchal days (*e.g.* Bethel, Gn. 28).

12. *You shall set bounds.* This verb, as it stands, has *the people* as object; the Israelites are 'confined to camp'. But the Samaritan version is probably correct in reading 'mountain' instead of 'people' here as object. The area of the mountain itself was 'sealed off' by some kind of markers. Since the mountain was holy (not permanently, or in itself, but on this occasion, and rendered so by the descent of God), then anything or anyone that touched it would also become 'holy' or devoted to God. For a living creature that meant sacrifice, which, in turn, meant death.

13. *No hand shall touch him.* Lest the very executioner should be caught in the same net, he must kill by stone or dart, without touching the doomed body himself. This concept, as well as the plentifulness of stones in Israel, probably accounts for Israel's normal method of execution of criminals by stoning. *The trumpet*: Hebrew *yôbēl* (giving English 'jubilee') is probably the ram's horn, whose blowing marks the advent of a festival in later Israel. Perhaps however, in earlier days, its purpose was to announce the advent of God, whether to save or to destroy (*cf.* Jos. 6:8, the trumpet-blast at Jericho, and Rev. 8:6, the seven trumpets of doom).

19:16-25. The theophany. 16. Whether Mount Sinai was a volcano or not, this verse quite explicitly refers to *thunders*, *lightnings* and storm *cloud*, all the adjuncts of a thunderstorm, not uncommon at certain times of the year on these mountains. The terror of the Israelites at the manifestation of God's presence is a motif taken up at a later stage.

18. *Fire*: understand 'of God' (as expressed in 2 Ki. 1:12). This may mean lightning. Bushfire was also dreaded in these dry lands and could be a symbol of God (like earthquake and typhoon, as in 1 Ki. 19:11,12) but it does not seem to be intended here, in spite of the *smoke* mentioned. Harmonists can point out that lightning can start bushfires, but not of course if it is accompanied by thunderstorms and rain. The whole phenomenon is compared to the appearance of *a kiln* or smelting-furnace: fire and smoke escape through the conical chimney. Those who follow the Midianite/Kenite hypothesis make much of this simile as derived from the metal-working activity of the Kenites. It is known that there were copper mines in the Arabah, presumably in Midianite territory. This 'smelting-furnace' then would be an object well known to Moses. But the simile is as old as Genesis 19:28, describing the destruction of Sodom by volcanic activity.

The whole mountain quaked greatly. Those who hold that Sinai was volcanic will point as proof to the fire and smoke, as well as to the earthquake denoted here by *quaked* (the same word as had been used of the Israelites above in verse 16). However, the whole may be metaphorical, an 'impressionistic' picture of the effect of a heavy thunderstorm (see Ps. 18:1–15). The LXX (with some 9 Hebrew MSS) escapes this difficulty by making 'the people' the subject of 'quaked greatly' instead of 'the mountain' – the reverse of the process suggested above in verse 12.

19. *Moses spoke, and God answered.* This may be the source of the description of Moses as one with whom God talked 'face to face' (Ex. 33:11). God's answer was explicitly given in the thunder on this occasion at least. Was Moses speaking in the blast of the ram's horn, to which the thunder was a reply? However, the text may merely mean that Moses spoke at this point of time.

21. *Lest they break through.* The danger was rather lest the people 'tear down' the artificial barriers erected around the mountain: crowd control is no new problem. Sheer idle curiosity would have been the motive, not any deep desire to be close to God. Some scholars have felt that the following verses are unnecessary and repetitious, and have seen in them descriptions of the same event, coming from different sources. But this is to ignore the anthropomorphisms and the artless style of the Pentateuch, especially in narrative, which frequently leads to repetition.

22. *The priests.* There is no evidence for priests, as such, existing in Israel until after Sinai. In Exodus 24:5 it is the 'young men' who offer sacrifices. Perhaps the word stands for 'elders', to whom there has been reference already (18:12) in a religious context. If 'priests' be kept, in the full sense, whoever are meant, the point is that, on such a solemn occasion, even those who stand in peculiarly close relationship to God have need to purify themselves, and cannot presume on their position.

24. *Bringing Aaron with you.* Usually it is Moses alone who climbs the mountain: but in Exodus 24:1 he is also accompanied by Aaron (along with Nadab, Abihu and seventy sheikhs).

25. *And told them.* The sentence ends abruptly. Moses' words are lost (a fairer translation would be 'and said to them . . .'), unless the reference is to 'reported speech' in chapter 20.

b. The ten words (20:1–17)

On this whole section, see Hyatt's excellent discussion, especially on the nature of the commandments. This short passage is one focal point of the Torah (another being the passover in chapter 12) and indeed of the whole of the Old Testament. Scholars differ as to whether the 'ten words' (to use the typical Hebrew phraseology of Ex. 34:28) are, as it were, the original kernel of the Torah, around which the whole of the rest may be grouped as expansion, or whether they are a later distillation of the Torah, a summing up of the whole in a few lucid sentences. It would seem from the book of Exodus that the former is the biblical picture: the 'ten words' are at once the beginning and the heart of the Mosaic revelation. Around the 'ten words' it is possible to group most of the provisions of the 'book of the covenant' in chapters 21–23, and around the book of the covenant in turn to group the rest of the Torah.

For the purpose of description, the Torah may be, and often is today, divided into various law 'codes' (although there is no proof that these ever existed separately). For example, the so-called 'book of the covenant' (Ex. 21–23) and the book of Deuteronomy are clear self-contained units. At least seven such codes have been isolated. Of these, the 'ten commandments' or 'ten words' form both the most important and the most fundamental code. It occurs twice in the Pentateuch (Ex. 20 and Dt. 5), with slight variants in the explanatory additions to the commandments, suggesting that, while these explanations may well be Mosaic, they are not part of the original form. This view is reinforced by other considerations. Israel's law has long been divided into 'apodeictic' (also called 'categoric') and 'casuistic'. The first is an abrupt and absolute command (usually in negative form) admitting no exceptions, while the second begins with an 'if' or 'when'.

The second variety is well known outside Israel from the legal codes of ancient Western Asia, and is generally considered to be 'case law', later decisions dependent on great early principles. The first type (rare outside Israel) embodies these principles, and may therefore be assumed to be earlier. It is stern desert law giving no reason for its commands, and allowing no exception or argument.

It therefore seems likely that the commandments antedate the rest of the law, and that the original form of the commandments, as written on the two tablets (maybe, as suggested, and as not unusual at the time, duplicated on either tablet) was simply the categoric 'You must not . . .' without fuller explanation. Some hyper-critical scholars have claimed that both the ten words and the book of the covenant appear somewhat abruptly and break the flow of the narrative, which is resumed immediately after (Ex. 24). Therefore thay have, on these grounds, divorced the commandments from the theophany at Sinai, and from the subsequent convenant-making, both of which they admit to be central to the story. But to take this view is to ignore the whole stress of Exodus, which is that God reveals Himself precisely in those moral commandments. To Israel, the 'book of the covenant' is a definition of the terms under which God, as a great monarch, accepts Israel as His subjects under a 'suzerainty treaty' (see notes on the book of the covenant 20:18 – 23:33, below). We therefore must accept both commandments and book of the covenant as integral parts of the final form of the narrative in which they are embedded.

Some scholars have also argued that the commandments have no connection with the great theme of exodus from Egypt (or deliverance at passover, if the event is seen from another angle). But if the preamble in Exodus 20:2 to the 'ten words' is taken at its face value (and there is no reason to do otherwise), then the whole is set against the background of redemption. It is because of His redemptive work that God has the right to command.

The question of the numbering of the commandments is interesting. There is a universal early tradition that there were ten (witness the common title), although tradition is not agreed as to how to divide the material so as to make this ten. There seems to be no special sacredness about the number ten, although the Hebrews, like most of mankind, counted to the base of ten, probably because the possession of ten fingers made this an easy task. The institution of the 'tithe' (Gn. 28:22) shows how this basis of ten could take a religious meaning. Twelve would have been the obvious number to choose, in view of the tribal basis of early Israelite life: therefore, if ten is the traditional number, it must be original. Other groups of ten or twelve commandments occur elsewhere in the law: Noth cites Exodus 34:14–26 and Deuteronomy 27:15–26 as examples, but the mathematics are somewhat artificial. Exodus 34 (where Noth might well have started with the prologue in verse 11) is the so-called 'ritual decalogue'. This title is fair in that its major concern is not (as in the 'ten words') with basic moral principles, but with the outward religious forms by which these may be expressed. It will be discussed under the appropriate chapter below.

A final general question is that of the place of the ten commandments in Israel's organized religious life later. A passover-story was no doubt narrated at the appropriate annual festival: but when were the ten commandments recited? That they are couched in a form suited for recitation is clear enough. Those who hold that Israel held an annual festival of 'covenant renewal', when they celebrated God's kingship over Israel, think of this as a suitable occasion for the proclamation of the terms of the covenant. While it is true that later Judaism celebrated annually at Pentecost the giving of the law, there is, in the view of the present writer, insufficient biblical evidence to justify the assumption of such an annual festival of covenant renewal. However, Scripture makes plain that such renewals of covenant did occur from time to time: *e.g.* at Shechem, after the conquest (Jos. 8:30–35); at Shechem again, before Joshua's death (Jos. 24), as well as later under the kings (*e.g.* 2 Ki. 23:1–3). Such occasions would certainly be suitable, but can hardly have been the only occasions when the commandments were read or recited in public. That they were known (even when broken) to every Israelite seems clear from subsequent history.

1. *All these words.* In Hebrew, *words* is deliberately connected with the verb *spoke* with which the verse begins. The whole stress is that these commandments are words of revelation from God. The emphasis is primarily on their source, secondarily on their purpose, and only thirdly on their content, although this is naturally governed by God's nature. It has been well said that the commandments are God's nature expressed in terms of moral imperatives: and it is significant that God chose to reveal Himself so, rather than in terms of philosophical propositions. So, to the Israelite, He is the God of history (verse 2) and of daily life (verses 13ff.) rather than the God of speculation. This is not to say that philosophy and speculation are illegitimate; but they are not our primary channels of certain knowledge of God, and they can be based only upon what God has done and said.

2. *I am YHWH . . . who brought you out.* To Judaism, this is the first commandment, enjoining belief in God, and, at that, not belief in God in general, but belief in the living God who had acted on behalf of Israel. To make the traditional number of ten, Judaism then groups verses 3-6 together, to make the second commandment forbid the worship of other gods, and the use of images of any kind, presumably whether of the true god or of false gods. Roman Catholic theologians also traditionally group verses 3-6 together, but make them the first commandment, instead of the second, as in classical Judaism. They then divide the tenth commandment into two, to make up the required number. But the earlier Jewish tradition, represented by Philo and Josephus, takes the view since followed by most Protestant theologians, that this opening verse is the preface or preamble, common in secular covenants of the day, and is the basis and reason for all that follows. There is no theological point involved; the whole divergence simply suggests that, while the number of ten was traditional, the division and distribution of the matter, so as to make up this total, was quite uncertain. We may compare the similar uncertainty as to the exact names of the twelve apostles, or the mathematical difficulties in trying to identify twelve and no more as names of Israel's tribes.

Whatever the literary form of this sentence, whether it be statement or command, it is the credal basis of all Israel's later faith. It embraces the great divine Self-disclosure contained in the new name YHWH, which affirms the personality of God in direct terms: it also shows Him as living, dynamic and active in Israel's history. The succeeding verses will go on to show that His nature can be understood by man only in moral terms. So we have the summary of Israel's faith: a God who speaks and a God who acts.

Further, this clause is very valuable as linking the exodus-theme with the Sinai-theme: nor can it be dismissed as an editorial addition. Our new understanding of the process of covenant making in early Western Asia (see Mendenhall) has shown conclusively that such a self-proclamation is an integral part of any covenant making. Although Mendenhall's evidence is largely from Hittite sources, no doubt the Hittites are simply reproducing what was the wider pattern throughout the whole area. The 'great king' stated his identity, outlined what he had done for his prospective vassal, promised future protection and, on the grounds and basis of this, demanded exclusive loyalty and laid down certain obligations for his subjects. Often lists of curses and blessings are appended: these too are familiar from the Old Testament. This is not of course to say that Israel's law is deliberately imitating Hittite suzerainty treaties, but that both are faithfully reproducing the common literary and structural patterns of the time, just as Paul's epistles show formal and outward similarity in structure to the secular letters of the day. So we can say that this introductory sentence, rich in meaning, is an integral part of what follows, whether we call it preamble or first commandment. Law is firmly set in the context of grace, from its very origins.

3. *No other gods*: possibly 'no other god', if the so-called 'plural of majesty' is used, as always when describing YHWH. Much argument has raged as to whether Israel's faith was true monotheism, since she could visualize the possibility of 'other gods' to serve. But to quibble about this is to expect too much self-analysis: monolatry (the exclusive service of one God) is demanded of Israel here in no uncertain terms. Israel lived in the midst of a polytheistic world: this terse prohibition deals with one of the dangers that came from living in just such a world. These commandments were after all addressed to the ordinary Israelite, not to the religious *élite* of the day: they are expressed in strong simple terms, understandable to all, and deal with the temptations of the common man, not of the theologian.

Before me: literally, 'to my face'. This slightly unusual phrase seems also to be used of taking a second wife while the first is still alive. Such a use, of breach of an exclusive personal relationship, would help to explain the meaning here. It then links with the description of God as a 'jealous God' in verse 5. Some modern commentators point out that 'before

YHWH' or 'the presence of YHWH' elsewhere in the Torah seems to denote the altar of YHWH (Ex. 23:17). Therefore they see a cultic reference: no other god may be worshipped simultaneously with YHWH at a common sanctuary as, for example, was common in Canaanite religious practice. This is undoubtedly true, but seems, in itself, an inadequate explanation. In whatever detailed way we understand it, the main thrust is clear: because of YHWH's nature and because of what YHWH has done, He will not share His worship with another: He is unique. For various other interpretations of the phrase, see Hyatt.

4. *Graven image* (NEB *carved image*): the Hebrew means something hacked or chiselled into some 'likeness'. These are primitive days; such idols are normally of wood (though the word could cover stone carving as well), usually with some precious metal covering. The 'cast metal' image is also implicitly forbidden (Ex. 34:17), but it is not mentioned here because it belongs on the whole to a later age (yet *cf.* the golden calf, Ex. 32:4).

A question arises as to the original form of the commandments, in view of the repeated explanatory clauses in this verse, and the motivation in verse 5. To judge from the minor differences in explanatory matter to be found in Deuteronomy 4 and the present passage, the original form of these negative 'apodeictic commands' was simply the short, sharp 'you must not'. Therefore the original or essential form of this commandment was probably only the first four Hebrew words, translated by the English 'you must not make for yourself an idol'. Similarly in the next verse, the core of the command would seem to have been 'you must not bow down to them'. That would mean that the commandments were brief, pungent sentences, easily written on small stone tablets, fitting within the palm of a hand.

This condemnation of images clearly includes images of the true god, for images may well have been in use among Israel's ancestors (even orthodox Jewish tradition allows that Terah, Abraham's father, was an idol-maker). Laban's 'household gods' may, it is true, have had legal rather than religious significance (Gn. 31:30) but what Jacob is reputed as burying in the sanctuary at Shechem were certainly religious objects (Gn. 35:2). This was before the law-giving: even after that date, images were known in Israel (see Jdg. 8:27, Gideon;

Jdg. 17:4, Micah; 1 Sa. 19:13, David). But the existence of images later in Israel does not prove that there was no law against their use.

Archaeology shows clearly that the horde who destroyed most of Canaanite culture in the thirteenth century BC were basically 'aniconic', using no images in worship. It is often argued that the cherubim above the ark were such images: but they were not objects of worship so much as symbols of the angelic beings serving God, rather like the temple guardians at the gate of an Assyrian temple. They were the throne for the invisible presence of God above. However, if the making of cherubim was permitted, then the prohibition of the 'image' will refer only to the making of direct objects of worship, not to the representation of any living object, as sometimes understood later. Stricter Judaism or Islam therefore confined itself to abstract designs and patterns in all forms of art. Also by Hebrew 'paratax' (the placing of two ideas side by side, rather than the introduction of a formal logical link between the two, as in syntax), this command must be very closely associated with the one immediately before it, so that the true translation of the sense would be 'You must not have any other god in my presence: you must not make any such image' (*i.e.* of such a god). As well as the cherubim, the law enjoins the embroidery of lilies, pomegranates and other natural objects on the curtains of the meeting-tent, so that there cannot have been a complete ban upon the representation of natural objects in early days.

This raises the question as to why such image-representation of the true God (even by human form) was forbidden. Perhaps the reason is that no likeness could possibly be adequate, and that each type of image would imprint its own misunderstandings. For instance, the young bull was a symbol of strength, but also of virility and sexual powers: such an association would be blasphemous to the Hebrew. The nations who pictured their gods in human forms imputed all too readily their own human weaknesses to the divine prototypes. To the Hebrew, man had been created in God's image, after God's likeness (Gn. 1:26): but that emphatically did not mean that God was like man (Is. 55:9). The localization and materialization of God was another danger inherent in idolatry. Even Israel in later days tended to believe that God's presence was localized and contained in ark or temple;

how much more so, if there had been an image? Finally, there would have been the danger of quasi-magical attempts to placate or control God through possession of some such localization of His presence, such as we can see in connection with the ark in 1 Samuel 4:3.

In Deuteronomy 4:12ff., the reason is given as the fact that, at Sinai, Israel saw no shape or form: she only heard the voice of God. This corresponds to the dominant position, right through Israel's faith, of the 'word of YHWH', spoken or written.

5. *A jealous God*: 'zealous' might be a better translation in modern English, since 'jealousy' has acquired an exclusively bad meaning. Like 'love' and 'hate' in the Old Testament (Mal. 1:2,3), 'jealousy' does not refer to an emotion so much as to an activity, in this case an activity of violence and vehemence, that springs from the rupture of a personal bond as exclusive as that of the marriage bond. This is not therefore to be seen as intolerance but exclusiveness, and it springs both from the uniqueness of God (who is not one among many) and the uniqueness of His relationship to Israel. No husband who truly loved his wife could endure to share her with another man: no more will God share Israel with a rival.

The third and the fourth generation. This is a typical Semitic phrase denoting continuity, not to be understood in an arithmetical sense. Further, it is applied to those who 'hate' God, who refuse to live their lives in accordance with His will. Since this is God's world, and since we are all involved with one another, breaches of God's law by one generation do indeed affect those of future generations to come. Slavery, exploitation, imperialism, pollution, immorality are all examples of this principle. What we call 'natural results' are just an expression of God's law in operation, punishing breaches of His will.

6. *Showing steadfast love*: Hebrew *ḥeseḏ*, a typical 'covenant' characteristic. By Semitic speech-forms, the stress of this sentence lies in the second part. True, God will punish those who do not conform to His will, but the negative aspect is but a frame for the positive. Again, the test of 'loving' is that they *keep my commandments*, further showing that to Israel hate/love is an attitude and activity rather than a mere emotion. The word *thousands* is used vaguely, like 'myriads' in English, to indicate the limitless extent of the mercy shown by God.

7. *You shall not take . . . in vain.* In later Judaism, this covered any careless or irreverent use of the name YHWH. It was pronounced only once a year by the high priest, when giving the blessing on the great day of atonement (Lv. 23:27). Originally the commandment seems to have referred to swearing a lying oath in YHWH's name (Lv. 19:12). This seems to be the true meaning of the Hebrew. To bless or curse in the name of YHWH was permissible under the law (Dt. 11:26); it was virtually a proclamation of His revealed will and purpose to different categories of men. To swear by His name was also allowed then, although forbidden by Christ (Mt. 5:34). Indeed, to swear by His name (and not by the name of another god) was the sign of worshipping Him (Je. 4:2) and was laudable.

A deeper reason for the prohibition may be seen in the fact that God is the one living reality to Israel. That is why His name is involved in oaths, usually in the formula 'as surely as YHWH lives' (2 Sa. 2:27). To use such a phrase, and then to fail to perform the oath, is to call into question the reality of God's very existence.

For YHWH will not hold him guiltless. The explanation, though correct, probably formed no part of the original abrupt apodeictic command.

8. *Remember the sabbath day* (*cf.* Ex. 16:23,26). The command about the rest-day is the first to be framed in a positive form, although still brief and apodeictic. Verse 12 contains the only other positive command in this series, but elsewhere in the law this form is not uncommon (a closely related form of positive command is the type found in Gn. 9:6). This alternation between positive and negative commands is not unknown in ancient codes, but if we want to find a negative form of the command for the sake of consistency, it is in verse 10, 'You shall not do any work'. Deuteronomy 5:12 is very similar to verse 8, though it has 'observe' for 'remember'. However, the reason given for the observance is completely different in Deuteronomy, as will be seen in verse 11.

11. *YHWH . . . rested the seventh day.* Exodus gives the reason for sabbath observance as being the memory of God's 'rest' from His great work of creation. Deuteronomy 5:15 regards sabbath as commemorating the 'rest' that came to the

Israelite slaves in Egypt, when freed by YHWH, and (typical of Deuteronomy) as offering an opportunity of similar 'rest' to Israel's slaves now (Dt. 5:14). These explanations are not mutually exclusive, since both deal with 'rest'; but they do tend to reinforce the view that the shorter form of the commandment was the original, perhaps 'Remember the sabbath day' alone. In either case, in the sabbath observance, as in all Hebrew festivals, an act of God is commemorated. Argument has raged as to the origins and date of sabbath observance: later Jewish commentators tried hard to find evidence of sabbath observance in patriarchal days but, apart from the law, the earliest references are 2 Kings 4:23 and Amos 8:5. The passage from Kings suggests worship as well as cessation from work, as being an early feature of the day (as it certainly was in post-exilic times). Babylonian parallels are not very helpful: the corresponding seventh days there were merely regarded as 'unlucky' for business, but this may have deteriorated from an original religious significance. It is highly likely that the origins of sabbath (like the origins of tithing and circumcision) go back well beyond the law, even though there is no direct biblical evidence for its observance.

12. *Honour your father and your mother.* Like verse 8, this is a 'categoric' command put in positive form. For the same principle, in another form, see Exodus 21:15,17: 'whoever strikes/curses his father or his mother shall be put to death'. This is called 'the first commandment with promise' (Eph. 6:2), and so it is, in the strict sense of the word, although verse 6, where God shows 'covenant love' to those who love and obey Him, is also virtually a promise. Nevertheless, God's promise is clearer here, and works itself out in human societies. Those who build a society in which old age has an honoured place may with confidence expect to enjoy that place themselves one day. This is not a popular doctrine in our modern world, where youth is worshipped, and old age dreaded or despised. The result is the folly by which men or women strive to remain eternally youthful, only to find it an impossible task. This commandment is part of the general attitude of Israel to old age (as symbolizing and ideally embodying the practical wisdom of life) commended throughout the Old Testament (Lv. 19:32), and found in many other ancient peoples, notably the Chinese. Whether it is connected with the idea that, since life is sacred and is the gift of God, the human givers of life are to be treated with respect, is uncertain: perhaps a Hebrew would not have analysed the commandment in this way.

That your days may be long. Sometimes over-sensitive souls have queried the morality of a promise attached to a commandment. But the Hebrew does not necessarily imply that the promised blessing is our motive for keeping the commandment, while it certainly assures us that it will be the result. Others query the material nature of the promise. But, in Old Testament days, God's promises are usually couched in material terms, understandable by those who are still, as it were, in God's school. To those who had as yet no sure knowledge of a future life, 'length of days' (understood as long life in this world) meant possibility of extended communion with God, and was of great importance. Others, however, regard it as a promise of security in the tenure of the land that God will have given them: this in turn will be glorifying to God, as showing His faithfulness to His promises. We, with a fuller revelation, may fairly 'spiritualize' such a promise without evacuating it of content. This commandment is the point at which attention shifts from relations with God to relations with the community that He has created. So the total contents of the ten commandments must be summed up in two 'words', not one: love to God and love to our neighbour (Dt. 6:5; Lv. 19:18). Again, there is no contradiction: the reality of our stated love to God is shown by the reality of our expressed love towards our fellow men (Je. 22:16).

13. *You shall not kill.* The next three commands are apodeictic law at its tersest. Only two words are used in Hebrew, as blunt as the order 'no killing' would be in English. Hebrew *rāṣaḥ* is a comparatively rare word for 'kill', and usually implies violent killing of a personal enemy (Hyatt): 'murder' is a good translation (RV, NEB). The command is stated in its most general form, but the law clearly distinguished between planned and accidental or unpremeditated killings (Ex. 21:12–14). Certainly this command was never seen by Hebrews as ruling out the death penalty (Ex. 21:15), although this is usually expressed by a verb corresponding to 'put to death', not by 'kill'. Also, there were no pacifists in Old Testament days. Whether the fuller light of the New Testament demands such conclusions or not, they cannot be proved from the Old Testament alone. As in verse 16, the prohibition seems addressed in the first place towards killing of a 'neighbour', a member of the same covenant-community. In any case, the sanctity of life, as God's gift, is established: hence 'blood-guiltiness' is an awful reality, from the time of Cain onwards (Gn. 4:10).

14. *You shall not commit adultery.* The law allowed polygamy (perhaps a necessary social institution to secure the protection of unattached women), but it never allowed polyandry (the taking of several husbands simultaneously by one woman). For a man to have intercourse with another man's wife was considered as heinous sin against God as well as man, long before the law, in patriarchal times (Gn. 39:9). Perhaps this command is connected with the 'stealing' and 'coveting' forbidden in the two commandments below, since the wife belonged to another. Perhaps this also explains one aspect that is most puzzling to us who live under the New Covenant: while men are never commended for intercourse with prostitutes, it is never forbidden in the law (although the Israelites are forbidden to allow their daughters to engage in this degrading practice, Lv. 19:29). Presumably this is not infringement of another man's rights, as adultery was. It is clear nevertheless (see Mt. 19:4–6) that monogamy was God's purpose for man in creation: and doubtless, like divorce, polygamy and even fornication were tolerated in Mosaic times because of the hardness of men's hearts (Mt. 19:8). In Christ, they become unthinkable (1 Cor. 6·15). So far from abrogating this commandment, Christ instead intensified it, for He included under 'adultery' much of what is not only tolerated but justified by our permissive society (Mt. 5:28). Similarly, He included angry thoughts under the prohibition of murder: the commandments are aimed at thought and motive, not merely deed (see under the tenth commandment).

15. *You shall not steal.* Here again, this prohibition is to guard the fellowship of the covenant community. Perhaps the original prohibition was mainly directed against kidnapping for slavery (see Joseph's experience in Gn. 37), but no doubt all sorts of theft are included. The covenant code makes details clear (*e.g.* Ex. 22:1–4), so no expansion is felt necessary here. In a peasant society where life is hard, any theft of property may lead to death, so theft is a very serious crime. There is a clear relation between this and the tenth commandment.

16. *You shall not bear false witness.* Since, in a simple desert society, nearly all crimes were capital charges, successful 'false witness' would be equivalent to murder. To safeguard against it, a witness must also be the executioner (Dt. 17:7), so that he might incur blood-guiltiness if he was lying. False witnesses figure largely in the Old Testament (*e.g.* 1 Ki. 21:10), as in any land where extreme poverty exposes men to the temptation of bribery. No doubt the command could be generalized into the prohibition of tattling and tale-bearing (Lv. 19:16), particularly of untrue and unkind gossip which could damage one's neighbour.

17. *You shall not covet*: Hebrew *ḥāmaḏ*, 'desire', is in itself a neutral word. It is only when misdirected to that which belongs to another that such 'desire' becomes wrong. It is sometimes claimed that this is the only one of the ten commandments which prohibits an attitude of mind rather than an outward act: but to make this distinction is probably to misunderstand Hebrew thought. As in the case of 'loving' and 'hating', 'desiring' is an activity, almost equivalent to 'seeking to acquire'. This same identification can be seen in the behaviour of young children. *House* means 'household', in the early sense of the word, and the thought of 'wife' is primary. This is made explicit in Deuteronomy 5:21, where the wife is named first. *Ox* and *ass* are the typical wealth of the bronze-age peasant or semi-nomad, for whom the perplexities of developed society have not yet arisen. 'Slaves' are the only other form of movable property. Ultimately to desire, and to try to obtain, the property of another is to be dissatisfied with what God has given, and thus to show lack of faith in His love. Further, the envy which this encourages will lead sooner or later to the hurt of one's neighbour, and this is inconsistent with the primary duty of love.

Alt, quoted by Hyatt, sees the eighth commandment as prohibiting the kidnapping of an Israelite man, while the tenth would prohibit kidnapping of his wife or theft of his possessions. This seems an unnatural division: if a contrast must be seen, it would be better to see it between 'act' (8th) and 'motive' (10th), though, as stated above, even this must not be exaggerated.

c. The book of the covenant (20:18 – 23:33)

This section gains its name from the supposition that it represents the actual terms upon which the covenant was ratified, as recorded in 24:7 (although some would restrict the terms to the 'ten words' themselves). It certainly is a homogeneous whole, dealing with the simple problems of bronze-age society. Because of this, even extreme critics usually allow an early date for this section (the period of the judges at latest), even if they are reluctant to see it as Mosaic as it stands.[1] The reference to writing 'all the words of YHWH' in 24:4 (*cf.* 17:14) is generally taken as applying to these chapters. If so, this 'book of the covenant', along with the 'ten words', would be Israel's earliest codified and written law book. Attempts have been made to see the book of the covenant as an extended commentary on the ten commandments: this seems far-fetched. In many respects, the legislation of Deuteronomy is supplemental to this 'covenant code'.

20:18-21. The background. This returns to the vivid description of the phenomena associated with the theophany on Sinai recorded in 19:16-25. Whether it is intended as a retrospect and summary of the past, or whether it looks forward to the following section (as assumed here), is not however certain.

18. *Lightnings.* The word here is unusual and might be translated 'torches', meaning 'flashes' or 'fireballs'. This is the word used for the symbol of God's presence that Abraham sees at the making of God's covenant with him (Gn. 15). Its use here may therefore be a deliberate reminiscence. The reading 'they were afraid' (RSV) is to be preferred to 'they saw', in the second half of the verse.

19. *Let not God speak to us.* This is the first appearance of the theme of Israel's reluctance (because of consciousness of their own sin) to enter God's presence, or even to hear His voice. Even a saint may and must feel this (Is. 6:5), but what Israel dreaded was what Moses coveted (Ex. 33:18).

20. *To prove you.* This is another frequent theme of Exodus. Presumably the 'testing' was to see if they had that true fear of God, which would lead to the avoidance of evil. In other

[1] Since 'apodeictic' and 'casuistic' laws are mixed, Noth and Alt would place it in the post-conquest period.

words, their present reaction was basically right, human nature being as sinful as it is.

20:22–26. Ritual regulations. (*Cf.* 23:10–19.) Davies points out that most ancient codes begin with santuary or altar laws: this is no exception.

22. *I have talked with you from heaven.* Some see this as the basis of the command not to make images, since images would be incompatible with the heavenly nature of God. But possibly the reference here is rather to the majesty, reality and power of the living God, all of which are His authority for giving the commands which follow. The actual code will begin at Exodus 21:1, 'these are the ordinances'. Note that YHWH is regarded as speaking *from heaven*: Sinai is only the locale of the revelation.

23. *To be with me* seems the correct interpretation of the Hebrew, which would therefore explain the 'before me' of the corresponding commandments (Ex. 20:3). *Gods of silver* means 'silver images': it may be a naïve form of expression, originally corresponding to the belief that the god actually resides in the image. Alternatively, it can have abusive force (see Kaufmann): these are only silver gods, compared with the living YHWH (*cf.* Ps. 135:15). Naturally, images of YHWH were forbidden: but the strict wording here suggests images of other gods. *Gold* and *silver*, in Hebraic fashion, is meant to cover all precious materials.

24. *An altar of earth* may imply patriarchal origins, in an area such as Mesopotamia where stones are not abundant, as they are in Palestine. Hyatt argues for an altar of sun-dried mud brick, as at many Canaanite sites. Some have argued that it denotes settled agricultural life, but that does not necessarily follow. Noth has argued strongly that it and the following regulations stem from very primitive Israelite society and times. The only alternative form of altar envisaged (verse 25) is one of loose natural stone. Either type of altar is a wanderer's altar, raised and used when needed and then abandoned, and either suggests a flat steppe area, without any 'hill tops', which were a favourite Canaanite site. At a later stage, wooden altar frames, sheathed in copper, would be used (Ex. 27:1–8). *Your burnt offerings and your peace offerings.* The latter is better translated as 'communion meals'. These two particular types may be mentioned as being the most

primitive types of sacrifice, or the commonest, and therefore
typical. In these early days, with no fixed altar and no priesthood, the 'whole burnt offering' covered the later concept of
'sin offering' as well (eaten by the priest). *In every place.* In
spite of some versions (which read 'the place', referring to one
single sanctuary) this seems correct. It was certainly the
practice of Israel in early days to worship God at more than
one place. But even if there were several places where sacrifice
could be performed, they were not chosen at random. They
were all places of God's revelation in patriarchal days. Perhaps
cause my name to be remembered refers to the new title of the 'god
of the fathers' usually annexed to such a fresh revelation and
place in patriarchal days (see Gn. 22:14).

25. *You shall not build it of hewn stones.* This 'cyclopean' type
of altar, of unhewn stones, unlike the earth altar, reappears in
Joshua 8:31, where undressed stones are obediently used. It is
quite unnecessary to see in this the belief that spirits reside in
stones, and could be driven out by hammering; the text
specifically says that the stone would be defiled, and thus
made unfit for YHWH's use, if any human hand lifted a
chisel to it. The term for *hewn* or 'squared' *stones* refers to the
well-cut Phoenician 'ashlar' masonry, first used widely in
Israel under Solomon.

26. *Steps* were an adjunct of altars in the ancient world,
either to increase the majesty of the occasion, or (more likely)
to reproduce the idea of some mountain 'high place' (as the
'ziggurats' of Mesopotamia did on a large scale). In Temple
days, Israelite altars had steps, but long before then priests
wore special linen breeches, so that the old reasons of modesty
would not apply (Ex. 28:40–42). Ritual nakedness was a
feature of early cults, whether with fertility-cult significance
or as an example of extreme religious conservatism. On either
score it was strictly forbidden to Israel: God made clothes for
Adam and Eve (Gn. 3:21) when they lived in a fallen world.
It is interesting that both prohibitions (against 'gods of gold'
and ritual nakedness) were ignored by Israel in the incident
of the golden calf (Ex. 32). This, however, only proves that
such regulations were needed, not that the regulations did not
exist. Bad theology and bad morals usually seem to go together
(Rom. 1:18–32): certainly this was true of Baal worship.

21:1–11. The Hebrew slave. As in the book of Proverbs,

there is no reference in this section to any distinctly Israelite covenant-bond as the grounds of merciful treatment of the slave by his master. But a bond there is: both master and man are 'Hebrews', an early term of wide descriptive range (Ex. 5:3).[1] These laws may therefore be patriarchal, dating from long before Moses: Abram too is described as a Hebrew (Gn. 14:13). Naturally, we have no written code of early 'Hebrew' law or customs, so there is no way of checking this. In any case they are 'casuistic' laws, not 'apodeictic' (*i.e.* deduced from principles, rather than the principles themselves), of the type common in Western Asia. Israel however regards both types of law as stemming from God. Napier stresses the appropriateness of commencing the covenant code with a section on slavery. Israel herself had been a nation of slaves, freed by YHWH's mighty act. Leviticus 25 and Deuteronomy 15 specifically make this experience of salvation a motive for kind treatment of slaves by Israel. We have already considered Daube's view that the whole exodus-story is recounted in language deliberately intended to recall the process of manumission of an Israelite slave (Dt. 15:13,14), especially with reference to the capital compensation paid for the years of servitude.

2. *A Hebrew slave.* He was, more properly, an 'indentured labourer', bound for *six years*. When his *seventh* year came, he must go free: if the 'double seventh' of the jubilee year came first, he might apparently go free in any case (Lv. 25). The link with the concept of 'sabbath rest' seems obvious. A foreign-born slave, or one 'born in the house', might, however, serve for ever (Lv. 25:46). *Free*: Hebrew *hopšî* should probably be translated as 'freedman', for it seems to denote a definite class in society (known also in Canaan) lying between 'nobles' and 'slaves'. It is not the same as the word translated 'for nothing', meaning that no redemption price need be paid. E. C. B. MacLaurin has suggested a meaning like 'professional soldier' or 'liable to military service', on the grounds of Arabic *hubshu* (verbal communication).

3. *Single*: literally 'with his back', *i.e.* 'bare back and nothing more'. The phrase is vivid and unique, but the meaning is clear. This provision may seem hard to us, but the wife was presumably a perpetual slave, and therefore the master's own property. Some see relics of a neolithic matriarchal society

[1] This would be to identify 'Hebrew' with the wider cultural term *Habiru* or *'Apiru.* Hyatt rejects this wider meaning, but seems mistaken.

here, with the relationship to mother closer than that to father. But at least there was provision for the husband to stay, if he so chose: he was not compelled to leave wife and children behind.

6. *Bring him to God*: that is, to the sanctuary (to render 'to the judges', with some editors, is explanation, not translation). The approach to the sanctuary is presumably to make a solemn declaration (swearing by YHWH), in the presence of witnesses, as to the status of the slave. Whether *the doorpost* is that of the sanctuary or of the home is, however, disputed. The latter seems preferable, in view of the nature of the ceremony, which made the slave a permanent member of the household. To *bore the ear* is probably to earmark as private property (as with animals today). There is, however, no clear ancient evidence that a pierced ear as such denoted slavery. The other possible connotation seems to be that of obedience (Ps. 40:6). On consecration, the priest's right ear was smeared with blood, presumably with much the same significance (Ex. 29:20). *For life*: a correct translation of the Hebrew 'for ever'. The Israelite was practical, not philosophical, in his approach to life.

7. *She shall not go out.* The case of the Hebrew slave-wife is quite different. She does not automatically go out like the man, because her master-husband still has duties towards her.

8. Even if he has wearied of her, he cannot sell her to another master: that would be a breach of marriage obligation to her. Instead he must allow her own relatives to buy her back. The verb 'to deal faithlessly' (or 'treacherously') is often used of breaches of marriage: it is applied to unfaithful Israel in Jeremiah 3:7,8.

9. *He shall deal with her as a daughter.* She is virtually his foster-child. The old Chinese custom of buying a slave-girl, as wife for the son in days to come, is an exact parallel. Probably the origin of the custom was the same in either case: to avoid paying a higher bride-price at a later age, and to rear the future daughter-in-law within the family, ensuring that she 'fitted in'. Such an attitude to slaves abolishes slavery, except in name.

10. *Her food, her clothing, or her marital rights.* These three provisos read like an old legal formulation. The word translated *food* should perhaps be rendered 'meat': it means, say the commentators, the wife's fair share of luxuries, not mere subsistence allowance, which any slave would get. Meat was probably a rare item on the average Israelite table, except after sacrifice. See Hyatt for the suggested translation 'oil, ointments' instead of 'marital rights'.

11. *She shall go out for nothing.* Should the master-husband default in any of these three areas, she goes out free. In such circumstances, there was no need for her relatives to pay the 'ransom price', which was presumably equivalent to the initial purchase price of the slave-wife. Alternatively, the 'three things' could refer to the three ways of dealing with her – taking her as wife, giving her to his son as wife, allowing her to be 'redeemed'.

21:12–17. Stern desert law. The next group of laws are an intermediate 'participial' type, neither categoric nor casuistic, but closer to the first. All end with a strong Hebrew phrase which may be translated 'he must be put to death'. Verse 12 states this in its tersest form; 13 and 14 explain and define exceptions and limits to the general rule.

13. *God let him fall into his hand.* This may be a vague phrase to cover 'without malice aforethought'. More probably it expresses the strong theological position found elsewhere in the Old Testament (*e.g.* 1 Sa. 24:18). This involves a feeling that the man's death is a deserved punishment, as well as the belief that all events are directly under YHWH's control. *A place*: Hebrew *māqôm*, better 'holy place', for verse 14 shows that this is the sanctuary where YHWH's altar is. The suppliant would catch hold of the projecting 'horns' of the altar (1 Ki. 2:28). This was tantamount to dedicating himself to YHWH, like any animal sacrifice bound with ropes to the altar horns. Any innocent blood shed at YHWH's altar would be sacrilege, but not the execution of a guilty man. Presumably the *place* in question is one of the 'cities of refuge' mentioned in Numbers 35:6. As these were Levitical cities, they may be assumed to have had altars and to have been centres of worship. The distinction between premeditated and unpremeditated killing is both early and remarkable: primitive blood-feuds had taken no account of this. Here, as so often, the law imposes strict limits on the rough and ready justice of the day (*cf.* verses 23–25).

15. *Strikes* often means 'kill', but here it may be applied to a mere blow. Such an act is a specific breach of Exodus 20:12, the command to honour parents, and, as such, was punishable by death. Verse 17 should be taken closely with this, for cursing parents was also a capital crime. Since to curse was to will and pray the downfall of the other with all one's heart, it represented the attitude from which sprang acts like striking or murder. Although the death penalty was exacted in these circumstances on several occasions in church history, this literal fulfilment seems foreign to the spirit of the New Testament. Nevertheless, respect for parents is still enjoined in the New Testament (Eph. 6:1) and the great principle remains the same. Nothing but the overmastering claim of Christ has a higher position than family ties (Mt. 10:37).

16. *Whoever steals a man.* Kidnapping for slavery was common in the ancient world: Homer regards it as a common occupation of Phoenicians (that is, the earlier Canaanites). Joseph is an example from the pre-Mosaic days (Gn. 37), and there may be hints of the same practice in the warnings of Deuteronomy 17:16. As mentioned, possibly Exodus 20:15 was primarily aimed at this form of theft, at once the most lucrative and the most possible, in a poor society. *Or is found in possession of him* should be translated 'and is caught with the money in his hand'. Unexpectedly large bank balances are still hard to explain to the Income Tax department of our own day.

21:18–27. Quarrels and injuries. These are less serious offences, and the death penalty is not demanded except in exceptional circumstances.

18. *With his fist* is how the LXX understands the obscure word, probably correctly, rather than 'stick, cudgel' with the Targum and some versions. In any case, the nature of the impromptu 'weapon' shows that the blow was not 'malice aforethought' but a hasty unpremeditated act. Had he intended the deed, he would have carried a knife.

19. *Walks abroad with his staff*: that is, 'comes to convalescence'. All that is now needed is 'workman's compensation' and 'health benefits': these the guilty party must pay, in very modern fashion.

20. *He shall be punished.* The great advance on ancient thinking is that a slave is considered here as a person. His master has no right to beat him to death deliberately, even though the slave may be his 'property'. But, if the slave lingers a while before dying, the supposition is that his master intended only to correct him, not to kill him. This is 'accidental homicide', and the financial loss incurred by his master in the death of the slave is considered punishment and lesson enough.

21. *The slave is his money.* Probably the best interpretation is that given above, unless we take the meaning as being 'the slave is his own purchased property': and therefore he has the right to beat and correct him. If we think that even this concedes too much to the master, we should set alongside it the limitation of verses 26–27, where the knocking out of a slave's eye or tooth by his master ensures his immediate emancipation. The Torah accepts slavery as an inevitable part of ancient society, much as Paul did, but the new humanitarian approach will ultimately be the death-knell of slavery. In any case, slavery in Israel was rural, domestic and small scale. Not for her were the terrible 'slave pens' of imperial Rome, although the mining and building activity of Solomon may have necessitated something of the kind at a later date than Moses.

22. *A woman with child*: only accidentally involved in the men's brawl (unless she intervenes to protect her husband, like the woman of Dt. 25:11). But nevertheless, if there is a miscarriage, monetary compensation must be paid. It has sometimes been claimed by those in favour of abortion that the unborn child is not really considered as an individual here: but that is not the point of this passage, which is primarily concerned with injury to the woman. The destruction of the unborn child was regarded by the Hebrews as an instance of the most barbarous cruelty, calling down God's judgment (2 Ki. 15:16).

24. *Eye for eye.* This is the famous *lex talionis*, tit for tat, but it is to be seen as restrictive. No more can men avenge themselves sevenfold (Gn. 4:24), for this law imposes a strict limit of justice. In Leviticus 24:19,20 and Deuteronomy 19:21, the same principle is used by a judge, as a deterrent to malicious injuries and false witness. Noth says that this is a legal principle to guide judges in decisions, not a rule to govern personal relationships of man to man. But popular Judaism must have so interpreted it, or Christ's rejection of the common interpretation (Mt. 5:38,39) would have no point. This is another area where the New Testament transcends the Old, by applying the law of love in all personal relations.

21:28-36. Injuries by animals. This means injury by

oxen, since the Israelites kept no other animal that was capable of killing a human: horses were foreign luxuries.

28. *The ox shall be stoned*: like a human being, for the ox has incurred blood guilt (Gn. 9:5). That is why its flesh may not be eaten: it is not merely to punish the owner by financial loss of the meat, which cannot be sold on the market.

29. *Its owner also shall be put to death.* Punishment of the careless owner shows acumen, again distinguishing clearly between guilty and innocent, instead of the automatic 'blood-guilt' of early days.

30. *A ransom* and *redemption* are important words for the later theology of salvation. Both are used in the strictly literal sense here, applying to the man convicted of 'culpable homicide' though not of 'murder'. Probably this explains (as Driver points out) why it is that only here and in verse 32 does Hebrew law allow 'blood-money', so common in other countries (*cf.* Nu. 35:31).

32. *If the ox gores a slave.* In the case of a free man, relatives might agree to accept a 'blood-price': in the case of a slave, they must do so. This is one of the few differences between bond and free that still existed in Israel. *Thirty shekels of silver* was the standard price for a slave at the time. The sum reappears in Zechariah 11:12, probably with scornful reference to this passage, and as the blood-price of Christ's betrayal by Judas in Matthew 26:15. However, whether slave or freeman had been gored to death, the ox had incurred blood-guilt, and its flesh must not be eaten. Even in Israel, a slave was still a man: his blood brings blood-guilt, like that of any other man.

33. *A pit*: more likely to be for grain storage than water storage. Pits were also used as traps for animals (2 Sa. 23:20) or prisons for men (Gn. 37:24). Such pits were a feature of Canaan in disturbed times: the growing measure of security can be gauged by their gradual disappearance in later days.

35. *Divide the price.* The concern for 'fair dealing' seen in the prophets has its roots in the Torah, and ultimately lies in the very nature of God. To a struggling Israelite farmer, fair payment for the death of an ox might mean the difference between life and death, or at least between freedom and slavery for debt. Many of these rules are standard practice among desert bedouin today, according to Doughty, as quoted in the modern commentators.

22:1-17. Civil laws on robbery. There is some uncertainty as to the exact order of the opening verses, as RSV footnotes explain. This commentary will follow the arrangement of the RSV. The sense is the same in any case. The Hebrew text, for instance, has verse 1 RSV as verse 37 of the last chapter: but all chapter divisions are arbitrary.

1. *Kills it or sells it.* There is a heavier fine for this, since such action presumably shows deliberate intent to steal. To keep the animal in his possession would show that theft might have sprung from sudden covetous impulse. Reparation for an ox is fivefold (as against fourfold for a sheep), since a trained ox is not only more valuable, but harder to replace. The ox to the Israelite was what the family water buffalo is in South-east Asia – almost a member of the family. Like a horse, an ox takes years to train.

2. *No bloodguilt for him.* To kill a thief digging through the mud-brick wall (Ezk. 12:5) is justifiable homicide, if done after dark. He may be an armed murderer, for all the householder knows. His death may even have been accidental, in the blundering fight in the darkness. But in the daylight, the householder has no excuse for killing: besides, he can identify the man. It is typical of Israel's merciful law that even a thief has his rights. This type of 'justifiable homicide' (bringing no blood-guilt) is used as a metaphor in Jeremiah 2:34.

5. *To be grazed over*: the same verb is used for 'kindle' in verse 6, but the context seems to make the meaning distinct. However, the NEB may be right with 'burn off' here. It is a sound principle of law that restitution must be *from the best*. The case under consideration is a common cause of friction where two cultures meet, the pastoralist and the agriculturalist. It must have been particularly vexatious during the years when Israel was changing her own patterns of life from the desert to settled land.

6. *When fire breaks out.* Bushfires were dreaded in Israel, with its Mediterranean vegetation and dry hot summers. Any Australian will appreciate how quickly dry thorns will catch, and grass or stubble burn. The *thorns* are probably used for a hedge, to keep cattle out (like cactus today), and burn with fearsome crackles and explosions, aptly compared to brainless guffaws (Ec. 7:6). In Palestine they were and are used for fuel by the poor.

8. *Come near to God.* As before, the meaning must be 'to the sanctuary'. The man must take a solemn oath in God's name (see verse 11), declaring his innocence. As this is equal to 'trial by ordeal', it must be accepted by the plaintiff. If the defendant has sworn falsely, the curse that he has invoked will fall upon him, and he will be sufficiently punished. Perhaps the point of 'whom God shall condemn' (verse 9) lies here. The man who suffers the effect of the curse has clearly been shown guilty by God, and must then repay double to the plaintiff in addition. Since the word used for *God* is the general Semitic word, and not YHWH, the specifically Israelite title (except in verse 11), some feel that these laws were borrowed from Israel's neighbours. More cogent is the suggestion that these, with their general similarity to Mesopotamian law, are pre-Mosaic. They would then be part of the 'customary law' of Israel's patriarchal ancestors, before the name YHWH, after the revelation to Moses, became the distinctive usage in Israel.

9. *This is it.* An object has been lost: the owner later sees a similar object in possession of his neighbour, and claims it as his own. The Israelites apparently did not follow the Anglo-Saxon dictum of 'finders are keepers': a lost object remains the possession of the original owner, who can claim it on sight.

10–13. *Ox, ass* and *sheep* (including goats, as a minor sub-division) represent the common domestic animals, as well as the commonest form of wealth in the Bronze Age. *It dies or is hurt or is driven away.* Cattle-raiding by enemies and destruction by wild beasts were the commonest of dangers in a wild 'border' society. If these disasters could be proved, either by oath or by production of the carcase, no man was held culpable or suspect of committing the theft himself. Production of the carcase would show that, while the shepherd could not prevent the kill, he was alert enough to stop the devouring of the prey (Am. 3:12). Jacob complained that, in spite of doubtless similar laws, Laban had made him pay for these excepted items (Gn. 31:39). Joseph's blood-stained coat was accepted as similar evidence of killing by wild beasts (Gn. 37:33). See Hyatt for the suggestion that 'or is driven away' should be omitted here, on textual grounds: the eventuality is mentioned in verse 12 anyway.

14. *Borrows*: literally 'asks'. This is the word used of Israel 'asking' jewelry from the Egyptians in Exodus 3:22. In itself, it leaves open the question of whether the object is to be returned, though such a return is assumed here. There is another more technical verb here which means 'lend' or 'borrow' at interest.

15. *It came for its hire.* The phrase is succinct and obscure. If the RSV translation is correct, the sense is that the hirer took the risk of damage when he hired it out. But, since the word rendered 'hire' usually means 'hired man', and not 'something hired', Noth and others would translate 'if the man (through whom the damage came) is a hired man, the damage is charged to his hire'. If this is so, the passage becomes one of several in the Bible where stress is laid on the carelessness of the 'hired man' as opposed to the 'owner' (*cf.* Jn. 10:12). This is a shrewd psychological observation, true today also.

16. *If a man seduces a virgin*: this comes under the general heading of robbery. An unmarried girl was, in a sense, her father's property, and he would in due course receive a *marriage present* or 'bride-price' for her. The handing over of such gifts marks the official 'engagement' to this day in many parts of the world. Naturally such 'engagement' is almost as binding as marriage, being a financial arrangement, and seduction of an engaged girl by another man is treated as adultery, and so punished (Dt. 22:23,24). This accounts for Joseph's quandary in Matthew 1:19. But, in this instance, since a man has taken a girl without paying bride-price, bride-price he must pay, for who else will pay it now? Also, he must acknowledge her as his wife, unless her father refuses. Even if he does, the price must still be paid: this both recompenses the father and punishes the man.

17. *Pay money*: literally 'weigh out silver', which was the custom until coined money was introduced long afterwards by the Persians, who borrowed the custom from the Lydians (*cf.* Gn. 23:15,16).

22:18–27. Categorical imperatives. These have no common subject, and may be grouped together purely because of their form. In verses **18–20** three pieces of desert law occur, stern and puritanical, marking out Israel's faith from the lush corruption of Canaan. All three are fundamentally religious offences in Israel's eyes: the prohibitions spring from God's revealed nature. No witch must live: bestiality is a capital offence: the sacrificer to any god but YHWH comes under the *herem*, the sacred 'ban', that condems him to destruction, along with all that he has.

18. *You shall not permit a sorceress to live*: see 1 Samuel 28:9 for obedience to this command. Israel is forbidden to peer into the future, since God has given her other means of finding His will (Dt. 18:9–15). At a deeper level, we might say that to desire to know the future shows lack of faith, while to desire to control the future is even worse. With the decline of religion in the western world, 'magic' has today taken on a new fascination as a substitute. Witchcraft is equally condemned in New Testament days (Acts 13:10; 19:19), but in spite of the practice of the church in the Middle Ages, there is no hint in the New Testament that mediums or witches should be put to death. We may assume that the Exodus 'rule of thumb' was designed to preserve the integrity of God's community from such dangerous influences, alien to faith, in early days, and to show for all time God's abhorrence of these things.

19. *Whoever lies with a beast.* This was a capital crime in Israel, as was homosexuality (Lv. 20:13). Bestiality was not only an obvious perversion: it figured so often in the Canaanite cycle of 'Tales of Baal' that it probably had a religious significance for the Canaanites. Our attitude to perversions of God's natural order can hardly vary from those of the law, while our treatment of offenders will be very different today.

20. *Utterly destroyed.* Alt, quoted by Hyatt, by a slight emendation, makes this read 'Whoever sacrifices to *other* gods shall be put to death', where 'other' takes the place of *utterly destroyed*, as in the Samaritan and some MSS of the LXX. As it stands, however, the strong wording is only explaining Exodus 20:3 in terms of sacrificial worship. The man guilty of this sin comes under the sacred 'ban': he must be destroyed, as the Canaanites were to be destroyed before Israel.

Verses **21–27** deal with the protection of the 'underprivileged' classes; aliens, widows, orphans and poor folk in general. It is striking, as Noth says, that all this is apodeictic, not casuistic; that is to say, it is basic to Israel's law, not a deduction from it. Israel must care for the poor and helpless, because YHWH cares for them: that is His very nature.

21. *You were strangers.* This clause directly relates the obligations to Israel's experiences in Egypt, in a thoroughly 'Deuteronomic' manner (*cf.* Ex. 23:9). The *gēr*, *stranger*, is a 'resident alien' ('within your gates', Ex. 20:10) not a mere 'foreigner', for whom a different Hebrew word is used.

24. *Your wives shall become widows.* This is a divine application of the *lex talionis*. This too could be illustrated from their Egyptian experience. Egypt afflicted Israel, God's first-born (Ex. 4:23), so Egypt's first-born died, and Egypt's wives were left widowed by the disaster at the Sea of Reeds. The society that lacks social justice will itself come under God's judgment.

25. *You shall not exact interest.* Not only are exorbitant rates of interest condemned here, but all interest on money lent to a poor man (Dt. 23:20 extends this rule to money lent to any fellow-Israelites). Anyone who has lived in underdeveloped countries will know the crippling burden of exorbitant rates of interest, especially in an agrarian society where the farmer is dependent on seasons. These laws clearly date from long before the economic development of Israel as a trading power under Solomon. The reason for the prohibition is presumably that the poor man borrows in his need. The loan is seen as assistance to a neighbour, and to make money from his need would be immoral. Christ commands us to go still further along the same road, and forbids even the attempt to recover the principal (let alone the interest) in such cases (Lk. 6:34,35). The interest-free loan to a brother in need has now become an outright gift. These great spiritual principles remain equally true in our 'affluent society', however applied in detail.

26. *Restore it to him before the sun goes down* is an example of how Israel's understanding of God softens the application of the law, while maintaining its letter. Even an interest-free loan to a fellow-Israelite needed some pledge or security. Such a pledge was permitted, though even here Deuteronomy 24:10,11 sets restrictions. The most obvious pledge (probably the only movable possession of any value) was the 'poncho' or shepherd's cloak, which functioned as a blanket at night, and a 'swag roll' by day (Ex. 12:34) for every Israelite. The general custom of taking clothing as a pledge for debt is illustrated by Amos 2:8. But if this cloak had to be returned each night (when its use was necessity, not luxury), its value as a pledge was minimal: it became purely a vexatious reminder of the debt. The verb changes continually between singular and plural in this passage (AV 'thou' and 'ye'), a fact not apparent in the *you* of the RSV. Such alternation is, however, found elsewhere in legal matter.[1]

---

[1] It is certainly no reasonable ground in itself for postulating different sources, as some scholars do. On the whole matter, see Kitchen.

22:28–31. God's dues from His people. 28. *Nor curse a ruler.* This is the famous verse quoted by Paul at his trial before the high priest (Acts 23:5). *God* and *ruler* seem at first a strange pair, for the verb used in either case (RSV *revile* and *curse*) is the same. It is just possible that the word 'God' should be translated 'judges' here: in several other passages of the Old Testament, this would fit the sense. But if reverence towards God makes the cursing of parents a capital offence (Ex. 21:17), so also the cursing of the tribal chief appointed by God. The Hebrew *nāśî'* meant a patriarchal clan chief in early days, with a representative and almost a religious position, as can be seen from Numbers 17:1–6. In later days, it became a vague term usually translated 'prince', as in Ezekiel 46. This reverential attitude to authority rings strangely to our modern ears, but it is in tune with the teaching of Romans 13:1 and the general principle of mutual subjection in 1 Peter 5:5. Of course, this does not rule out conscientious withholding of obedience to authority for Christ's sake (see Mt. 22:21).

29. *From the fulness of your harvest and from the outflow of your presses. Fulness* and *outflow* are the only words expressed in the Hebrew, but the RSV is probably correct in its translation. Since we know that 'fullness' usually applies to wine, it is likely that 'outflow' (literally 'tear') applies to olive oil. The Mishnah however applies it to the juice that oozes naturally from the over-ripe grapes, in which case the two clauses will be strictly parallel. *The first-born . . . you shall give to me.* This is the bare principle. It does not follow that the author knew nothing of the Israelite custom of redemption or substitution (Ex. 13:13), so clearly laid down elsewhere in the Pentateuch.

31. *Men consecrated to me.* All Israel was virtually in the position of priests (Ex. 19:6). It was unthinkable that a priest should defile himself (and so defile God) by eating carrion, which had not been ritually slaughtered, and would therefore contain blood in it.

23:1–9. Humanitarianism in daily life. This next passage bears certain resemblances to the 'ten words', being categorical law interspersed with 'Deuteronomic' explanations of reason and motive (so called as being most frequently found in that book).

1. *A malicious witness*: better translated 'witness in a charge of violence', for the thought is that a verdict will be fatal to the defendant. The law then becomes an explanation of Exodus 20:16.

3. *A poor man.* By changing *dāl* to *gāḏôl*, most editors read 'a powerful man', arguing that to favour such a one is a real temptation, and that verse 6 would be repetitious otherwise. But this is to ignore a more subtle temptation than that of considering the rich and powerful as always right: it is that of considering them as always wrong. This is a real danger in our modern society, and must have been an equal danger in egalitarian Israel. Strict justice will not allow this, any more than the other.

4. *Your enemy's ox. Enemy* in this context probably means 'legal adversary'. Justice demands that we treat him like any other neighbour, and certainly that we do not 'take it out' of his helpless livestock. It is only a short step from this practical concern for the good of our adversary to the 'love your enemy' of Matthew 5:44.

6. *Your poor:* '*eḇyôn* is the common biblical word for 'poor', frequent in the Psalter with the sense of 'pious poor' (*e.g.* Ps. 9:18). It later gave the name of the Jewish-Christian sect of the Ebionites ('God's poor'), and had perhaps been used before as a title of the Jerusalem church (Gal. 2:10).

8. *You shall take no bribe:* as above, always a danger in a marginal society. It was important for any Israelite judge to be able to establish his position on this (1 Sa. 12:3). Samuel's own sons failed at this point (1 Sa. 8:3).

9. *You shall not oppress a stranger:* a common temptation, since the stranger had no kin to protect him. Here again is the Deuteronomic phrase that reinforces the command by giving the reason. Love for the resident alien is not based on mere humanitarianism, but on a fellow-feeling which comes from a deep personal experience of God's saving grace, when in a like situation. *The heart of a stranger:* the Hebrew is not the usual word for 'heart' but *nep̄eš*, which can be translated 'life' or 'self'. Here it seems to have more the meaning of 'desires and longings'. However it be translated, the verse is indicative of deep and true sympathy, alike the Jewish and Christian duty (Rom. 12:15). Perhaps we might translate: 'you know from experience what a stranger yearns for.'

23:10–19. Ritual regulations. These are still apodeictic laws, but more ritual than humanitarian in this section, though both alike have religious motivation. In some cases, humanitarian motives are adduced for what appear at first sight to be mere ritual regulations.

11. *Let it rest*. From the Hebrew verb used here comes the noun used in Deuteronomy 15:1 for 'year of release'. In Deuteronomy, it applies to a remission of debts: here, it has its simplest meaning of 'leaving ground fallow'. The parallelism between the seventh year and the seventh day (of rest) is made explicit in verse 12. The only stated purpose of the 'fallow year', however, is so that the poor may eat and, after them, the wild beasts. To let a field *lie fallow* every seventh year is wise agriculture, and would increase its fertility (especially when little fertilizer is available for addition to the soil); but that was not the reason for Israel's observance, while it may well have been the result (compare the hygienic aspects of the law of Moses, probably unsuspected by those who first kept it). Some hold that the purpose of the 'sabbatical year' was to allow God's earth to return to its original uncultivated state, and so to glorify the God of nature. Others hold that it was simple conservatism, looking back to the days when man was a food-gatherer or a pastoralist, not an agriculturalist. On the religious level, its observance was a practical exposition of Israelite faith in the God who would provide their needs, as was the weekly observance of sabbath.

The wild beasts may eat. This is not a primitive taboo, but deeply theological. The glory of Israel's faith is the belief that God preserves both man and beast (Ps. 36:6) and feeds the wild animals every day (Ps. 104:21). Christ tells us that God cares for the sparrows on the roof (Mt. 10:29) and feeds the ravens (Lk. 12:24). We do not know whether the sabbath year was intended to be observed simultaneously all over the country, or whether it was to be a different year on each farm, according to the date at which the land had been initially taken in. In Maccabean days, such a year was observed universally and simultaneously. In early days, it was probably not observed at all on a wide scale. Later prophets saw the seventy years of the exile as a punishment for four hundred and ninety years' neglect of this 'sabbatical' rule (counting from the initial occupation of Canaan).

12. *On the seventh day you shall rest*: as in the ten commandments, but with a difference. The weekly sabbath here is not merely a reminder of God's creative work (Ex. 20:11) or of

Israel's deliverance from Egypt (Dt. 5:15). It is to be a cessation from labour for Israel, physical rest for the animals, and refreshment for the workers in slave or semi-slave status, for whom there was presumably no religious obligation.

13. *The names of other gods.* The Hebrew says 'name' in the singular, so perhaps we should translate 'another god's name'. It is probably a reference to swearing by another god's name instead of by the name of YHWH: this would of course indicate lack of faith in YHWH. Paul seems to refer to this verse in Ephesians 5:3.

Verses **14–17** contain an account of the three annual festivals in Israel that required a pilgrimage to God's holy place. All adult males must go, presumably because such occasions are a gathering of YHWH's war-host, though we know from 1 Samuel 1 that women could and did go up with their husbands. It is, however, plain that even the greatest of the three (passover) was observed only sporadically or on a limited scale during the time of the kingdom (2 Ki. 23:22), though no doubt kept regularly after the exile, when Ezra and Nehemiah were able to enforce the law in a small close-knit community. This of course does not prove that the regulation did not exist earlier.

15. *The feast of unleavened bread*: *cf.* 'harvest' (or 'first fruits') and 'ingathering' in verse 16. Because these names are agricultural, some have thought that the feasts were borrowed from the settled Canaanites after the conquest. This does not necessarily follow: the names may instead be far older than Moses. Festivals with these names may even have been observed by Israel's ancestors, whether in patriarchal or Egyptian days. There would then have been no need to learn anything from the Canaanites. But all these three feasts were associated in post-Mosaic days not merely with the round of seasons and with God's gift of a fruitful land, in fulfilment of His promise to the patriarchs. They were also associated with His saving acts in history, shown in the salvation of Israel. Here *unleavened bread* is kept as a memorial of the deliverance from Egypt, while in Leviticus 23:43 (under its other name of 'booths') the third feast is also commemorative of the same event. By New Testament times (and probably therefore long before) the feast of weeks (here called 'harvest') was commemorative of the law-giving at Sinai, another 'act of God' in history.

It is strange that 'unleavened bread' should be used here as a title rather than passover, if the two feasts were contiguous (see notes on Exodus 12 for possible explanations of the reason for this). Perhaps it was because the seven days of unleavened bread made the one day of passover seem a mere preliminary: or perhaps it was because in early days the passover was more a family meal than a central religious activity. In any case, it is significant that, even as early as this date, 'unleavened bread' is given no other justification in Israel than as a memorial of a past historical event, Israel's redemption from Egypt.

Empty-handed. Since each feast corresponded to some harvest activity, this command was easy to fulfil, by the general rule of offering of first-fruits (verse 19). Unleavened bread, for instance, fell at the beginning of barley harvest. Harvest, or 'weeks', was seven weeks later, squarely in wheat harvest. Ingathering (or 'booths', or 'tabernacles') was the 'harvest home' in autumn, when grapes and olives were all gathered in. The agricultural calendar ended then, with the cessation of all agrarian activity for the winter.

18. *Not . . . with leavened bread* may be either a general sacrificial regulation, or a specific reference to passover. Leaven seems to have been a stock symbol of evil (Mt. 16:6) since, like fermentation of grapes, it symbolized corruption. *The fat of my feast*: that is, the special portion of the victim that belonged to God. Were it left till morning, it might be rancid, and so unfit for sacrifice. Any unused portion of the passover victim must be burnt in the same night (Ex. 12:10). Compare the parallel verse in Exodus 34:25, and the general rule of Leviticus 19:6.

19. *You shall not boil a kid in its mother's milk.* The Canaanite texts show this to be a magic spell, so the prescription is more ritual than humane. Some tradition of this spell must have survived: Maimonides, the mediaeval Jewish scholar, warned us that the rite was connected with fertility-magic, and Driver suggested the same thing, sixty years ago, showing how scholarly acumen is sometimes later vindicated by archaeology. Had we more detailed knowledge of Canaanite religion, it would no doubt explain many a taboo in the law. For instance, the ban on pig was probably ritual, because of its use outside Israel in sacrifice: the ban on donkey almost certainly so, because of its place in Amorite religion (*e.g.* in covenant sacrifice).

23:20–33. The 'Deuteronomic promise'. This title may well be given to the present passage because its hortatory style and theological approach are so close to that seen best in Deuteronomy. Traces of this outlook can be found in Leviticus (19:9–17). We should therefore see it as a 'strain', a way of understanding God and His dealings with Israel. It runs right through the Old Testament, because it corresponds to one aspect of God Himself.

As regards the form of the passage containing the promises and warning, Driver points out that this is a suitable ending for the book of the covenant. Both Leviticus and Deuteronomy likewise end with exhortation, blessings and curses. Indeed, such an ending seems to have been the usual conclusion of the secular 'covenants' of the day.

20. *An angel.* It is better to translate the word by the neutral 'messenger', and leave it to the context to decide the messenger's nature. It could be argued that Moses or Joshua was originally intended here: but the following verses seem to suggest a supernatural messenger, *i.e.* what we would call 'an angel' in the full sense of the word. *To the place which I have prepared*: the reference is clearly to Canaan. The word *place* is probably to be taken in a general sense, not in its frequent sense of 'holy place', as though God were leading Israel to His sanctuary at Shiloh or elsewhere. Christ may be alluding to this verse in John 14:2,3.

21. *Do not rebel against him.* Whether the messenger is human or divine, rebellion against God's messenger is the same as rebellion against God (*cf.* Ex. 16:8). No man can accept God's salvation except through accepting God's Saviour. This can be seen in relation to Israel and Moses (Acts 7:35) and, even more clearly, in relation to the world and Christ. *My name is in him* seems to translate the 'messenger' into the supernatural realm, for God's 'name' is the equivalent of His revealed nature. 'Angel' may indeed be here a reverent periphrasis for the presence of God Himself. Other suggestions are that the 'messenger' means the column of cloud or fire, which traditionally led Israel (Ex. 13:21), or the ark, called 'YHWH's ark' and thus bearing God's name, and symbolizing His presence with His people (Nu. 10:35,36). See also Exodus 32:34; 33:2. Whatever the exact nature of the 'angel', every such reference reminds us at once of God's transcendence and His immediacy.

22. *If you hearken.* God's blessings are conditional on faith and obedience. This is not an arbitrary rule, but essential, because only obedience is an expression of that new relationship of dependence on God, which ensures His will of blessing for us. *I will be an enemy to your enemies*: a fulfilment of the promise to Abraham in Genesis 12:3, 'him who curses you I will curse'. Put in another way, it is not so much that God will be enemy to our enemies, as that we will be enemies to God's enemies. For this identification, see Psalm 139:21,22. What is a physical reality in the Old Testament becomes a spiritual reality in New Testament days.

23. *I blot them out* cannot be the correct translation of the verb, or it would contradict the verses below, which suggest a gradual reduction. Some lighter meaning is required, perhaps 'make them disappear'.

24. *Their pillars*: literally 'standing (stones)' or 'orthostats'. These upright stones are often found in groups of ten at the Canaanite sanctuaries (Gezer and Taanach, for instance). In Exodus 24:4 Moses set up twelve, to symbolize the twelve tribes of Israel. In patriarchal days their use had been innocent enough (Gn. 28:18), but not now, in the context of Canaanite Baal-worship. As in Hinduism, the stone probably represented the male principle in the fertility cult, while the tree represented the female-principle.

25. *I will bless.* God's blessing is here couched in material terms, easily understandable by ordinary men. The Creator promises food, health, fertility, and long life, to those who obey His laws. As a rough 'rule of thumb', this can be tested and found true at any level of civilization. While it is not universally correct that 'honesty is the best policy', in any stable society honesty does demonstrably bring its own rewards, even in this life. God's law, if obeyed, ensured fair distribution of food in Israel. Considered as an hygienic code, God's law ensured a health standard for Israel far higher than that of neighbouring lands, such as Philistia or Egypt, where plagues were endemic (Ex. 15:26). Respect for old age, and in particular for parents, ensured that the old had a secure and honoured place in society. A psychologist would say that, in the stability of Israelite married life, the psychological stresses and strains that sometimes inhibit child-bearing would be absent. All this, be it noted, does not explain away God's promised blessing: it simply shows some ways in which God's blessing comes.

However, when this 'rule of thumb' is seen either as universal or as independent of man's response, then it gives rise to a theological problem (the 'suffering of the righteous') faced in Job, Ecclesiastes and some of the Psalms. Gradually, it becomes clear to God's saints that the deepest of God's blessings are spiritual, not physical (Hab. 3:17,18): this brings us to the dawn of the New Testament.

27. *My terror* explains the method that God will use to subdue the Canaanites before Israel: a divine panic will grip them. For an illustration, see Joshua 2:11, which gives Rahab's account of the terror of the settled population of Canaan before this horde of invaders.

28. *I will send hornets.* This could be understood literally. In South-east Asia, for instance, few things are dreaded as much as hornets, and several deaths are caused each year by them. Deuteronomy 7:20 and Joshua 24:12 use the same Hebrew word in the same context. It seems better, however, to understand it metaphorically, either of a plague, or of some attacker, whether human or superhuman. By slight vocalic alterations, some commentators translate the word either as 'leprosy' or 'discouragement' (see Hyatt): but this seems unnecessary. Isaiah 7:18 uses 'the fly' as a symbol of Egypt's armies, and 'the bee' as a symbol of the armies of Assyria. Since the bee or wasp was a heraldic symbol of the pharaoh, probably the best explanation is that 'hornet' refers to the Egyptian army, steadily raiding Canaan year after year, and so weakening her before Israel's advent.

29. *I will not drive them out . . . in one year.* At first sight, the book of Joshua might seem to indicate a complete and easy conquest, while Judges shows a ding-dong struggle. Here, from the start, not only is the conquest envisaged as long and gradual, but a practical reason is given for its protracted nature. For the real possibility of multiplication of *wild beasts*, see 2 Kings 17:25, where the lions represent a major danger to the 'Samaritan' colonists of Israel, the so-called 'proselytes of the lion'. In Malaysia, during the communist 'emergency' in the years following World War II, tigers increased alarmingly in some areas, since no hunter had leisure or opportunity to peal with them. Additional reasons for the gradual nature of the conquest are given in Judges 2:20 – 3:4 (to teach succeeding generations to fight: to test their faith: and so on).

31. *I will set your bounds*: the ideal boundaries of Israel, attained only briefly under David and Solomon, and possibly for the second time under the united rule of Jeroboam II and Uzziah of Judah. *The Red Sea* (literally 'Sea of Reeds') must clearly be the Gulf of Aqaba here (whatever area of water is meant in Exodus 14), because it is considered as the eastern border, as opposed to the Mediterranean in the west. *The wilderness* is then the southern frontier, and *the Euphrates* the extreme northern border. 'The river' in the Bible is always 'the great river', *i.e.* the Euphrates, just as 'the sea' is normally the Mediterranean (the Dead Sea, the Sea of Reeds and the Sea of Galilee are distinguished by epithets).

32. *You shall make no covenant.* This is the end of the 'book of the covenant', giving the terms upon which God's covenant was to be made with Israel. The next chapter moves on to the actual establishment of YHWH's covenant. In view of the exclusive nature of this relationship, it is right that this chapter should end with the forbidding of any other covenant, human or divine, for Israel. Such a provision was common in the treaties of the day.

33. *It will surely be a snare to you.* As Driver points out, *snare*, in Hebrew thought, is a symbol, not so much of falling into sin, as of falling into destruction: so is 'stumbling-block' in the New Testament. The warning is therefore more stern than the English would suggest.

d. The covenant ratified (24:1–18)

24:1–11. Making the covenant. 1. *You and Aaron, Nadab, and Abihu.* This verse gives the *dramatis personae*, which will be taken up again in verses 9–11. *Nadab* and *Abihu* are the two sons of Aaron, whose death, under God's judgment, is recorded in Numbers 3:4; the actual story is in Leviticus 10. This explains their failure to reappear later. It also assures us of the authenticity of the tradition, for no-one would have inserted their names here in the account of such an important event. By contrast, 'Aaron and Hur' (verse 14) are known as a 'pair' together from Exodus 17:12, the battle with Amalek. *Seventy of the elders* is a loose traditional number, representing either the twelve tribes of Israel or Jacob's seventy descendants (Nu. 11:16 and Lk. 10:1). Perhaps these 'sheikhs' were a permanent feature of Israel's later tribal structure, like the twelve clan-chiefs (Nu. 1).

2. *Moses alone* goes up to the summit. The scene in Gethsemane is similar (Mt. 26:36-39), and perhaps denotes degrees of nearness to God. The common people remain at the foot of the mountain: even the others come only part-way: only Moses is at the top, with God.

3. *All the words . . . ordinances*: *words* would be categorical law (like the 'ten words') while *ordinances* (better 'judicial decisions') would be 'case-law'. Since the book of the covenant contains both, the distinction is not important. It does however render it unlikely that the ten commandments were considered as the only terms of the covenant (apart from the wider range of material contained in the book of the covenant).

4. *Moses wrote all the words of YHWH*. Any covenant involved public recital and acceptance of its terms. Next, some permanent outward form must be given to these 'treaty obligations', and so they are written down. It is unthinkable, in this millennium, that any treaty should exist without some written form: but the extent of the written formulation on this occasion is a moot point. It could be either more or less than our present 'book of the covenant'. There are not many places in the Pentateuch where contemporaneous recording of events or laws in writing is stressed in the tradition: but compare the writing of the 'ten words' (Ex. 31:18) and the account of the war on Amalek (Ex. 17:14). *An altar . . . twelve pillars*. Here the 'standing stones' are symbols of the twelve tribes of Israel, while the *altar* clearly symbolizes YHWH Himself in the ceremony that follows. However, to show that this is only symbolism, not superstition, in the blood-ceremony the blood is dashed over the people themselves (verse 8), not over the pillars that represent them.

5. *Young men*. This is a primitive touch, coming from before the time of a specialized priesthood (see Ex. 32:29 for Levi's later 'ordination'). There is nothing magical in the choice of young men for the task: it is purely a practical consideration. To bind cattle to a stone altar required strength and agility. As a young man was a natural warrior, so he was a natural 'priest'.

6. *Moses took half of the blood*. Blood-ritual of some kind is common to most forms of covenant: witness the custom in many lands of making 'blood-brothers' by allowing the blood from two persons to mingle and flow together in one. No explanation of the covenant ritual is given here. It may be that God and people are reckoned as of 'one blood', and that God declares Himself to be their 'father' and 'redeemer-kins-man' or 'blood-avenger' (Ex. 6:6). Abraham's covenant had been made by a still more primitive blood-ritual, by which both parties passed between severed pieces of sacrificial animals (Gn. 15, an archaism revived in the later days of Jeremiah, Je. 34:18). The blood-ritual may have been the equivalent of invoking death on oneself if the terms of the covenant are not kept, but again there is no evidence. It does not appear that this particular shedding of blood was connected with the forgiveness of sins (Lv. 17:13), although it may well have symbolized the laying-down of life.

7. *Read it in the hearing of the people.* The reading of the terms from an official written copy now seals and solemnizes the verbal acceptance so far given. It is from this verse that the title 'book of the covenant' is derived and used to cover the chapters immediately preceding, probably correctly.

8. *The blood of the covenant.* This phrase reappears in the solemn phraseology of the Last Supper (Mt. 26:28). Christ Himself would be, on the cross, not only the mediator of a covenant (like Moses), but also the sacrifice that initiated that covenant.

9. *Moses and Aaron, Nadab, and Abihu.* Verses 9–11 continue the anecdote of verses 1,2, but there is no need, because of this, with some editors to see verses 9–11 as an alternative account of the covenant-making already described. The reason for climbing the mountain on this occasion, to judge from verse 1, was purely worship. It is true that a shared meal (especially if involving salt) was a common way of sealing a covenant, from biblical times till modern days. However it is also true that any form of worship which involved the sacrifice of 'peace offerings' (verse 5) would be naturally followed by a sacrificial feast. What else would be done with the meat? Any 'burnt offerings' would have been of course totally consumed in the sacrificial fires as an offering to God: but the phrase 'ate and drank' (verse 11) probably refers to 'peace offerings' which usually followed 'burnt offerings'.

10. *They saw the God of Israel.* At first sight, this is a contradiction of Exodus 33:20. But it will be remembered that even there Moses was to be allowed to see God's 'back' (33:28). In this verse it is equally stressed that the elders did not dare raise their eyes above His footstool. Naturally, there is deep spiritual truth in these anthropomorphic metaphors, a truth which finds expression in Moses' hiding of his own face (Ex. 3:6) and Isaiah's cry (Is. 6:5). No mortal man can bear to see the full splendour of God; it is only in Christ that we can see Him mirrored (Heb. 1:3). The phrase *the God of Israel* is not uncommon in the Old Testament, although it has an a archaic flavour here. The miracle, as outlined in verse 11, was not merely that the elders had the vision, but that they were unharmed by it, and could therefore join in the fellowship meal.

A pavement of sapphire stone. According to Noth, this type of pavement is known particularly in Mesopotamia. It may be a reference to the blue 'lapis lazuli' which was favourite there from early times. If correctly translated, *sapphire* would imply a deep blue, and a better description of the vault of the sky could hardly be found. After all the thunders and lightnings, now there is a transparent azure; yet even this splendour is only God's lowly footstool. Ezekiel 1:26 sees God as seated on a sapphire throne, over a crystal 'firmament' (verse 22), and the thought is taken up again in the book of Revelation (4:6).

11. *The chief men*: literally 'corner pegs', an unusual and archaic word, whose meaning is clear from the context. Similar metaphors will be used elsewhere in the Old Testament (Is. 22:23; Zc. 10:4).

24:12–18. The tablets of stone. 12. *The tablets of stone, with the law*: better translated 'stone tablets, that is to say the law and the commandment'. This description must surely, in view of the sequel, refer here to the ten words alone. Elsewhere these tablets are called 'the tablets of the testimony' (Ex. 31:18) or 'the tables of the covenant' (Dt. 9:9).

13. *Joshua*: first mentioned in 17:9. He will assume increasing importance in connection with the meeting-tent later (Ex. 33:11).

16. *The glory of YHWH settled on Mount Sinai.* The symbols of God's manifested presence or 'glory' are all there; cloud and fire, and the voice of God. *Settled*: the Hebrew verb is *šāḵēn*, 'dwelt'. It is used in a technical sense later of God's 'shekinah', the outward manifestation of His presence to men. In the New Testament, assonance suggests the Greek word *skēnē*, 'tent' (AV 'tabernacle') and so the corresponding Greek verb is used of the 'tabernacling' of the Word in the midst of men (Jn. 1:14).

18. *Forty days and forty nights* may be a symbolic period (*cf.* Israel's forty years in the desert, and Christ's forty days of temptation), but it clearly indicates a prolonged stay. The period is intended to cover the giving of all the ritual instructions about the meeting-tent, priesthood and worship contained in chapters 25–31. It is not until chapter 32 that Moses and Joshua come down from the mountain, to face the apostasy of Israel.

e. Covenant worship (25:1 – 31:18; cf. 35:1 – 39:43)

In chapters 25–31, detailed directions are given to Moses on Mount Sinai as to Tent, furnishings, priesthood and so forth.[1] Chapters 32–34 are a historical interruption, covering the idolatrous rebellion of Israel, the reiteration of the covenant, and the final handing over of a second set of stone tablets, engraved with the commandments. Then in chapters 35–40 comes a virtual repetition of the detail of the earlier chapters. This time, the emphasis is on the execution of the commands, and the full obedience of Moses to the 'pattern shown him on the mount' (Ex. 25:40; Heb. 8:5). Apart from changes in the persons and tenses of the verbs, and some minor shortenings and omissions, there is so little alteration that no fresh commentary will be required. There are however some new statistical details about the Tent and its materials, and these will be examined under the later section.

i. Ark, table and lampstand (25:1–40)

25:1–9. Introduction. This is an introductory passage, explaining as it does the source of the materials used later in the construction of the Tent and its equipment. There are three fundamental spiritual principles exemplified here, which remain eternally valid. The first (in verse 2) is that giving to God must be voluntary, not forced (2 Cor. 9:7). God's grace will prompt men to give: and man will then give his most costly treasures gladly to God. This is clearly the meaning of the list of contributions in verses 3–7, whatever uncertainty

---

[1] Critics such as Wellhausen have always regarded this section as completely unhistorical, a 'back-projection' to wilderness days of Solomon's Temple. On the other hand, Cross argues strongly for the archaic nature of much of the material: see Hyatt and Henton Davies for attempted reconciliation of these views.

there is about detailed interpretation. Secondly, it is God's aim and purpose to live in the midst of His people (verse 8): that is the whole reason for making the Tent. Thirdly, obedience in carrying out God's master-plan is essential (verse 9). This last point is the great stress through chapters 35-40, as mentioned above.

2. *Every man whose heart makes him willing.* The Hebrew says, picturesquely, every man 'whose heart makes him vow': he cannot help himself.

3. *Gold, silver, and bronze.* The last word is better translated 'copper': it is certainly not 'brass', as the older translations. Driver points out that there is a definite principle by which the closer to the presence of God, the more precious the metal used. The Arabah, to the south of the Dead Sea, was rich in copper mines: gold was also found in the Sinai Peninsula. If, as is probable, the Midianites were a mining people, Israel had easy access to metals: in addition, the 'looting' of Egypt, when they left, should be remembered (Ex. 12:35). Because a nomadic people live in tents, it does not follow that they do not own costly objects: witness the rare carpets in some eastern tents today. In spite of Hyatt, it is probably indicative of an early date that there is no mention of iron here.

4. *Blue and purple and scarlet stuff.* The first of the three words used, *t^eḵēleṯ*, is Akkadian for 'violet dye' (*i.e.* yarn dyed that colour). The second word, *'argāmān*, in Sanscrit means a reddish purple; the 'red worm', the third term, is the cochineal insect or kirmiz (Arabic), giving our English word 'crimson'. It is probable that the three words are used together loosely, to denote any rich dye in the red-to-purple range. *Fine twined linen*: *šēš* is an Egyptian word. Egypt excelled in the production of linen, especially *twined linen*, where every thread was twisted from many strands. The Hebrew slaves must have learned many Egyptian arts and crafts, such as metalwork, spinning, weaving and embroidery during their stay in Egypt. Linen was the dress of the noble and the priest in Egypt, chosen both for coolness and cleanliness. Cloth made from *goats' hair* was the usual material for nomadic tents, then as now, giving hard-wearing dark fabric, resistant to rain. Felt would be the modern equivalent.

5. *Tanned* ('reddened') *rams' skins*: presumably this was to make the leather 'tent bags'. RSV *goatskins* (*t^eḥāšîm*) are either 'dugong skins' (from the Red Sea; *cf.* NEB *porpoise-hides*) or just a transliteration of an Egyptian word for 'leather' in general, which is more likely. *Acacia wood* is a typical desert wood, hard and aromatic, but spindly. It is however reputed to be good for cabinet-making: see Hyatt.

6. *Spices*: balsams are the great product of Arabia all through the Bible days. Precious stones (verse 7) are also a noted local product: the turquoise mines of Serabit-El-Khadem were particularly famous in the peninsula.

8. *A sanctuary*: the word literally means 'holy place', and can be used later even of the Temple itself (Je. 17:12). The purpose of the *sanctuary* is defined here as being so that God may *dwell* among Israel. The same Hebrew root is used (in a derived form) in verse 9 to give the name 'dwelling' or 'tabernacle'. See also the notes on Exodus 24:16. Davies has a good discussion of this 'theology of the presence' (of God) which he sees as dominating the book of Exodus, and which, for the Christian, is culminated by the coming of Christ to earth.

9. *The pattern* means almost 'architect's model'. Gudea of Lagash (3000 BC) claims that he saw in a dream the very model of a Temple, which he later built meticulously. Moses is commended for similar obedience, both in Exodus (39:5) and Hebrews (3:2–5).

25:10–22. The chest. 'Chest' (rather like a small seaman's chest, or a Chinese camphorwood box) gives the meaning of *'ārôn* better than the older translation 'ark'. A different word is used for the 'ark' of Noah and Moses. This chest was a yard long and eighteen inches in other directions, made of acacia wood, but gold-plated and plain, except for the golden 'cover' (translated 'mercy seat', verse 17) to which were soldered two small golden 'cherubim' facing inwards. Golden rings were to be fitted at the corners, and into these rings gold-plated acacia poles were to be inserted for carrying. Essentially, the chest itself was a sacred box, easily portable, to contain the two stone tablets engraved with the law. The 'covering', overshadowed by the wings of the cherubim, was also seen as a throne of the invisible God, who would meet with, and speak to, Israel there (verse 22).

11. *Pure gold* was used for anything closely connected with God's immediate presence, in accordance with the principle mentioned above. Otherwise, silver or copper might be used.

Probably the reference is to overlaying with gold leaf: but see Hyatt for the possibility of gold inlay.

16. *The testimony*: 'the witness', in modern English.[1] This is a common name for the law (or at least for that part engraved on the two tablets), presumably as being a witness and reminder of the nature of God.

17. *A mercy seat*: this is an interpretation, not a translation, of Hebrew *kappōreṯ*. It could mean either 'lid' or 'cover' in the literal sense (though this meaning is not found elsewhere in the Old Testament) or 'that which propitiates', in the metaphorical sense of 'covering'. This sense must certainly be included, in view of phrases like 'day of atonement' which came from the same root (Lv. 23:27; literally 'day of covering'). Such 'atonement' was not usually performed at the ark, but by the blood shed at the altar (Lv. 17:11): however, the transference is easy and natural.[2]

18. *Two cherubim.* These were most likely human-faced winged sphinxes, to judge from the visions of Ezekiel 1 and Revelation 4 as well as Egyptian usage (although cherubim are mentioned in Gn. 3:24, they are not described). In Assyria, the *karubu* (same root) has the function of a temple-guardian. In Israel, *cherubim* symbolized God's attendant and messenger spirits (Ps. 104:3,4) and so were not considered a breach of Exodus 20:4, since no man worshipped them. Figures of 'cherubim' were embroidered in vivid colour all around the inner curtain of the Tent (Ex. 36:35), so their appearance over the chest was not an isolated instance. Solomon's Temple had two enormous cherubim of gilded olive wood, fifteen feet high, freestanding from the chest (2 Ch. 3:10). This is only one of many points in which Solomon's Temple was more elaborate than the plans outlined here for the Tent.

22. *There I will meet with you . . . I will speak with you*: from His throne, above the cherubim (1 Sa. 4:4). The chest was always regarded as the visible symbol of God's presence and, as such, in Mosaic days it was hailed when going out or coming in (Nu. 10:35,36). Under Eli, it was wrongly regarded as a magic 'charm' ensuring divine protection (1 Sa. 4:4). David

[1] Hebrew *'ēdûṯ* may perhaps be connected with the Akkadian *ādū*, which is frequently used in treaty-covenants. In view of the relationship of law to covenant in Israel, this may be significant as a parallel.

[2] The one time in the year when blood was actually sprinkled on the *kappōreṯ* itself was the day of atonement (Lv. 7), but this scanty use could be explained by the sacredness of the spot.

refused to abuse its protection in this way (2 Sa. 15:25) and Jeremiah foresaw the day when such a symbol would no more be needed (Je. 3:16). It presumably perished in the sack of Jerusalem in 586 BC. In later temples a symbolic block of stone took its place, and in modern Jewry the carved wooden cupboard that houses the scroll of the law bears its name. The holiest place of all in the Tent was the resting-place of this sacred chest, which to touch was death to a commoner (2 Sa. 6:7). It is however typical of Israel's faith that neither chest nor cherub was an object of worship: the chest, by containing the law, merely witnessed to the nature of the God who was worshipped there.

25:23–30. The table. Most sanctuaries have a table for offerings, and Israel's is no exception. Again, the table is of acacia wood, gold-plated, with rings and rods so that it is portable, as all Israel's sacred objects must be, in desert days. For the construction, see below.

30. *The bread of the Presence.* The characteristic use of the table was to display the 'bread laid before God', as this phrase might be paraphrased. Twelve flat cakes, arranged in two piles (Lv. 24:6), were put out fresh-baked each morning, and removed each evening, to be eaten by the priests only, in normal circumstances (1 Sa. 21:6). The symbolism is not explained: perhaps it was grateful acknowledgment that the 'daily bread' of the twelve tribes came from God. There certainly seems to be some link here with the origin of the well-known phrase in the Lord's prayer (Lk. 11:3).

We are fortunate in having, on the Arch of Titus, a carved representation of this table (as well as of the golden lampstand). The model pictured is that from Herod's Temple but, to judge from the description in Exodus, it followed closely the Exodus pattern. On the table still rest some of the golden cups used for incense, or for libations poured at the foot of the altar (verse 29), while a few priestly trumpets lean against it. The technical terms used in Exodus to describe the construction of the table are not all certain because of their rarity. The table seems to have had supporting struts and claw feet, like modern tables, to judge from the Ark of Titus.

25:31–40. The golden lampstand. 31. *A lampstand*: the m⁽nôrâ that has become a symbol of Israel today (older translations have 'candlestick'). This had a practical function: in Eli's day, a 'lamp' was still kindled in the dark shrine (1 Sa. 3:3). Solomon had ten such in his great Temple (2 Ch. 4:7).

32. *Six branches.* Zechariah 4:2, in a vision, seems to refer to a lamp consisting of one oil-bowl whose rim was 'pinched' together in seven places at the side to allow seven wicks (Albright reports this type of lamp in terra cotta from Mizpah, according to Davies). But, if we compare the description here with the carving in the Arch of Titus, a different picture emerges. This is a seven-branched lampstand, of solid gold (gold-plated acacia wood cannot be used here). It is highly decorated with carving and moulding of almond blossoms and supports seven small single-wick lamps at the top. A glance at any reproduction of the Arch of Titus will make the main outline plain, although the exact metaphorical sense of some of the technical terms used is not quite clear.

33. *Three cups made like almonds.* If the references to the almond-tree are to be taken as literal designs used for decoration (and this seems the obvious interpretation), then we are reminded of Aaron's almond rod that budded (Nu. 17:8) and Jeremiah's vision (Je. 1:11,12). It would seem from Jeremiah that the almond, as the first tree that blossomed in the springtime, was an appropriate symbol of God's wonderful care over His people, and of His fulfilment of the promises made to their forefathers. But all this is guesswork, and we do well to tread cautiously. Some technical terms are of doubtful meaning, but do not affect the main sense. The *capital* of verse 34 is the usual word for 'Crete' in the Bible, so probably indicates the source of this decorative motif.

37. *So as to give light*: to the otherwise dark 'holy place' in front of the curtain. However, we are not told the further meaning of the symbolism. Some feel that the lampstand stood for Israel's task as a light to the Gentiles (Is. 60:3). Certainly 'seven' is always a symbol of perfection: while oil, at least later, becomes a picture of God's spirit (Zc. 4:1–6). The symbolism might be that of the light which God's presence brings to His people (Nu. 6:25), remembering that light, in the Old Testament, is also a symbol of life and victory (Ps. 27:1).

38. *Snuffers . . . trays.* The first is a pair of tongs or tweezers, for adjusting the wick: the second may be either a tray for preparing the oil (Noth) or a firepan (Driver). In either case, they are objects connected with the lamp.

ii. The Tent (26:1-37)

Again, while there are certain obscurities, the main pattern is plain, and the reader is advised to consult an illustration in any Bible dictionary.

1. *You shall make the tabernacle* (*tent*). The structure is roughly that of any nomad's home: an inner tent (corresponding to the women's section) with an outer tent for men, and possibly an 'enclosure' beyond that, for stock. As befits a tent for God, the dimensions are much greater than for an ordinary tent. In Solomon's Temple, even these dimensions are multiplied by two, giving a far greater size. The basic shape seems to be that of a 'coffin-tent', with flat roof and no ridge pole, supported on a light wooden frame. *Ten curtains . . . with cherubim*. The fabric of the Tent is *fine twined linen* (see note on 25: 4), richly inwoven with figures of cherubim. These would be seen on the roof and walls inside the Tent, by the light of the golden lampstand. From outside they would of course be invisible (see verse 7).

7. *Curtains of goats' hair.* The linen is protected from the weather on the outside by an ordinary tent fabric of black goats' hair, giving no hint of the brilliant colours beneath and within.

14. *A covering of tanned rams' skins and goatskins.* It seems that some form of leather 'tent bag', or wrapper, was provided for transportation. Some think that the phrase denoted a third (or even fourth) tent of leather, placed over the tents of goats' hair and linen, but this would seem to be impossibly heavy and unnecessary. For the materials, see verse 5. The fabric was woven in a series of curtains, rather like the 'brailing' of a modern marquee. These long curtains were then fastened together at the edge by hooks and loops, forming one huge sheet, which could be unhooked and rolled up for transport. An additional length of this material, suspended from poles, divided the Tent into two parts, in the inner of which rested the chest.

15. *You shall make upright frames*: or "supports', making a vertical framework (so RSV, following Kennedy: older translations had 'boards' or even 'beams').[1] This frame was made of acacia-wood spars (three inches thick, according to Josephus)

[1] The root *kāraš* means 'cut off' in other Semitic languages: in Ugaritic, the noun is used of the 'pavilion' of El (see Hyatt), which might suggest 'framework' here.

fitting into sockets, and forming a light trellis support, over which the curtains were draped. Horizontal bars locked the frame securely in position at the back, and special precautions were taken at the corners. In the Canaanite tradition, El's palace was also of 'trellised' construction, and Assyrian military tents had a similar, if much less complex, wooden framework. As it was only a wooden scaffolding, the embroidered cherubim could be seen from the inside of the tent between the poles. If the older translation of 'boards', instead of 'poles' or 'spars', had been correct, all this elaborate decoration would have been invisible, except upon the ceiling, since the Tent would have been completely panelled with boards within. Possibly, at a later stage of the sanctuary's history, when it was at Shiloh (1 Sa. 1:9) or Gibeon (1 Ki. 3:4), such actual solid 'boards' were used, making something halfway between a tent and a wooden building. But the argument still holds good that if the spars were as thick as the later Jews believed, then they would have been square beams, and their bulk and weight would have made carrying of the structure very difficult.

33. *The veil shall separate for you . . . the most holy*: cutting off about one-third of the area. The Tent was small (say 45 feet by 15 feet) compared with any modern church. It was also airless and dark, apart from the light from the golden lampstand and any accidental light that appeared temporarily when the flap over the door was raised to permit the entrance of priests. This lampstand was in the 'holy place': the 'most holy place' beyond the curtain or veil was always in pitch darkness. But the darkness and coolness inside would be great relief after the blinding heat of the desert outside (note how often YHWH's 'shadow' is mentioned as a symbol of refreshment and salvation, *e.g.* Ps. 17:8) and the very blackness itself, from the time of Sinai onwards, was a fitting symbol of God (1 Ki. 8:12). The small size was not a disadvantage, since only priests entered the main portion of the Tent, while the innermost shrine, always in total darkness, was entered by the high priest only once a year, on the day of atonement (Heb. 9:7). Herein was the significance of the tearing of the great Temple curtain at the time of Christ's death (Mk. 15:38). The congregation normally worshipped in their tent doors, looking towards God's Tent (Ex. 33:8), as a Muslim today turns towards Mecca to pray. If they came near at all, they only watched from outside what the priest did inside the 'courtyard' or great enclosure that surrounded the actual Tent. The various materials detailed here as to be used in making the Tent have already been mentioned in the list of offerings (Ex. 25:1–7).

iii. The altar, courtyard and night-light (27:1–21)

27:1–8. The altar. As Napier points out, there is a steady movement outwards, in the order of description of objects. First comes the description of the chest, in the holiest part of the Tent, and of the lampstand, in the main body of the Tent. Then the movement pauses for a moment, to describe the actual construction of the Tent itself. Once outside the Tent, we move on to the altar, and the courtyard in which it is set. As we move further out from the centre, the materials become less precious, and the structure less complex: again, the symbolism is clear.

1. *The altar of acacia wood.* To allow it mobility, it is made of acacia planks sheathed in copper plates. It is a square of $7\frac{1}{2}$ feet approximately, much smaller than the copper altar later built by Solomon, 30 feet square and 15 feet high (2 Ch. 4:1). Probably the 'earth' or 'unhewn stone' altars previously enjoined (Ex. 20:24,25) were for local use only, unless, with some editors, we assume that the space inside this framework of wood and copper was filled with earth or uncut stones, to the appropriate height, so that the altar would still be preserving the rules of the book of the covenant.

2. *You shall make horns*: hornlike projections at the four top corners, like most other ancient altars. These may have once represented the actual 'horns' of the beasts offered in sacrifice. Later they served the useful purpose of projections to which the bodies of the sacrificial animals might be bound (Ps. 118:27) or supplicants might cling. Since the altar was a 'sanctuary', a miniature 'city of refuge', the suppliant would grasp these horns in his hands, making himself a living sacrifice, devoted to YHWH, and so under His protection.

4. *A grating.* It is not sufficiently clear from the description what the purpose and position of the *network of bronze* was. Like most ancient altars, it was hollow (verse 8). The bronze grating perhaps then rested on a ledge inside the altar, halfway up. If so, the meat was virtually 'barbecued' on this, allowing the fat and ashes to drip down below. This explains both the way in which Jeroboam's new altar at Bethel 'burst open', spilling ashes everywhere, much to the king's discomfiture (1 Ki. 13:5), and also why pans and shovels were provided for 'raking out' the altar, as we might rake out a garden incinerator (verse 3). This also explains why it was possible to use a wooden altar without it being burnt. The fire did not directly contact the wood, which was only a hollow scaffolding. Most editors, however, follow Driver in assuming that the 'bronze grating' was the lower section of the outside wall of the altar, to give 'draught' to the fire.

This was the only altar of sacrifice in Israel's sanctuary in early days: blood would be smeared on its 'horns' in ceremonial atonement, and on it 'holocausts' or 'whole burnt offerings' would be laid. Libations were poured at its side, and blood dashed over it. It is usually called, in English translations, 'the brazen altar', in view of its outward appearance, although its actual construction was wood. Incense, on the other hand, was offered on another smaller altar, which appears, almost as an afterthought, in Exodus 30. This was also made of acacia wood, but plated with gold, not copper or bronze.

27:9–19. The courtyard. 9. *The court of the tabernacle.* This outer enclosure perhaps, as suggested, corresponded to something like a 'stock yard'. As far as the Tent is concerned, the court marks the outward limits of holiness (*cf.* the markers set all round Sinai on the day of God's descent and revelation there, Ex. 19:12). The later Temple at Jerusalem would have a stone wall, marking off its 'courts'. Corresponding to this in the desert, there is a series of poles with lengths of material stretching between, as we might screen off a cricket pitch today. The purpose was to provide a large open air area (150 feet by 75) where sacrifice could take place, and other sacred rites of a public nature might be performed. As the Tent itself took up only about one-fifteenth of the area of the courtyard, there was plenty of room, especially as the law knows nothing of the vast crowds that thronged the Temple courts in later days (Is. 1:12). Like Chinese temples today, men went to YHWH's Tent only for some specific purpose, and usually only on some festal occasion. In later days, the number of 'courtyards' was multiplied: here there is only one.

18. *The height five cubits*: the 'screening' around the court seems to have been 7½ feet high (too high to peer over, again like the cricket pitch), but it had an opening in one side, to act as entrance.

19. *All its pegs*: tent pegs make the whole firm, as they do the 'brailing' of a modern mess-tent or marquee. See Isaiah 54:2 for a reference to tent pegs and guy ropes, very familiar objects in Israel's early days, still used metaphorically centuries later.

27:20,21. The night-light. 20. *That a lamp may be set up to burn continually.* This is seen as a sort of 'perpetual light', burning all night in the outer part of the Tent, in front of the 'curtain' that shut off the holiest place of all, with the chest inside. It is not clear whether it is the same as the golden lampstand of Exodus 25:31 or not. At first reading, it certainly sounds like something much simpler, more like the lamp tended by Samuel at Shiloh (1 Sa. 3:3). The ultimate meaning is the same: it must never be completely dark before the curtain that shuts off the presence of God, and nothing but the finest of olive oil is good enough for YHWH's service. *Beaten* olive oil, so the Mishnah tells us, refers to the method of production of the very best oil. The olives are beaten only lightly with rods to produce this variety, not crushed completely, as they are to make lower grades of oil.

iv. Priestly robes (28:1–43)

Now follows the description of the semi-royal garments for the priests of Israel. Aaron is 'the priest' *par excellence*, and most of the description is of the splendid vestments to be made for him. By contrast, his 'sons' (whether meant literally, or as a priestly 'caste', the Semitic sense of the word) dress comparatively simply. The full priestly dress is very complex, and the exact meaning of some of the words is no longer as clear to us as to contemporaries. The writer of Exodus assumes that he deals with well-known objects, and therefore does not describe them, but concentrates on details: this makes interpretation difficult. But fortunately the main outline is clear: the garments are *holy*, *i.e.* set apart from others, and they are *for glory and for beauty* (verse 2). Apart from this, no special liturgical significance is given to the individual pieces. They are made of the finest materials (like the curtains of the Tent) but with gold thread worked in as well, to give added splendour (verse 5).

On the shoulder-pieces of the priestly ephod were two precious stones engraved with the names of the twelve tribes of Israel: the same names were also engraved on precious stones on a pouch of embroidered material that lay on his heart. In twofold symbolism he bore Israel's name before God, whenever he entered the Tent, a picture perhaps of his representative, if not intercessory, position. In the same pouch he carried the two oracular stones, used when casting lots to determine God's will in a given instance. On the very turban wound round his head, he had a gold plate (or ornament) inscribed 'Holiness to YHWH' perhaps as a reminder of his and Israel's position. As Napier says, the priestly garments are not ends in themselves, as might appear. By their symbolism, they testify to God's presence among His people, and to God's willingness to forgive and to guide. Even in Old Testament days the great prayer was not merely that YHWH's priests should be vested correctly, but that they should be 'clothed with righteousness' (Ps. 132:9). In the days of the new covenant, the old has been 'fulfilled', when all are truly priests to God (1 Pet. 2:9) and all such adornment is that of the spirit (*e.g.* 1 Pet. 5:5). Nevertheless, although we cannot find a literal counterpart in Christian days, this remains a noble picture from the past, and the spiritual principles embodied in this 'ABC' of God's instruction to His people remain eternally valid.

28:1–4. Introduction. 1. *Nadab and Abihu*: already mentioned as going up the mountain with the elders (24:1). They died by fire (Lv. 10:1,2), and so it was *Eleazar* who succeeded his father Aaron (Nu. 3:4). The later Zadokite high priests at Jerusalem traced their geneaology to him (1 Ch. 6:3–8), while Eli's house, including David's priest Abiathar, traced their ancestry to *Ithamar* (1 Ch. 24:3).

2. *Holy garments*: that is to say, different to, and set apart from, common clothing, as being worn in the service of God. They too are briefly described as *for glory and for beauty*, the reasons for their use.

4. *A coat of chequer work*: see Driver for detailed discussion on the type of fabric meant here. See also his discussion on the three different types of embroidery mentioned in Exodus.

28:5–14. The ephod. 6. *They shall make the ephod.* The

extent of our puzzlement is shown by the fact that we do not
know whether the ephod was a waistcoat or a kilt, to use
modern terms. In either case, it was apparently made of rich
material (though elsewhere in the Old Testament it is merely
described as a 'linen ephod', perhaps as being the common
material). It was the typical priestly garment, and was
supported by two shoulder-straps to which were attached seal-
stones carved with the names of the tribes. Most modern
editors prefer the translation 'kilt' to that of 'waistcoat', in
view of the description of David in 2 Samuel 6:14. The boy
Samuel wears a linen ephod (1 Sa. 2:18), as do all the men at
Nob, the priestly town (1 Sa. 22:18). On the other hand, when
David wants guidance, he asks Abiathar the priest to fetch the
'ephod' (1 Sa. 23:9). Since the pouch containing the sacred
oracular lots was worn on top of the ephod, the reference is
probably to the pouch itself here. Also, the 'ephod' is clearly
an euphemism for 'idol' at times, but the reason for this is
completely unknown (Jdg. 8:27; 17:5).

12. *Stones of remembrance*: cf. verse 30. Aaron bears Israel's
names before God whenever he enters the Tent, identifying
himself with them.

28:15–30. The oracular pouch. 15. *A breastpiece of judgment*: 'breastpiece' is pure guesswork for Hebrew *ḥōšen*. If the
translation is correct, Noth quotes a striking parallel from
bronze-age Byblos. This is a rectangular gold plate, set with
jewels, hanging from a gold chain: it apparently was a breast
adornment for a local king. With the exception that the
Israelite work is in cloth, not metal, and is double (forming a
flat pouch or bag for the lot-stones), the similarity is remarkable. Basically, the idea is very simple: the priest carries the
precious objects (whatever they are) in a bag tied around his
neck: and this bag is suitably adorned with symbols of the
tribes of Israel on the outside.

29. *Aaron shall bear the name of the sons of Israel*: cf. verse 9
with reference to his shoulder-straps. This reiterates the concept
of bearing the tribes before YHWH already expressed in
verse 12, whether the idea is bearing their guilt, or simply
interceding for them in prayer.

30. *The Urim and the Thummim*: the correct spelling is
'Tummim'. This explains why the garment may be called the
'breastpiece of judgment', since it contains the two oracular

stones, by means of which God's 'judgment' might be made known. Their names mean 'lights' and 'perfections' which, if taken literally, might be a reference to the nature of the God whose will they reveal. But they may be used in the sense of 'alpha and omega', beginning and ending (Rev. 1:8), since the words respectively begin with the first and last letters of the Hebrew alphabet. These sacred 'lots' were used to solicit divine guidance, usually of the 'yes' and 'no' variety: the clearest example is in the case of Saul's query (1 Sa. 14:41). It is quite uncertain what they were: two precious stones seem to be the most likely suggestion, but the manner of their use is not clear. To judge from further analogies, one stone was withdrawn (or shaken out) from the bag, and the answer 'yes' or 'no' depended on which stone it was. There is no biblical evidence for the use of this method of obtaining guidance after the time of David, but presumably priests still continued to wear the oracular pouch, with the conservatism of all religions. The system of 'drawing lots' after prayer, as a means of seeking guidance, reappears in Acts 1:26.

It is perhaps worth noting that by no means the only function of the Israelite priest was to sacrifice. As Driver remarks, he was also to give 'torah' or instruction (Dt. 33:10), to decide by Urim and Tummim (as here), and to give decisions 'before God' at a sanctuary (Ex. 22:8,9). Nor indeed were 'Urim and Tummim' the only accepted way of asking for God's guidance even in early days (1 Sa. 28:15). We may assume that, as prophetic activity grew in Israel, the need to use such 'mechanical' means of guidance lessened. In the New Covenant, it is no accident that, after the coming of the Spirit (Acts 2), there is no instance of the use of 'lots': God guides His people directly.

28:31-43. The minor vestments. 31. *Make the robe . . . all of blue*: 'violet' is a better translation. This 'robe' is presumably worn under the ephod and pouch, with the neck specially strengthened.

32. *That it may not be torn.* Since it seems to have been slipped on and off over the head, like a pullover, this was a sensible provision, as any housewife knows. John 19:23 seems to refer to this robe: it is John's oblique way of pointing to Christ's high-priestly position.

33. *Bells of gold.* The tinkling bells were presumably so that the people outside could trace the movements of the priest within, who was of course invisible to them. By this they would know that his offering had been accepted, and that he had not been struck dead. The *pomegranates* (symbols of fruitfulness) were either hanging as 'bobbles' between the bells, or else embroidered on the fabric.

36. *A plate of pure gold.* The *plate* (something like a 'flower', to judge from the Hebrew) was tied to the turban by a diadem of violet ribbon (verse 37), like that used later by the 'Great King' of Persia. It was inscribed *Holy to YHWH* as a reminder of his, and Israel's, position. See Hyatt for a justification of the rendering 'a diadem of pure gold': 'flower' is virtually a synonym for 'crown' here (*cf.* NEB *rosette*).

39. *The coat,* or 'tunic', was the usual garment of men of rank (Gn. 37:3), but it is hard to see what relation it had to the other priestly garments. The *turban* (literally something wound around: the Talmud tells us that eight yards of material were used) and the *girdle,* a 'sash' (perhaps an Egyptian word), might be worn by kings or high officials as well as by priests.

42. *Linen breeches*: what we might today call 'underwear', to ensure modesty of dress at all times. As in Exodus 20:26 (the prohibition of altars with steps), this is probably a reaction against ritual nakedness in other religious. *Linen* was common material for Israel's priestly dress (as in Egypt), both for beauty and hygiene.

v. The installation of priests (29:1–46)

In a sense, this chapter could be regarded as a supplement, for all the earlier chapters dealt with the making of objects or garments for the Tent. This alone contains details as to a ritual, but it could legitimately be considered as the culmination of all that has gone before. In addition, the last few verses contain details of the daily offerings to be continued henceforth in Israel (29:38–42), the main task of the priests.

Amid much that was temporary, and no doubt much that was similar to the rituals of other peoples round about, certain principles stand out as eternal. The priest must be cleansed symbolically, both by washing and by his sin-offering, before he can be installed in his new robes: he must be solemnly anointed for his task: hand, foot and ear must be dedicated to God. Then, and then only, can he make sacrifices that are pleasing to God. All this ritual must be repeated daily for seven days, both to emphasize its sacred importance and to give the sense of completeness.

29:1-9. Washing and anointing. 4. *Wash them with water.* The appendix in Exodus 30:17-21 tells of the construction of the bronze laver, for this and other ritual washings, the forerunners of Christian baptism (Tit. 3:5; Eph. 5:26).

7. *Take the anointing oil*: see Exodus 30:22-33 for details of the composition of this special oil. It seems from this verse that only Aaron (not his sons) was so anointed (but see Ex. 30:30). In later days, kings (as almost priestly figures) might share the rite (1 Sa. 10:1), but the word is used only in a metaphorical sense of the appointment of prophets (1 Ki. 19:16). Anointing denoted God's choice and designation for a special task. In the early days of kingship, it was often accompanied by charismatic gifts of the Spirit (1 Sa. 10:6) and may therefore have come to symbolize these gifts. In later times, 'God's anointed' and 'God's chosen one' (Ps. 89:3) become almost synonymous. For the Christian, 'anointing' has become rich with new meaning in the concept of Jesus 'the Christ' (that is, 'the anointed'), not only king but also high priest for evermore in a greater and heavenly tent (Heb. 9:11).

9. *Ordain*: 'fill the hand' is the technical Semitic term (as old as the Mari texts), probably coming from the idea 'induct them into the rights and privileges of their position'. Here, however, the word is obviously used with no such nuance: nevertheless, 'install' (NEB) is better than 'ordain' as a translation.

29:10-28. The animal sacrifices (for installation). These include sin-offerings (verse 14), whole burnt-offerings (verse 18), the peculiar blood ritual of verses 19-21, as well as the symbolic 'wave-offerings' of verses 22-28. These do not differ in essential from the same type of offering on other occasions (with the exception of the arresting ritual of verses 19-21) and therefore do not require detailed exegesis here.

10. *Lay their hands upon the head of the bull.* As usual in the case of all sin-offerings, the laying on of hands signifies identification. This clearly means that the death of the animal is accepted as the equivalent of the death of the individual. This sacrifice is followed by the blood ritual, in which some of the blood is smeared on the horns of the altar (as a visible lasting sign) while the rest is dashed against sides and base of the altar to run away (verse 12).

20. *Ear*, *thumb*, and *toe* are symbolically cleansed and dedicated to YHWH. The priest will hear and obey: hand and foot alike will work for God. To lose thumbs and big toes was the symbol of impotence and uselessness (Jdg. 1:6): so to dedicate them to God was to dedicate all one's strength. For the 'ear-marking', see Exodus 21:6. It seems to be the mark of a perpetual slave's willing obedience.

29:29–46. Allied regulations on priestly matters. These concern the handing down of priestly garments from father to son (verse 29); the sacred meal (virtually a 'peace-offering') that sealed the priests' appointment (verse 33), for only as priests could they eat 'holy flesh'; the atonement that must be made even for an inanimate object like the altar, by a sin-offering (verse 36); and lastly the regulations for the daily offering upon the altar by the newly-installed priests (verses 38ff.).

33. *With which atonement was made*: the Hebrew verb is *kuppar*, coming from the same root as that used for the 'cover' or 'mercy seat' of the chest. It might be best to translate 'with which sin was covered' (impersonally), for there is no necessary thought of propitiation, but simply of dealing with sin, or expiation. It is better not to translate as 'propitiate' unless both subject and object are expressed, and both are personal.

36. *A sin offering for the altar*. Perhaps it is regarded as being initially 'defiled' since it is the product of human hands, unlike the natural stone or earth altar enjoined in 20:24,25.

38. *Continually*. This is the *tāmîd* or 'perpetual daily sacrifice', the heart of the later worship of Israel in the Temple (Acts 3:1). For the same word in the sense of a 'regular custom', see Exodus 27:20. In later days, this daily sacrifice was seen as the heart of the law, and its involuntary temporary intermission in emergencies was viewed with the greatest of horror (Dn. 8:11). The Bethlehem shepherds of Luke 2:8 were probably concerned with the raising of the seven hundred lambs required annually for this temple sacrifice alone, apart from the many others demanded by the law.

40. *Flour . . . oil . . . wine*: cereal-offerings and libations of wine accompanied the animal sacrifice, in an ancillary capacity. Perhaps the thought was that a complete burnt-offering to God ought to include every element of an ordinary domestic meal (meat, bread, wine).

46. *They shall know that I am YHWH . . . who brought them forth.* Here the passage ends with a strong statement of God's purpose to live among His people. Indeed, it states bluntly that this was His great purpose in rescuing them from Egypt initially. The section concludes with the triumphant all-inclusive claim (so often given in Leviticus as the sole justification for a law or command), *I am YHWH their God.* As in Exodus 20:2, such a pronouncement is adequate reason and justification for every claim and demand made by God on His people, for it sets out God's nature, and His relationship to us, expressed in gracious act. This verse, then, is the sum and crown of all that has gone before.

vi. An appendix (30:1 – 31:18)

This deals with many diverse matters, between which it is hard to see any connection (unlike chapter 29, which at least, though heterogeneous, followed closely on 28 as still dealing with priestly matters). It is better therefore to see it as an appendix of mutually unrelated subjects. Some of these topics however either fill gaps in the previous account (incense-altar), or explain points assumed before (anointing oil, incense and laver).

30:1–10. The incense altar. 1. *An altar to burn incense upon*: of a type and size well known in the ancient world. It had the shape of a small truncated pilaster, with miniature *horns* on the corners. Like the other objects in the Tent, it was made of acacia wood, overlaid with gold, and had rings fitted through which staves could be slipped to make it portable (verse 4).

6. It stood in the 'holy place', inside the Tent, but in front of the curtain that shut off the holiest place (Heb. 9:4 locates the incense altar inside the curtain, near the chest; this is less likely). By way of contrast, the altar for sacrifice must, of course, stand in the open air, in the middle of the great courtyard. As it is further from God's presence, it may be sheathed in bronze (Ex. 27:2).

7. *Aaron shall burn fragrant incense*: twice a day, incense was to be offered on this miniature altar by the priest, while he was tending the wick and oil of the sacred lamp. The special composition of the sacred incense (forbidden to others) will be described in verses 34–38. Of course, as Numbers 16:17 shows, incense could be offered apart from any altar, upon 'fire pans' or 'censers'; but this particular altar was to be used for nothing but incense. In view of its position inside the Tent, and not in the open air, this was a wise provision.

10. *He shall make atonement for it once in the year*: cf. 29:36 for atonement for an altar. This is a most important verse, since it casually refers, in passing, to the ritual of the day of atonement, elsewhere mentioned only in Leviticus (23:27), and often assumed therefore to be a late innovation.

30:11–16. Census and poll-tax. 11. *When you take the census*. Such a census is recorded in Numbers 1, and indeed gives its name to that book. The experience of David's day showed how dangerous such an activity was considered (2 Sa. 24); in view of this regulation, it is hard to see why, unless the provision of verse 12 had been deliberately disregarded.

12. *Each shall give a ransom*. It was already a principle in Israel that every first-born son belonged to God, and must be redeemed by a sacrifice (Ex. 13:13). It was also accepted that all Israel collectively was God's first-born (Ex. 4:22) and thus belonged to God, although God had accepted the tribe of Levi in lieu of all the first-born (Nu. 3:12). This passage is an extension of the same principle of 'redemption'. When there was a census of what was virtually God's army, each adult male must give a 'ransom' for himself.

13. *Half a shekel*. The symbolic nature of the ransom is clear from the small and invariable amount demanded of every person, rich and poor alike. Typically Israelite is the practical application of this money for the upkeep of the Tent (verse 16). Later, the 'half-shekel' became an annual temple-tax (Mt. 17:24). See also Nehemiah 10:32 for its collection in the post-exilic period. In days of economic stress, Nehemiah had to rest satisfied with one third of a shekel. *The shekel is twenty gerahs*: the 'gerah' is a Babylonian weight. Its use here cannot mean that the passage dates from a time when the weight of a shekel was forgotten (the shekel was still being used in the days of the Second Jewish Revolt). It is in explanation of the unusual term 'shekel of the sanctuary' or 'sacred shekel' (the same as the 'Tyrian Shekel', according to the Talmud). This was to distinguish it from the ordinary shekel: for exact weights, see Driver.

30:17-21. The laver. 17. *You shall also make a laver of bronze*: to be consistent, we should translate 'copper'. It was probably *bronze* (copper and tin), but Hebrew has no separate word to denote this metal. The need for ritual washing for the priests before consecration and approach to God has already been mentioned in Exodus 29:4. This was only one of numerous such occasions, mentioned here (verse 20). The *laver* (no dimensions are given) was probably of modest size: if only Aaron and his four sons are envisaged as using it, this would be quite adequate. By contrast, Solomon had ten lavers of bronze in the Temple, in addition to his brazen 'sea', some larger receptacle (see 1 Ki. 7). This is only one of the many areas where the plan of the Temple departed from that of the Tent. In Exodus 38:8 some tantalizing details are given about the source of the metal for the laver, which also would suggest small size, but apparently solid casting from metal (no wooden frame).

18. *Between the tent of meeting and the altar.* The laver then was to stand in the great courtyard, before men entered the Tent itself. After washing and cleansing, the priest could enter to offer incense in worship. Priests must certainly have needed to wash after sacrifice and blood ritual, so it had practical value as well. It is a little strange that the laver was not mentioned along with the bronze-covered altar of sacrifice and the courtyard in chapter 27. Perhaps this passage has become dislocated from an earlier position in the book. The same might perhaps be said about the description of the incense-altar, which is not in the most logical place in our present texts.

30:22-33. The anointing oil. 23. *Take the finest spices.* This oil was a special mixture, forbidden for other uses under pain of death (verses 32,33). The spices used are rare, costly and aromatic, mostly coming from lands as far away as India by way of trade: for Arabia was not only a producer of spices, but also a great spice-mart. For the interpretation of the words (by no means certain) see the larger commentaries. *Cinnamon* and balsam of various species are the main ingredients, giving a very sweet-smelling oil. In view of the frequent use of fragrant oils in the ancient world for toiletry (Est. 2:12), revelry (Ps. 23:5) and medicine (Lk. 10:34), the prohibition against lay or profane use was very necessary.

26. *Anoint with it the tent of meeting.* It appears from this passage that not only were Aaron and his sons to be anointed on their installation to the priesthood, but also the Tent, and all the furniture of the Tent as well (verses 26–28).

29. *Whatever touches them will become holy.* The effect was to impart 'holiness' to them, as set apart for God's service. As in Exodus 19:12, this 'holiness' was transmissible by touch, in the sense that whoever touched them (apart from the priests) was doomed to die. See 2 Samuel 6:7, the story of Uzzah, as an illustration of this principle in action.

30:34–38. Incense for the altar. This passage fits well in the vicinity of the description of the incense-altar: it also fits naturally into the context of a similar description as to the manufacture of anointing oil. Davies points out that, while the oil was 'holy' (verse 31), the incense is described as 'most holy' (verse 36), because nearer to the presence of YHWH, as symbolized by the chest. This linguistic distinction is not accidental: it can be found elsewhere in the description of articles used in the Tent.

34. *Take sweet spices*: *stacte, onycha* and *galbanum* are clearly rich and rare spices, but not altogether identifiable. Similar ingredients today are used in Egypt for the production of women's cosmetics. This uncertainty somewhat nullifies the results of Knobel's experiment in reproducing the recipe and finding it to be 'strong, refreshing and very agreeable' (see Driver). To a Jew, such an experiment would have meant death.

35. *Seasoned with salt.* This 'salting' of the mixture was probably designed to secure rapid burning, through the addition of sodium chloride. Perhaps it was also done for the preservative value of the salt, since verse 36 makes plain that a large amount of incense was mixed at the one time: subsequently it was broken down and used gradually, as needed. The salt may of course also have had a symbolic value. Perhaps this was derived from some of its physical properties, or from its position as an essential ingredient in all meals, since it formed part of all sacrifices and could in itself seal a covenant (Lv. 2:13–this last was true outside Israel as well). See Numbers 18:19 and 2 Chronicles 13:5 for a 'covenant of salt', meaning 'sure covenant'. For New Testament application, see Matthew 5:13 and Colossians 4:6.

36. *Put part of it before the testimony*: the meaning is 'burn a portion on the incense altar, before the chest'. The purpose of burning incense is not discussed here. Perhaps, like sacrifice, it was such a basic part of religion in those days that it was taken for granted. In early days in Hebrew, 'pleasing odour' was the term applied to the thick white smoke yielded by the burning fat of animal sacrifice. The pungent smell so produced was considered to be pleasing to God (Gn. 8:21). Perhaps, at first, incense was a substitute for sacrifice, or a symbolic sacrifice, since it too produced a sweet smell and clouds of smoke. Incense would also have a very practical value in a hot climate, with animal sacrifice continually taking place nearby, and doubtless numerous rank smells as competitors (blood, dung, burning hide, burning meat and fat). Whatever the origins of the use of incense, it clearly accompanied and symbolized worship, as here. It accompanied intercession (Nu. 16:46) and in this sense could 'make atonement', like an animal sacrifice. In the imagery of Revelation 8:3,4, 'incense' may again have this atoning sense: it certainly is that which is supplied by God, added to the prayers of the church, and makes such prayers acceptable to God. It has been suggested that the cloud of incense, rising straight up in the still desert air, may itself have been a symbol of prayers ascending God-wards. Of the employment of incense in the literal sense, there is no hint in the New Testament church: its use, to a Jew, would be unthinkable except in the Temple, and any connection with that was soon gone for evermore.

31:1–11. God's craftsmen. It is an extraordinary instance of survival of tradition that the names of these two artificers should have been remembered. Like the names of the Hebrew midwives in Exodus 1:15, the two names 'Bezalel' and 'Oholiab', preserved here, are archaic, neither containing the new title YHWH as a formative element. There is no conceivable reason for their insertion, since neither reappears (except in the parallel passage in Exodus 35): therefore there are no grounds at all to question their genuineness. Even those commentators, such as Davies, who do not see the passage as Mosaic, feel compelled to date these two craftsmen as working on the Davidic Tent (1 Ch. 15:1), and thus before Solomon's Temple, since Solomon's artificer had a different name (1 Ki. 7:13), likewise preserved by tradition.

2. *I have called by name* means special choice for a particular purpose, though the one chosen may be ignorant even of the fact of the divine choice (Is. 45:4). *Bezalel* means perhaps 'in El's shadow' (*cf.* Ps. 91:1), using the old general name for God, current (with other titles) in Israel before the Mosaic revelation. He was of Judah: and Driver shows that both his name and those of his ancestors (Hur, Uri, Bezalel) occur in 1 Chronicles 2:20 as 'Calebite' names in the tribe of Judah (not of course necessarily referring to the same people). *Oholiab* (verse 6) seems to be Bezalel's assistant: at least, he has not such a prominent place in the account. His name is also archaic and West Semitic. Driver quotes parallels from several other languages. The meaning must be 'My tent (*i.e.* shelter) is the Father-God' (for the thought of God hiding men in His tent, see Ps. 27:5). Hyatt sees a further appropriateness in the name, in that Oholiab is a craftsman of 'God's tent'. Elsewhere in the Old Testament, a similar form 'Oholibamah' occurs as a Hivite woman's name (Gn. 36:2), while Ezekiel symbolically names Judah and Israel 'Oholibah' and 'Oholah' respectively (Ezk. 23:4).

3. *I have filled him with the Spirit of God.* In early Old Testament days, every form of skill and strength and excellence is directly and bluntly credited to 'the Spirit of God'. This is because God is rightly seen as the source of all wisdom. As the Old Testament proceeds, with further revelation as to the nature of the Spirit as 'holy', moral and spiritual qualities would be increasingly attributed to Him, without denying the above theological truth. Hyatt well defines the Spirit in the Old Testament as 'the outgoing power of God'.

31:12-18. The sign of the sabbath. Here, in a section which reminds us strongly of Leviticus, the importance and place of sabbath (the seventh day, our Saturday) is stressed.

13. *You shall keep my sabbaths, for this is a sign.* For the *sabbath*, see Exodus 16:23; 20:8; 23:12. Here however the weekly sabbath has an additional significance as being *a sign* (like unleavened bread, Ex. 13:9) between God and Israel, a reminder of their peculiar relationship to God. For Israel, circumcision was the great 'sign of the covenant' made with their ancestor Abraham (Gn. 17:11). Like circumcision, sabbath seems to have been practised to some extent in other Semitic lands (at least as an 'unlucky day', avoided for business): but in Israel alone, as far as we know, it has this unique religious significance. Perhaps the sabbath injunction is introduced here to remind that, even in building the Tent, sabbath must be observed (so Hyatt).

14. *Shall be put to death*: the form is categorical desert law. Numbers 15:32-36 shows this death-penalty actually being inflicted on an Israelite in the desert age. John 5:16-18 shows Christ facing death on the same charge. We know little of the observance of the sabbath in pre-exile days (but see 2 Ki. 11:5 and Is. 1:13). Later Jews traced the exile as in part due to failure to keep sabbath in pre-exilic days (Ne. 13:17,18), and Nehemiah fought hard for its enforcement on the return (Ne. 13:19-22). Doubtless, like food laws and circumcision, it took on a new importance as a distinguishing mark when Israel was surrounded by 'Gentiles' who did not keep it. In the Maccabean age, it became a test of orthodoxy and point of martyrdom (1 Macc. 2:29-38): in the New Testament, an intolerable burden (Mk. 2:23-27). Christ insisted that works of love and mercy, or works of necessity, were alike permissible on the sabbath day, even under the Mosaic law. He also pointed out (against much orthodox theology) that the sabbath had been made for man, and not man for the sake of observing the sabbath (Mk. 2:27), as well as claiming that the Son of man was the sabbath's lord.

17. *On the seventh day he rested.* The reason given for sabbath here is the same as that in Exodus 20:11, the 'rest' of God. This is the key to Christian understanding of the principle involved. By faith the believer has ceased from his 'work' (in the sense of trying to earn his own salvation) and entered into that spiritual rest and peace of heart that comes to those who know themselves to be already accepted and justified by God (Heb. 4:10). The Christian's 'Lord's day' (Rev. 1:10) is not directly related to sabbath. It is the 'first day' of the week (1 Cor. 16:2), the day of light and creation, the day of the Spirit's coming; and it is the weekly memory of Christ's resurrection, when His people gather especially for worship (Acts 20:7). All their time now belongs to God, not merely one day in seven.

18. *The two tables of the testimony*: translate 'the two tablets that bore witness'. This verse rounds off the whole section. The two tablets however cannot be considered as containing the whole of the above system of ritual laws and instructions, nor even as containing the book of the covenant that preceded them. At most, we should probably think of the 'ten words', perhaps in an abbreviated form, as suggested above. *Written with the finger of God*: see Exodus 8:19, where the same metaphor is used of the plagues of Egypt, and Luke 11:20, where it is used of Christ's ministry. This is a strong statement of divine source and causation, but need not be pressed in a strictly literalistic sense.

IV. REBELLION AND RENEWAL (38:1 – 40:38)

a. Rebellion and atonement (32:1 – 33:23)

This is a very vivid passage, showing that the spiritual experience of Moses was not shared by his people. Even Aaron comes out badly: but he had neither had the vision at Sinai as a shepherd, nor had he had the unique preparation in Egypt that Moses had had. Only Joshua seems to share the mind of Moses, as does, at a lowlier level, the tribe of Levi. But even Israel we must not judge too harshly; they were a slave people, still with the minds of slaves, even if God had set them free. Paul makes the same complaint about Christians in Galatians 5:1. Indeed, much of his language in describing them seems drawn from the descriptions of erring Israel in the Old Testament. It is because Israel is so like us in every way that the stories of Israel have such exemplary value (1 Cor. 10).

The story moves on rapidly to God's anger, and Moses' self-less intercession. Aaron's weak excuses show both his fear of his brother, and his fear of the consequences. The shattered tablets speak of the shattered covenant. The Lord's judgment falls on the people, through the sword of the tribe of Levi, who win for themselves the priestly position by caring more for God than for their own kith and kin. Chapter 32 ends with another noble plea from Moses, this time a plea for God's forgiveness for Israel, even at the cost of his own exclusion. The following chapter shows the inevitable consequences of such sin in the new remoteness of God from Israel, symbolized by the site of the meeting-tent. But it also shows Moses' great yearning for closeness to God, and how that prayer was granted.

32:1-6. Israel's sin. 1. *Up, make us gods, who shall go before us.* Impatience lay at the root of this sin of Israel's. They cannot wait. Where has Moses gone? They must have visible gods. The plural *gods* is demanded by the plural verb: otherwise 'gods' might legitimately be translated 'God', treating it as the common 'plural of majesty'. Whatever Aaron may have thought, the Israelites were not thinking of YHWH at all. Not for them the higher levels of imageless worship, or even of monotheism. As later Israel wanted a human king, not the invisible divine king (1 Sa. 8:4-8), so now they want a god 'with a face', like everybody else. The last thing that they want is to be different, by their new relationship to God: yet this is God's aim (Ex. 19:5,6). *This Moses, the man who brought us up out of the land of Egypt.* The phrasing is deliberately employed to bring out the coarseness of this slave people. They do not regard the redemption really as YHWH's achievement at all: it was simply something that Moses had done.

2. *The rings of gold*: presumably, this was part of the loot taken from Egypt (Ex. 12:36). History records that, unlike their Midianite cousins, the men of Israel did not subsequently wear gold ornaments (Jdg. 8:24). But Genesis 35:4 mentions the wearing of such ear-rings earlier, in Jacob's day, and Exodus 11:2 mentions jewelry in connection with men as well as women. Exodus 33:4-6 traces the later Israelite taboo on ornaments to this sin at Sinai. In earlier days, therefore, Israel's men presumably wore such trinkets freely. Some have argued that the golden image must have been small, if made solely from ear-rings. That however depends on the number of the Israelites, and the size and weight of the ear-rings (often considerable, as in India today) and indeed on the construction of the image, as mentioned below. Gideon too made an idol (an 'ephod', Jdg. 8:24-27) from the ear-rings taken from Israel's enemies.

4. *Graving tool . . . molten calf.* The wording here certainly suggests that the image was first rough-cast in solid gold, with the details subsequently hand-carved. Alternatively (*cf.* Ex. 37:1,2) it may have been gold-leaf on a wooden framework, as 'burnt' in verse 20 would support. The first seems the most likely, in view of the phrase 'ground it to powder' in verse 20. 'Burnt' would then be used in the sense of 'melted down in an open fire' (*i.e.* not in a crucible, like the goldsmith). An easy vocalic emendation would yield the sense 'cast it in a mould' instead of 'fashioned it with a graving tool': this is better than Noth's 'tied it up in a bag' (Hyatt).

Calf is not a good translation of the Hebrew *'ēgel*. A young bull in his first strength is meant: for instance, the word can describe a three-year-old animal (Gn. 15:9). Compare the name of Eglon, king of Moab (Jdg. 3:12), which is clearly an honorific like 'John Bull'. This image can hardly be modelled on that of Apis, the sacred bull of Egypt. Apis was not worshipped under image form, but as a continually-fresh incarnation in the form of an ordinary bull, born with certain particular markings. Hathor, an Egyptian goddess, was symbolized by a heifer; but this is the wrong sex. Nor is it likely to be the bull of Hadad, who bore, enthroned on his back, the invisible presence of the Syrian storm god: although some have compared the invisible presence of YHWH, throned between the cherubim above the ark (Ex. 25:22). Such subtleties were beyond the ken of rebellious ex-slaves, reacting against aniconic worship. This is more likely to be the bull into which Baal used to transform himself, according to the Ras Shamra cycle of tales (Baal I. v. 18). If it be objected that later Canaanites seem to have depicted Baal as a human warrior armed with the thunderbolt, rather than as a bull, the answer could well be that Israel, in the desert, is at a far lower and less sophisticated culture level than Canaan, and may well be preserving earlier memories. The sacredness of the bull as the symbol of strength and reproductive power runs from Baal worship in Canaan to popular Hinduism in South India today, wherever religion is seen as a form of stockbreeder's 'fertility cult'. It is likely that, even during the sojourn in Egypt, Israel had already been corrupted by some such cult, images and all: she would now be 'reverting to type', after the stern demands of Sinai. That Baal was widely known and worshipped in the delta area we know from archaeology; and certainly he was worshipped by some Semitic peoples resident there.

Some editors have seen this action of Aaron's as proving that Israel's worship at the time still permitted the use of images, but this is totally to fail to see the point. Certainly the 'ten words' defined Israel's worship as aniconic (Ex. 20:4): the violence of Moses' reaction proves the historicity of this enactment (verse 19), as does the general evidence from archaeology of Israelite sites in the days of the judges. To use any image as symbol of God is misleading (Ex. 20:23). To use a bull as symbol of God is worse; further, it is blasphemy, if the 'new' god is called YHWH, as apparently it was on this occasion. In addition, verse 6 seems to show all the licentious Baal worship of Canaan (*cf.* Nu. 25:1–9). It seems impossible that, so soon after receiving such a lofty revelation, Israel could fall so low: but Christian experience today is often the same.

These are your gods: as in verse 1, the plural verb makes the RSV 'gods' the only grammatical translation of the text. Possibly the plural is used derisively by the writer to show the inevitable polytheism that would stem from the introduction of idolatry (if a bull-form, why not other forms as well?). Alternatively, it may be to point out the similarity between what Israel did now and what Israel was to do later under Jeroboam (1 Ki. 12:28). It can be no accident that the same phrase is used, both here and under Jeroboam, as a call to worship.[1] But it is hard to see how one idol could be described as 'gods' by the original idolaters, however aptly the plural might be used of Jeroboam's two bull-statues. Either way, the phrase is a credal statement, parodying Exodus 20:2. Even in her sin, however, Israel's religion is still one of history, and therefore completely different from the fertility-cult of Baal in Canaan. She still looks for a god who acts, even if it be a false god.

5. *He built an altar.* There was as yet no altar of sacrifice, as later. Probably Aaron built a rough altar of earth or loose stones (Ex. 20:24,25), showing that this is not a casual incident: it is an organized cult, with statue, altar, priest and festival. *A feast to YHWH.* Did Aaron see this as the fulfilment of the promise made by God to Moses, that Israel would keep a 'feast' or 'pilgrim festival' at Sinai (Ex. 3:12; 5:1)? Or is the reference general? It is interesting to speculate whether the time of the year had any special significance. Later Jews associated the giving of the law with the feast of weeks or firstfruits (New Testament 'Pentecost'), so perhaps Aaron's feast was a rowdy agricultural occasion. This would account for the dancing and sexual licence associated with it, though we would have expected such abuse to be more likely at the autumn vintage festival (ingathering, or booths). Some editors

---

[1] Again, this could be seen as a derisive comment by the editor of Kings, pointing to the parallel between the apostasy of Aaron's day and that of Jeroboam's, rather than as an exact record of the call to worship in Jeroboam's day. For another suggestion of a more critical nature, see footnote to verse 5, below.

compliment Aaron on making a valiant attempt to 'contain' this reactionary movement within Yahwism, by annexing this festival to YHWH in spite of its trappings of Baal.[1] However, Exodus never credits Aaron with any such deep theological motives (verses 22–24). Besides, it was precisely this identification of YHWH with Baal that was the greatest sin; even open apostasy to Baal would have been less deadly than this 'syncretism'.

6. *Burnt offerings . . . peace offerings.* The outward forms of liturgical worship, whether of YHWH or of Baal, were doubtless not dissimilar, to judge from the Ras Shamra texts. That is why the later prophets found it easy to denounce the ritual worship of Israel, if devoid of spiritual reality (Is. 1:10–20) or moral demands. *Sat down to eat and drink, and rose up to play.* *Eat and drink* could be innocent enough, after a 'peace offering', but the verb translated *play* suggests sex-play in Hebrew (see Gn. 26:8) and therefore we are probably to understand drunken orgies. These, in a Baalized context, would have a religious, not an immoral, significance to the worshipper: but not so in YHWH's sight. In the context of the worship of YHWH, who, by the 'ten words', had expressed His very nature in terms of moral requirements, it was intolerable. Only a realization of the holiness of YHWH can explain the violence of Moses' reaction, and the terrible punishment of Israel that followed.

32:7–14. Moses at prayer. 7. *Your people, whom you brought up.* The change in the possessive adjective is deliberate, as though God were disowning them. Notice how Moses reverses this, in his prayer of verse 11. This is a deliberate 'anthropopathism', describing God's feelings in human terms, as being more comprehensible to us: see also verse 14 below.

9. *A stiff-necked people.* This phrase, common in the Bible, is a farmer's metaphor of an ox or a horse that will not respond to the rope when tugged. It is thus peculiarly apposite to

---

[1] Some scholars of a more critical nature go even further. Pointing out that Aaron's grandson was priest of the ark when it was at Bethel in early days (Jdg. 20:28), and that Bethel was later one of the two centres of iconic worship of YHWH, they claim that this was the 'foundation story' of the Bethel sanctuary, and originally favourable to Aaron. They claim that YHWH was worshipped at Bethel under the form of a young bull, long before Jeroboam. See Hyatt, quoting Newman, for these views, which of course involve a complete rejection of the biblical account.

Israel, who will not respond to correction, and may be fairly translated 'stubborn'.

10. *Of you I will make a great nation*: a real temptation to Moses (as real as the temptations of the Lord), or it would have lost its whole meaning. It was the fulfilment of God's promises to Abraham (Gn. 12:2) and to Jacob (Gn. 35:11), but the people would now bear the tribal name of 'sons of Moses', not 'sons of Israel'. The price was only to abandon his shepherd's calling, and to let Israel go. Their own behaviour had earned their rejection, as he is reminded here. But no true shepherd could do this: so comes the intercessory prayer of Moses (verses 11–13, taken up again in verses 31,32), reminiscent of the prayer of Abraham (Gn. 18:22–33).

11. *Thy people*. Moses appeals to God by His Self-chosen relationship to Israel, and by all that He has already done for them in the past. Next, he appeals to the need for God to vindicate His own name (verse 12). Lastly he appeals to the great patriarchal promises (verse 13). The third is a most important point. As clearly as the vision at the burning bush, it links the new name YHWH with the old patriarchal titles for God and the old patriarchal promises. It brings the saving acts of the exodus into direct lineal relationship with the acts of God done for Abraham. Put briefly, this prayer is an appeal to God by the consistency of His own nature, a declaration of confidence in His revealed will. Not even in New Testament days can prayer rise higher, though, in Christ, we have an even deeper knowledge of that nature and will, and therefore fuller grounds for appeal as well as for confidence.

14. *YHWH repented*. Another 'anthropomorphism' (more properly an 'anthropopathism') by which God's activity is explained, by analogy, in strictly human terms. The meaning is not that God changed His mind; still less that He regretted something that He had intended to do. It means, in biblical language, that He now embarked on a different course of action from that already suggested as a possibility, owing to some new factor which is usually mentioned in the context. In the Bible, it is clear that God's promises and warnings are always conditional on man's response: this is most clearly set out in Ezekiel 33:13–16. We are not to think of Moses as altering God's purpose towards Israel by this prayer, but as carrying it out: Moses was never more like God than in such moments, for he shared God's mind and loving purpose.

32:15–29. The aftermath. This section contains the breaking of the tablets (a significant ceremonial act, not a mere exhibition of anger), the destruction of the idol, the punishment of Israel, and the 'installation' of Levi as a priestly tribe.

15. *Written on both sides*: this is the only place in Scripture where this detail is recorded and emphasized. Noth maintains that this was most unusual for inscribed stones, *stēlai*, in the ancient world: it is therefore an interesting piece of early tradition. Usually one side of the stone was left blank, and one side only was inscribed. However, this scarcely applies to small stone writing-tablets, which is presumably what is meant here.

18. *Not the sound of shouting for victory.* This passage is rhythmic, a fragment of early verse. Not many scholars today would follow the older theory of Sievers, by which he held that the whole of the Pentateuch had been originally written in verse (like the Ras Shamra cycle), but certain poetic fragments do remain. Perhaps, like Numbers 21:14,15, this came from the lost 'Book of YHWH's Wars' (*cf.* also Nu. 21:27–30).

19. *The dancing*: perhaps 'the dancing bands'.[1] This probably implies a religious ceremony, with devotees whirling ecstatically before the idol and altar, as David danced before the sacred chest (2 Sa. 6:14). In Exodus 15:20 Miriam herself had led such a triumphal dance for YHWH. Here, however, in view of the bull-cult, there is probably an orgiastic undertone. Compare the verb 'break loose' in verse 25, which certainly covers morals as well as religion. Bad morals follow idolatry (Rom. 1:24,25). *Broke them at the foot of the mountain.* The breaking of the tablets is a repudiation by Moses (presumably acting on God's behalf, although we are not told this) of the validity of the covenant. Because of Israel's breach of the terms, it has been rendered null and void.

20. *Burnt it with fire and ground it to powder.* We may compare Josiah's treatment of the altar (and bull?) of Bethel (2 Ki. 23:15). Such treatment of the golden bull is symbolic, repudiating its claim (stated by its followers, Ex. 32:4) to be the one who had led Israel out of Egypt. In addition, it is the treatment of Canaanite gods demanded by the covenant terms (Ex.

---

[1] Although perhaps the plural *meḥōlōt* refers only to various different types of dance, or even the varying movements of the dance. It might even be a 'plural of indignation', as we might say 'such goings-on!'.

23:24). Finally, the gold dust sprinkled on the water of the wady, flowing down from the mountain, the water that Israel must drink, reminds us of the 'water of bitterness' to be drunk by the wife suspected of unfaithfulness (Nu. 5:18–22). As Israel has in fact been unfaithful to YHWH, her heavenly 'husband', so the curse will indeed fall upon her (verse 35; *cf.* Nu. 5:27).

21–24. These verses, containing Moses' stern rebuke of his brother, along with Aaron's absurd excuse, may contain some grim humour. Like Adam (Gn. 3:12), Aaron blames another. What he says of Israel (in verse 22) is perfectly true, but does not excuse him for acting in 'priestly' capacity at the worship of the bull-calf (Ex. 32:5).

24. *There came out this calf.* This seems designed to claim the production of the idol as a miracle, as being the work of no human hand. The Bible frequently makes merry at the absurdity of the craftsman worshipping something that he himself has made (*e.g.* Is. 44:9–20). Perhaps even Aaron is conscious of this absurdity and, by this lame excuse, tries to escape from it. In the ancient world, natural (*i.e.*, not man-made) objects were sometimes worshipped because of fancied resemblance to human or animal figures. The meteorite held sacred to Artemis at Ephesus is one biblical example (Acts 19:35): but Aaron could hardly claim the golden bull as another. On the other hand, it is possible that the verse is simply to be taken as eastern politeness, admitting the making of the idol, but couched in the vaguest terms.

26. *Who is on YHWH's side?* 'Who is for YHWH?' is the literal translation of the Hebrew. Presumably Moses calls upon all those who have not gone over to the new bull-cult, but who have remained faithful to the imageless worship of YHWH, with its strong moral demands. Thus they would be opposed to the new movement on two scores. Even though the 'great rebellion' of 32:1 is before the arrival of Moses down from Sinai with the two law-tablets in his hands (32:15), it is quite clear that the demands of God, as there expressed, were known to Israel already, so that neither Aaron nor the people could plead ignorance of these two aspects of God's law. Indeed Exodus 24:3–8 states that they, or similar material, were the initial basis of the covenant, both in oral (24:3) and written (24:4) form. But this seems to be distinct from the solemn acceptance of the tablets, foreshadowed in 24:12, and recorded in 31:18 – unless the text is out of chronological order.

All the sons of Levi. The tribe of Levi was of course Moses' own tribe. It has been claimed that this may have influenced them to remain loyal to Moses (as well as to YHWH), in spite of his prolonged absence up the mountain. If so, a closer bond with Moses than theirs does not seem to have had the same effect on Aaron. There is no evidence that the tribe of Levi as a whole had any priestly significance as yet, although Aaron's immediate family did (Ex. 28:1).

27. *Every man his brother*: as often, *brother* means 'fellow-Israelite'. It can hardly mean 'fellow-tribesman', in view of the statement that all of Levi responded to Moses' call. The same great principle was expressed by Christ, although the application is very different. No physical or natural relationship can be as close as that which binds us to Christ and His people (Mt. 12:46–50). Our love and loyalty to Christ must come first, even though this brings deep division where men would most hope for harmony and understanding (Lk. 12:51–53).

28. *Three thousand men.* The small number guarantees the historicity of the incident. They may have been ringleaders, but it seems more likely that they were chance worshippers, caught in the charge when Levi ran amok in the camp, as God's avengers. Nor were they necessarily more wicked than the others: Luke 13:1–5 shows that such 'restricted judgment' is of grace, and exemplary.

29. *You have ordained yourselves*: literally 'you have filled your hands'. So the versions read. The Hebrew is imperative: 'ordain yourselves'. Like the later slaughter of the Canaanites this was *ḥērem*, or sacred war. The dead were regarded as a sacrifice to God and in this instance as an 'installation-sacrifice' by which Levi was consecrated to the service of God (*cf.* Ex. 29). This service is presumably the *blessing* to which reference is made at the end of the verse. A similar act of zeal for YHWH is recorded of Phinehas, Eleazar's son and Aaron's grandson (Nu. 25:10–13). It met with a similar reward, the 'covenant of a perpetual priesthood' for him and his descendants. In both cases, it is important to realize that it was not the nature of the vengeance that secured the blessing. It was the wholehearted following of God (Jos. 14:8): it was the counting of other ties as nothing compared with that tie (Dt. 33:9) and the fact that both Levi and Phinehas were 'jealous with

YHWH's jealousy' (Nu. 25:11). Like the author of Psalm 139, they had made God's cause their own (Ps. 139:21). Since they shared something of the mind of God, they could not think that it was a light matter if Israel was openly unfaithful to God (Ex. 19:5). For the origins of the phrase 'fill the hand' (*i.e.* 'ordain' or 'install'), see the discussion in Hyatt.

32:30-35. Vicarious suffering and intercessory prayer.
30. *Perhaps I can make atonement.* Moses wishes to 'cover' (the same root as in Ex. 29:36) the sin of the people. He assumes that physical death will be their punishment, as often threatened in the law (Ex. 28:43), and he wants to save them from this.

32. *If thou wilt forgive their sin.* This usually means in the Old Testament that the punishment of death will be remitted (*cf.* David, 2 Sa. 12:13), although punishments of a lighter and disciplinary nature may well follow. But, if YHWH will not forgive, Moses offers either to die on behalf of his people (in which case compare Paul, Rom. 9:3) or along with his people. In this latter case, he is again rejecting the temptation of Exodus 32:10. *Thy book*: called elsewhere 'the book of the living' (Ps. 69:28) or 'the book of life' (Is. 4:3). This is a metaphorical way of expressing the idea of 'the world of living men', and at the same time stating the truth that every man's life or death is in God's hand. Census lists like those in Numbers 1 may be the origin of the expression (*cf.* Ezk. 13:9): the lists of God's people might well be called 'God's book'. In the New Testament, the concept becomes spiritualized, as meaning the roll of those who have entered, or will enter, into eternal life (Phil. 4:3; Rev. 3:5). Moses, God's servant (Ex. 14:31), is often portrayed in the Pentateuch (though not so described) as a 'suffering servant', and in this sense is a prototype of Christ. He endures what all faithful shepherds of the flock must endure, and that which the 'good shepherd' will sum up in Himself (Jn. 10:11).

33. *Whoever has sinned against me, him will I blot out.* In these words, the offer of Moses is refused. It would have been inconsistent with the pattern, taught generally in the Old Testament, of direct responsibility and of punishment by suffering. Individual responsibility for sin was taught and believed long before the days of Jeremiah and Ezekiel, contrary to common views. Vicarious suffering of this type will find a greater fulfilment later, after the examples of Job, Jeremiah, and the 'Suffering Servant' of Isaiah 42–53.

34. *I will visit their sin.* According to tradition, that whole generation died in the wilderness (Dt. 1:35). God's action was not arbitrary: on repeated occasions, of which this is not even the first (*cf.* Ex. 14:12), Israel had shown themselves utterly devoid of the faith and obedience by which alone it is possible to please God (Heb. 11:6). Had they been allowed to enter the promised land in this state of mind, they would not have had the necessary faith to overcome the Canaanites, so that the mere entry of Canaan would have done them no good. It could be said that God was actually sparing them, in allowing them to remain in the desert, just as He had previously spared them by not leading them along the Philistine Road (Ex. 13:17). They were not in any sense acting 'out of character' in worshipping the golden bull. Indeed, in so doing, they showed clearly their essentially unchanged nature, as they would again, given any future opportunity.

35. *YHWH sent a plague*: presumably this refers to a temporary and immediate punishment, of the type so common in the Pentateuch (*e.g.* Nu. 11:33). However, the verse could be a vague general reference to the subsequent punishment of the entire generation.

33:1–6. Israel and her ornaments. Throughout the whole of Exodus, the theme of the presence of God is stressed, and the same theme can be seen as dominating this chapter. How can Israel still experience God's presence, after they leave the holy mountain (*cf.* Peter's words in Mt. 17:4)? That is the first question. But there is a deeper question still: how can such a sinful people experience God's presence at all?

2. *I will send an angel before you*: God's messenger, a promise repeated here from 32:34. However, unlike the 'messenger' of 23:20,21, this promise is a virtual refusal of the direct presence of God (verse 3). Moses will appeal against this decision in verses 12–16 below.

3. *Lest I consume you.* This refusal is protective. If YHWH is too close to Israel when they sin, His wrath will blaze out and they will die.

4. *They mourned; and no man put on his ornaments.* As an outward sign of mourning the lost presence of God, Israel strips off her ornaments (verse 6). In mourning, this was a temporary custom, but, for Israel, it becomes a perpetual rule. See note on Exodus 32:3: no doubt another reason for discarding the ornaments was that they had been an occasion for sin. Israel, in many respects, must have seemed a nation of puritans in the ancient world, not only in worship and morals, but even in dress. Yet the very ornaments that could make a golden idol in the past could now be dedicated to God for the use of His sanctuary. Exodus 35:22 makes plain that such trinkets were a major source of the offering of gold by the people for the vessels used in the Tent.

33:7-11. Moses and the meeting-tent. 7. *Moses used to take the tent and pitch it outside the camp.* God will not be in the midst of Israel, yet He will not withdraw His presence altogether. This is symbolized in the pitching of the 'meeting-tent' outside the camp, and at a distance from it. Sanctuaries were usually built a little distance away from towns in the ancient world: Israel has therefore lost her uniqueness, as the nation among whom God dwells in the very midst. On the whole question of the meeting-tent, see Hyatt: the imperfects must show customary action in the wilderness period. *Every one who sought YHWH would go out.* To seek the presence of God (for guidance, or prayer, or praise, expressed by sacrifice) a man had to separate himself from his own people (Heb. 13:13). But once here, outside the encampment, there was a possibility of fellowship with God, and that of a close and unique nature (verse 11, describing Moses).

9. *The pillar of cloud would descend.* This column or 'pillar' (literally, a 'standing' thing) of cloud, whatever its nature, signified the presence of YHWH, and whenever Moses entered the tent the sign of God's presence was to be seen. Exodus 40:33,34 seems to describe the same phenomenon in connection with the completed Tent of later chapters, as a sign of God's 'residence' (like the flag over a royal palace). It is not quite clear whether this section is an anticipation of what will follow later, after the dedication of the great Tent of worship, or whether some very much simpler 'meeting-tent' was envisaged as being used by Moses even before the setting up of the main Tent of Exodus 40. In many ways, some much simpler structure would better suit the picture here. Only Moses goes out to it, and only Joshua 'serves' at the Tent, instead of the multitude of later Levites. There is not even a mention of Aaron and his sons acting as priests here. Further, Numbers 3 seems to postulate a tent set up in the middle of the encampment, while this one is pitched beyond the limits. Even those scholars of more critical views, who deny the existence of the elaborate Tent of the later chapters of Exodus (seeing it as a 'back projection' of a later Temple), usually admit the existence of this simpler 'meeting-tent' as being truly Mosaic. However (apart from other considerations) the numerous differences between the elaborate Tent and Solomon's Temple make their denial of the existence of the Tent unlikely.[1] Perhaps therefore all this activity is to be regarded as in the 'past tense', and in connection with a simpler form of tent than that envisaged in later chapters (Nu. 11:24 and 12:4 seem to preserve the same early memory). The common people, at this stage, do not come to worship: they prostrate themselves at their tent doorflaps, facing toward the meeting-tent from afar.

11. *Face to face.* Numbers 12:8 explains the meaning of this phrase. God will speak to Moses 'mouth to mouth', that is to say, not in dreams and visions, but clearly and directly. Moses had the gift of clarity of spiritual insight: he shared the very counsels of God. *As a man speaks to his friend.* Perhaps Christ was referring to this in John 15:15, where He says that the mark of the friend (as opposed to the servant) is that he knows the purpose and meaning of the commands given to him. In spite of this, however, the great title of Moses in the Old Testament is 'the servant of YHWH' (Dt. 34:5).[2] He thus stands at the beginning of a long process of God's revelation, which will culminate in the 'suffering servant' of Isaiah 52, and which will find its fulfilment in Christ.

33:12–23. Moses' prayer for the presence of God. Here, as Noth sees, the link with the preceding passage is still the theme of God's presence. This has been denied to rebellious Israel, but given to Moses and Joshua at the meeting-tent. Moses is now concerned to obtain both a guarantee of that

---

[1] Some scholars see the Tent as a back-projection, not of Solomon's Temple, but of Zerubbabel's, after the exile. This does dispose of some of the difficulties, but also introduces fresh problems, so that the main argument remains.

[2] However, in the Bible 'the king's servant' is a high position of state (1 Ki. 11:26), probably just as high as 'the King's friend' (1 Ki. 4:5). The distinction should therefore not be pressed in the Old Testament.

presence for his people, and also the enjoyment of a closer experience of it for himself. So much is clear amid much that is obscure, perhaps because it is metaphorical or poetic. Muilenburg (quoted in Hyatt) notes the six uses of the verb 'know' in five verses.

12–16. God's presence with the people. **12.** *Thou hast not let me know whom thou wilt send with me.* It is not clear whether Moses is concerned to know the 'status' of the promised heavenly messenger, or whether this is a prayer (like that of Nu. 27:16) that God will provide an earthly assistant and successor to him. If the latter, then God's choice of Joshua was the answer.

14. *My presence will go with you*: translated literally. 'My face . . . '. With this promise, Israel's ultimate 'rest' in Canaan will be assured. That means that the heavenly 'messenger' sent with them will now be 'the angel of his presence' (Is. 63:9), *i.e.* a full manifestation of God, as in Exodus 23:20.

16. *So that we are distinct.* Israel is always called to be distinct and different from other nations. Moses rightly sees that the chief distinctiveness of Israel lies here, in that God's presence is in her midst. All else is a commentary on this, and flows from it.

17–23. The prayer for the vision of God. **18.** *Show me thy glory.* God has just granted the petition for His continued presence with Israel. Now Moses' prayer is to see the *kābôd*, the manifested glory (literally 'weight') of YHWH. This is a prayer to see God as He is: but, in these terms, it is impossible. Mortal man cannot endure to see God (verse 20). In vivid pictorial language, the passage says that man may see only where God has passed by (verses 22,23) and so know Him by His past doings and acts. God as He is, in all His mystery, we cannot know or comprehend. For a full revelation of what God is like, man must wait until Jesus Christ (Jn. 14:9). There is no contradiction between this and Exodus 24:10, where the elders 'saw the God of Israel' (*cf.* Gn. 32:30). All they saw was the 'pavement of sapphire' that was 'under his feet': all that Isaiah saw was the skirt of the royal garments that filled the vast Temple courtyard (Is. 6:1).

19. *Proclaim before you my name.* God's revelation will be of His 'name' (that is, His nature) proclaimed in terms of His deeds to man. God's nature is here defined as 'goodness' (Heb. *ṭûb*), and this is further described in terms of 'grace' and 'mercy'. Driver rightly says that the object of this divine grace and mercy is sinful Israel: without this quality of 'loving-kindness' as God's basic characteristic, Israel would be utterly lost. See Hyatt for various meanings of *ṭûḇ* in the Bible. *I will be gracious to whom I will be gracious.* Romans 9:15 quotes this verse with reference to the sovereignty of God. Israel can only marvel that she has been chosen as an object for divine mercy, for she cannot explain it in any human terms. Commentators point out that the Hebrew phrase used here does not imply any abrupt arbitrariness on the part of God, as its English translation might suggest. It simply draws attention to the fact that these are qualities of God which may be seen in certain specific historic instances, without going into further detail.

b. The renewed covenant (34:1-35)

This chapter covers the giving of the new stone tablets; the proclamation of God's name; the making of the covenant; and the listing of demands that spring from the covenant. The chapter closes with an addendum describing, in striking language, the visible effect on Moses of close communion with YHWH.

Again, the passage does raise problems. Some scholars believe that, so far from being a renewal of the covenant-making that went before (necessitated by the breach of the covenant by Israel), it is actually another account of the same events. If they consider the first account (in Exodus 19–24) as based on the 'E' source, they consider this one as based on the 'J' source. But both verse 1 here, and Deuteronomy 9,10, insist that there was indeed a renewal of the original covenant. This 'renewal' aspect may account for much repetition of thought, if not words (*e.g.* in the revelation of God, in verses 5–7, and the terms of the covenant, in verses 12–25). The first of these is parallel to the early visions of Moses: the second (naturally) finds many parallels in the 'book of the covenant' (chapters 20–23). It is a little strange that the 'ten words' are not quoted at verse 10, as in Exodus 19 and Deuteronomy 6. However, verse 28 certainly assumes them, and we have seen that the same ambiguity exists in Exodus 20–23 as to whether the terms of covenant were merely 'ten words' or included the whole 'book of the covenant'. If the 'book of the covenant' can be seen to be an amplification and explanation of the 'ten words', then there is no contradiction. The terms of the covenant are a revelation about God and man, rather than a limited series of set legal obligations. It is possible, even probable, that from the start there were several shorter formulations or collations of this covenant law, not considered as in any way conflicting with each other. This absolves us from trying to construct a so-called 'ritual decalogue' from Exodus 34:11-26 (basis of the restored and renewed covenant, Ex. 34:27) as parallel or, worse still, as rival to the so-called 'ethical decalogue' of Exodus 19 and Deuteronomy 6 (the true parallel being Ex. 23). Noth is excellent on this whole question: he points out that the two sets of laws may show difference of interest, but in no sense show fundamental theological opposition (any more than the ten commandments in chapter 20 are opposed to the book of the covenant in chapters 20-23). In any case, if the 'ten words', although not expressed, are assumed in the present context, the problem does not arise. For somewhat artificial attempts to create a 'decalogue' from the material, see Hyatt.

34:1-4. The new tablets. 1. *Cut two tablets of stone like the first.* Here Moses is himself commanded to hew two stone tablets (*cf.* Ex. 32:16), and in verses 27,28 he is to write on the tablets himself the 'words of the covenant', defined as the ten commandments. *I will write.* The narrator sees no conflict between verses 27,28, where Moses does the writing, and this verse, where God says that He Himself will do the writing. To him, the two statements meant the same thing; they were alternative ways of describing the same pattern of events. This shows a strong theological position, a belief that the Torah is the very expression of the mind and nature of God: but it also shows that we need not interpret the phrases in a mechanical and literalistic way. Any interpretation of this event along one line, 'God wrote', must also leave room for the equally true 'Moses wrote'. Perhaps we might generalize this position, and apply it to the whole of the Old Testament. One exactly similar case occurs earlier with reference to God and pharaoh. Side by side, we are told that God hardened pharaoh's heart (4:21): that he hardened it himself (8:15): and that pharaoh's heart was hardened, with no hint of, or reference to, any agency at all (7:13).

3. *Let no flocks or herds feed.* The rules as to the sacredness of

the whole mountain, when God descends upon it, are apparently the same as before (19:12,13).

34:5-9. God's Self-proclamation. 5. *Proclaimed the name
of YHWH.* The *name* of YHWH expresses all that He is and
does, so this means proclamation of the saving acts of God.
That is what is meant, in New Testament days, by *kērygma*,
'herald's proclamation'. Here is God, in Self-revelation, pro-
claiming His very Self to Moses (as in 33:19, or as in the
introduction to the 'ten words' in 20:2). It is hard to believe
that *proclaimed* refers merely to a declaration made by Moses
about God, rather than a declaration by God to Moses.
That a revelation made by YHWH to men should be expressed
in the third person is unusual, but not impossible. Hyatt,
however, prefers to translate this phrase 'Moses called upon
the name of the LORD', and leaves YHWH's Self-proclamation to verse 6.

7. *Who will by no means clear the guilty.* The revelation is here
primarily one of a merciful and gracious God (see Ex. 33:19
for both aspects, to which are added here 'steadfast love' and
'faithfulness', two words typical of relationships within the
covenant). But, as in Exodus 20:5, the other side of God's
nature, in punishing as well as forgiving the sinner, is also
brought out. In the context of a renewed covenant, this whole
Self-revelation has an even deeper meaning, showing the
wonder of God's grace in relation to forgiven Israel. *To the
third and the fourth generation*: a common Semitic idiom to
express continuance (see note on 20:5). We who live in a
world full of legacies of hate between colours and cultures can
see only too clearly how sin in one generation affects those
who follow after. So at least Moses must have understood the
meaning: for he at once pleads both for pardon and God's
continued presence with His sinful people, as in 32:9-14 and
33:12-16.

34:10,11. The covenant preamble. It seems best to take
these two verses closely together, unlike the RSV which begins
a paragraph between the two verses.

10. *Behold, I make a covenant.* God not only promises to make
a covenant (the tense is vague), but also gives an idea of what
will be involved in this covenant both from His side and from
their side. This was characteristic of the secular covenants of

the Hittite empire, especially of the so-called 'suzerainty treaties' between the great powers and subject peoples. (For discussion of this matter at length, see Mendenhall.) *I will do marvels*: the same Hebrew word has been used to describe the plagues sent upon Egypt (Ex. 3:20). Here, the sense is explained by saying that God will do *a terrible thing* (better 'something of which men will stand in awe'). As in the case of Egypt, it was to be, at one and the same time, a work of judgment and a work of salvation. All God's doings partake of this twofold nature: to the Christian, both aspects are summed up in the cross, by which a man is either justified or condemned.

11. *I will drive out before you.* Here the nature of the 'marvel' in question is explained as the expulsion of the Canaanites and the gift of the land of Canaan to Israel. The races of Canaan are detailed, not as a mere ethnological list, but as showing the greatness of the miracle (Dt. 4:38) by showing the greatness of the difficulties involved. But, as condition of this victory, Israel must keep God's commands: this is the usual second part of such a covenant preamble. These conditions, or terms, will be outlined below, in what is sometimes (if unfairly) called the 'ritual decalogue' (*cf.* Ex. 23).

34:12-28. The terms of the covenant. Although this is a convenient phrase, and not an incorrect description of the material following, it should not be misunderstood. Whether this covenant was new or a repetition, it must have included the 'ten words' in some form (verse 28). On the other hand, the material given here is so close to that in the 'book of the covenant' (Ex. 21-23) that we can only conclude that both are excerpts from the same larger whole (of which the legal material of Deuteronomy is also part). Therefore we must not think of these 'terms' as exhaustive: they are but a brief summary of God's demands. Further, to use the phrase 'ritual decalogue' to describe the passage is doubly misleading. In the first place, the items can be reduced to ten (or even twelve) only by drastic surgery, which is not necessary if we do admit the parallel existence of the earlier 'ten words'. Secondly, the passage is by no means exclusively or even mainly ritual: it would be better to call it a 'Code of Festivals' (with parallels in Ex. 23). Festivals must be kept to YHWH and to YHWH only, three times a year: and some details of the necessary observances are given. Sabbath is included as a festival. Since they are thanksgiving for fruitfulness, it is fitting that there should be a mention of firstfruits (verse 26), and that Canaanite magical fertility rites should be condemned. Yet (typically Israelite) at least one of these feasts is linked to God's past redemptive act in history (verse 18), and to this general context of redemption belong what appear at first to be unrelated minor rules about 'redemption' of first-born.

12. *Lest you make a covenant*: a covenant with God rules out any covenant with the Canaanites.

13. *Cut down their Asherim*. The *Asherim* are the sacred trees or wooden poles (perhaps symbolic of a tree) that often stood by Baal's altar (Jdg. 6:25). Such 'maypoles' symbolized the goddess Asherah-of-the-Sea of the Ras Shamra texts, the 'Lady Luck' of the Canaanites.

14. *YHWH, whose name is Jealous*. As Napier says, this code is unique not in material, but in arrangement. This phrase, for instance, is a vivid commentary on, and explanation of, Exodus 20:5, by defining God's very nature in terms of His demand for exclusive relationship with Him.

16. *Play the harlot*: perhaps 'commit adultery'[1] would be a better translation here, since unfaithfulness to YHWH, Israel's 'husband', is meant. The metaphor is doubly appropriate, since it is in a context that also forbids literal intermarriage with the Canaanites, and also in view of the immoral nature of Baal worship (Ho. 4:13,14) and the liaisons formed there.

17. *No molten gods*: images of cast metal. This prohibition is doubly relevant here, so close to the making of the golden bull, also described by this contemptuous term (32:4). Some doubt exists as to whether metal statues of YHWH are intended (as the worshippers of the golden bull would claim that their statue was, 32:5) or statues of other gods. Ultimately there is no contradiction: to worship a statue while calling it YHWH is not to worship YHWH.

18. *The feast of unleavened bread*: this, rather than passover, is mentioned (but see verse 25 below). Reasons are to be found in Exodus 12: passover is not strictly a 'festival', but a ceremonial meal of the family. *For in the month Abib you came out*

---

[1] Although Hebrew *zānāh* in itself does not necessarily imply adultery, but only irregular sexual relationships: the marriage-analogy should therefore not be pressed, unless there is a clear reference in the context to pin the meaning down precisely.

from Egypt. As in the 'book of the covenant' (Ex. 23:15), the feast of unleavened bread is firmly linked with the historical events of the exodus, not with an agricultural season. To this context therefore is annexed, very properly, the redemption of first-born (verse 20). Indeed, the historical and commemorative aspect of the festival is further stressed by mention of passover itself in verse 25, for the association of blood sacrifice with unleavened bread is probably a specific reference to passover, not a general reference to sacrificial regulations.

21. *In ploughing time and in harvest you shall rest*: a very far-reaching demand, in an agricultural community. The farmer is told to observe the rest day even at the times of year when he is busiest, and when another day's work, humanly speaking, might mean success instead of failure. The abiding spiritual principle, in Old Testament and New Testament alike, is 'seek first his kingdom' (Mt. 6:33). Since in Israel to keep the sabbath was a test of faith in God's provision (Ex. 16:29), this amplification is merely an extension of the same principle, in circumstances where faith is even more difficult, since the consequences will be more far-reaching.

24. *Neither shall any man desire your land.* This is a needed word of reassurance to the man who obeys the command to attend the festival. The godly farmer may well fear that his less godly Israelite neighbour (hardly a foreigner, if these have been driven out) may move his 'landmark' (Dt. 19:14), and so steal his land, while he is absent on pilgrimage. This was a danger facing medieval Crusaders too (*cf.* the experience of King Richard of England). For the meaning of *desire* as being practically 'take', and the primitive and direct psychology herein displayed, see the commentary on Exodus 20:17, the tenth commandment. Sometimes it has been argued that the very existence of such a promise as that of verse 24 implies the necessity of a long journey to one central sanctuary, and that this implies a late date. But at least some sort of 'amphictionic sanctuary' was envisaged from the start (Jos. 21:2; 22:12) and a journey of twenty miles was a great matter in early days (1 Sa. 1:3). It is also argued that 'ploughing' and 'harvest' imply a sedentary and not a nomadic people. But Israel had been long settled in Egypt, and even the patriarchs had engaged in some sowing and reaping (Gn. 26:12), in pre-Egyptian days.

26. *The first of the first fruits.* Since all these festivals have some agricultural significance, by the calendar dating at least, the reference to 'first fruits' is appropriate here (as in the condemnation of Canaanite magic and fertility-rites). But the mention of the redemption of the first-born sons also has relevance: this too commemorates Israel's salvation, in picture at least.

27. *In accordance with these words*: this is the usual covenant peroration. On the above terms (and doubtless other similar laws) the renewed covenant is made. As is the case of the first 'covenant book', there is a reference to the recording in writing of the terms (Ex. 24:4,7). Another parallel would be Joshua's writing of at least part of the terms of the covenant in 'the book of the law of God' at the sanctuary of Shechem (Jos. 24:26). It is possible to assume that the writing of the 'ten words' upon the stone tablets (verse 28) is distinct from the 'writing' of the covenant terms in verse 27. In that case, there would be two formulations of covenant law, one brief and the other discursive, but both equally binding on Israel as terms of the covenant. Since both are essentially summaries of the same law, there is no contradiction between the two. Note that the covenant is made with Moses (as mediator) and with Israel: the 'with you' is singular in Hebrew (Hyatt).

28. *Forty days and forty nights*. Deuteronomy 10:10 makes this a second period of forty days. Moses is exactly reproducing the conditions of the giving of the first (broken) tablets. Otherwise we might have assumed the number to be a vague general reference to Moses' first stay on the mountain (Ex. 24:18).

34:29-35. The effects of fellowship with God. This passage, expressing the truth of the transforming nature of communion with God, is famous from Paul's use of it in 2 Corinthians 3:7–18. Paul, however, assumes that Moses put the 'veil' on his face so that Israel could not see that the reflected glory of God's presence was gradually fading away (verse 13). The text before us says simply that Moses did it because the Israelites were afraid to look at him (verse 30), just as they had been afraid to draw near to God themselves. Doubtless Paul is following Rabbinic exegesis in his interpretation. For the whole, we may compare Matthew 17:1–8, the transfiguration of Christ: Moses is the mediator of the first covenant.

29. *Moses did not know.* Like John the Baptist (Jn. 1:21) and Paul (1 Tim. 1:15), Moses was unconscious of his own stature. This is true spiritual greatness. Numbers 12:3 rightly describes him as meekest (humblest) of men: here is an instance of it. *The skin of his face shone.* This very old story contains two unusual linguistic usages, which guarantee its authenticity. The first is the verb translated *shone* here; 'shot forth beams' would be the better translation. Unfortunately, because the cognate noun also means 'a horn', the Vulgate mistranslated the verb as 'having horns', and so it is that Moses appears in mediaeval works of art as wearing a pair of horns. The second unusual usage is discussed under verse 33.

33. *He put a veil on his face.* The word for 'veil' (*masweh*) is unknown, except from this passage, but both the context and Jewish traditional interpretation make its meaning clear. It is quite gratuitous, with some modern editors, to translate it as a 'priest's mask' (although such are known from the ancient world), the more so as Moses is acting in a prophetic, not priestly, capacity in this context. The whole story suggests an *ad hoc* expedient, not a religious ritual.

34. *He took the veil off.* Moses saw the glory of YHWH with unveiled face (2 Cor. 3:18). So his prayer in Exodus 33:18 ('show me thy glory') is answered at last.

c. Execution of God's commands (35:1 – 39:43)

These five chapters reproduce almost verbally (with changes of tense and person only) the material of chapters 25–31. Because of this, some editors have considered it a mere accidental reduplication. This however it cannot be, because of certain interesting additions and rearrangement of material. If it is a reduplication, it is a deliberate one, to point the lesson of the faithfulness of Moses in carrying out God's instruction (Ex. 25:9). It also emphasizes the faithfulness of God; He will still dwell among His people, in spite of their initial failure. Two methods are used to point the moral. The first is the mechanical device of reduplication; the second is the sevenfold repetition, 'as YHWH had commanded Moses' (Ex. 39:1,5,7,21,26,29,31). This sevenfold repetition occurs twice in these chapters (see also Ex. 40:19,21,23,25,27,29,32), lest we should fail to notice it. However, because most of the material has appeared already, comment will be made only on any significant difference from the earlier account. For the rest, the reader is advised to turn back to the parallel passage, and the notes there. The LXX varies more widely from the MT in these chapters than anywhere else in Exodus: see Gooding for a detailed discussion.

35:1–3. Reiteration of sabbath law. This is, at one and the same time, a virtual reiteration of the sabbath commandment, and also of 31:12–17.

2. *Six days shall work be done.* The mention of sabbath presumably recurs here because the sabbath is a covenant sign (Ex. 31:16) and the setting is a renewal of the covenant. It may also (as above) be intended to show Moses' faithfulness in retailing commands that he has just received (Ex. 34:21). The sabbath law is here prefixed to the whole section, athough it closed the earlier section, in chapter 31. This can surely only be deliberate, and, if so, there is an obvious conclusion to be drawn. Even in their newfound eagerness to construct the Tent, Israel must remember to observe the sacred day.

3. *You shall kindle no fire.* This strict prohibition is not recorded elsewhere in the Old Testament. However, Exodus 16:23 seems to imply that the sabbath supply of manna must be cooked the night before: this implies the same rule. The kindling of a fire is still regarded by the orthodox Jew as 'work', and thus forbidden on the sabbath (even the lighting of gas stoves). Hyatt suggests that the prohibition may have been aimed at fires used for the metalwork required for the sanctuary.

35:4–29. Offerings of material and labour for the Tent.
10. *Let every able man among you come and make.* As in the earlier passage, everyone who is willing may donate materials for the Tent (verse 5). But now the invitation to the work is wider. Not only Bezalel and Oholiab may take part, but 'every able man' may share in the construction.

21. The pattern is now still further widened: every man can give a gift, even he who has no skill to work, whether it be articles of personal jewelry or raw materials.

24. The women could spin (Pr. 31:13) and the wealthier chieftains could bring the precious stones and spices (verses 27,28). All have a part in building the sanctuary for YHWH, and, without each playing his peculiar part, it cannot be completed (*cf*. Eph. 4:16). Here again is a message for us today.

35:30 – 36:7. Abundant supplies. 5. *The people bring much more than enough.* The craftsmen whom God had chosen had to dissuade the rest of the congregation from bringing further gifts, so generous was the response. This is the typical reaction of God's people to the saving grace and forgiving love of God. Compare the story of the anointing at Bethany (Mt. 26:7), and the generosity of the Philippian church (Phil. 4:14-19). It must have been both a disappointment and a frustration to those who had delayed their gifts because they could not bear to part with their treasures, and who now found that God had no further need of them. His work was finished, but they had excluded themselves from any share in it: God deliver any of us from such a frustration.

36:8–38. The construction of the Tent. This is a repetition of the instructions of 26:1–37, with the persons and tenses of the verbs changed. Such repetition is characteristic both of Israel's literature in general and, in particular, of priestly circles: the book of Ezekiel contains many examples, as does Chronicles. As an architect delights to pore over plans or blueprints, so the pious priest would have rejoiced in this meticulous re-listing of specifications already given.

37:1 – 38:20. The manufacture of equipment. This passage follows the logical order of the construction work, unlike the earlier section (25:31). Here, for instance, the Tent itself is constructed before any of the equipment to go with it. The incense-altar is mentioned along with the other articles placed within the Tent, and the laver is mentioned with the other furniture of the great open-air courtyard where it belongs. Both of these had been displaced appendices in the earlier section, contained in chapter 30. Finally, the incense is mentioned where it properly belongs, next to the mention of the incense-altar, and not in a supplement. All this shows careful and systematic re-arrangement of material, not thoughtless repetition.

37:1. *Bezalel made the ark.* There is no contradiction between this and Deuteronomy 10:3, where it is said that Moses made it (in the sense of 'caused it to be made'). Exodus nowhere claims that Moses himself had personal artistic ability or skill.

38:1. *The altar of burnt offering* is so described in this passage (unlike the earlier account) to distinguish it from the incense-altar, which has been mentioned in the immediate context here (37:25).

8. *From the mirrors of the ministering women who ministered at the door.*[1] This is an interesting new piece of information, as to the source of the copper used in the manufacture of the laver. If men gave armlets (35:22), woman gave *mirrors* (always made of burnished metal in early days). The verb translated *minister* is rare and interesting, and is used in only one other place of women in the service of the sanctuary (1 Sa. 2:22). It really means 'organized in bands for war', but it is used of ordinary Levitical service (Nu. 4:23, *etc.*). It therefore probably stands for some form of organized sanctuary service, whether cleaning or sweeping (in which case many a Women's Guild has its prototype here), or in singing and dancing at festivals (like Miriam in Ex. 15:20). Alternatively, in view of the reference to the *door*, they may have had the lowly task of doorkeepers (Ps. 84:10). Some see parallels to Canaanite 'temple girls' (dedicated to the sanctuary), because of the wording of 1 Samuel 2:22. But such immoral practices were totally forbidden in Israel, and the reference in Samuel stresses the enormity of the sin of Eli's sons in treating YHWH's handmaids as if they had been Baal's girls. Had these 'ministering women' been temple prostitutes in a Baalized form of worship, such behaviour by Eli's sons would occasion no comment. Once again, the outward form of dedication to the sanctuary is common to YHWH and Baal worship: but the nature of that service performed is poles apart (Is. 55:8,9). See Hyatt for a full discussion.

38:21–31. Statistics and costing. 21. *For the work of the Levites.* Their appointment is recorded in Numbers 3, where Ithamar (already mentioned in Ex. 6:23) also appears in this capacity as 'headman'.

24. *All the gold that was used.* Reckoned in round figures, all the amounts of precious metals mentioned run into tons (one ton of gold, four tons of silver, and three tons of copper). It

---

[1] Since 'the Tent' was not yet constructed, this must refer to some simpler earlier structure.

is possible that the figures have been incorrectly preserved in the manuscripts.

25. *The silver from those of the congregation who were numbered.* The total of silver (very high) is obtained by multiplying the number of adult Israelites listed in Numbers 1, by the half-shekel that each had to give in 'redemption' (Ex. 30:13). It is not thought of as part of the free-will offering. This also accounts for the total of silver being higher than the total of copper, contrary to usual proportions. For reference to the 'shekel of the sanctuary', see Exodus 30:13. Such references are interesting examples of early attempts at standardization of weights. Various samples of this *beqaʿ* or half-shekel weight have been found in Israel (see Driver for exact modern equivalents).

39:1–31. Making the priestly robes. 1. *As YHWH had commanded Moses.* This sonorous refrain occurs, as mentioned, seven times in this chapter and seven times in the next. The deliberate intention of the repetition is made clear, in stressing the exact and detailed obedience of Moses to every minute command of God.

3. *Gold leaf was hammered out and cut into threads.* This method (not mentioned elsewhere in the Old Testament) is an interesting technical detail, explaining how Israel produced the gold thread needed to work into the priestly fabrics to produce extra richness.

8. *He made the breastpiece.* Amid much that is the same as before, 'Urim and Tummim' are not mentioned here, although the 'breastpiece' that contained them is described in detail. Perhaps the two oracular stones are not mentioned because they were not manufactured, but were natural objects. Compare the way in which the stones of YHWH's altar must be natural (Ex. 20:25), not chiselled by human hand.

30. *The plate of the holy crown*: the golden 'flower' or plate inscribed with 'holiness to YHWH', which was bound to the priestly turban by the diadem of violet ribbon, is here described as a royal *crown* (*cf.* Ex. 28:36,37). This makes both its significance and appearance clearer. Alternatively, the Hebrew may be describing the combination of plate and ribbon as a 'crown'. Since the ribbon corresponded to the 'diadem' of eastern kings, this is possible.

39:32-43. Approbation of the work. The individual items of work are now all completed, and they are in turn brought to Moses for inspection (prior to the pitching and dedication of the Tent in chapter 40), rather as the animals are brought to Adam in Genesis 2:19 for inspection and naming.

38. *The golden altar.* To judge from the material of which it is made, this must be the small incense-altar. The 'bronze altar' of the next verse is the large altar for sacrifice, as can be seen from its material.

43. *And Moses saw all the work . . . and Moses blessed them.* There is probably a deliberate reminiscence of Genesis 1:31 here. Moses reviews the work: since it has been done in obedience to God's command, he recognizes it as good, and blesses it. In a sense, this is a new creation (*cf.* 2 Cor. 5:17), for worshipping Israel is born this day.

d. Consecration of the Tent (40:1-38)

40:1-15. Instructions for consecration. These verses, like chapters 25–31, are, strictly speaking, forward looking. Moses is again given instructions, not only about the pitching of the Tent and the placing of the various ritual objects in position, but also for the 'anointing' of Tent, furnishings and priests, and so for their perpetual dedication (verse 15). Compare Exodus 29:9 for the 'perpetual priesthood' of Aaron's line. The instructions given here will be carried out in the later verses of the chapter.

40:16-33. Carrying out the consecration. 16. *In the first month in the second year, on the first day.* It is one year after the exodus (12:2) and nine months after Israel's arrival at Sinai (19:1). When we take out the period spent by Moses on the mountain, this does not allow overmuch time for the manufacture of the various objects, if all dates are factual and not symbolic.

27. *Burnt fragrant incense upon it.* Compare verse 29, which seems to show full sacrifice as actually beginning, apparently with Moses himself acting in a priestly capacity. However, possibly the sense is vague and 'causative', in the sense 'had incense burnt'.

40:34-38. God's seal on the Tent. 34. *The cloud covered* *the tent of meeting.* Two thoughts are joined in this chapter. The first is that God shows His approval of the completed work by descending in the cloud of 'glory' that shows His presence (*cf.* 33:9). Indeed, He so covers and fills the Tent that now not even Moses, God's faithful servant (Nu. 12:7), dares to enter (verse 35). The second allied thought is that this same cloud, the symbol of the presence of YHWH, led the way by day and night all through the desert years of Israel's experience (verse 36).

38. *Throughout all their journeys the cloud of YHWH was upon the tabernacle.* Driver notes that the book ends with the fulfilment of the promise of Exodus 29:45. YHWH is living among His people: the theology of the presence of God has become the fact of His presence. Davies adds to this the thought that the book ends with a confident look ahead. The God who lives among His people is the God who will lead and guide to Canaan, in fulfilment of His promise to the patriarchs. To speak of a journey is to look for an arrival: He who has begun a work of salvation for Israel will complete it (Phil. 1:6): that is at once the hope and the confidence of the people of God, as they move forward from Sinai, and therefore it is our hope too.